Children, Teachers and Learning Series
General Editor: Cedric Cullingford

The Nature of Learning

The Nature of Learning
Children, Teachers and the Curriculum

Cedric Cullingford

CASSELL

Cassell Educational Limited
Villiers House
41/47 Strand
London WC2N 5JE

First published 1990

British Library Cataloguing in Publication Data
Cullingford, Cedric
    The nature of learning. – (Children, teaching and
    learning series)
    1. Learning by children
    I. Title   II. Series
    155.413

ISBN 0-304-32287-3 (hardback)
          0-304-32284-9 (paperback)

Typeset by Fakenham Photosetting Limited, Fakenham, Norfolk
Printed and bound in Great Britain by Biddles Ltd, Guildford
and King's Lynn

Contents

For David and Linda Winkley

Foreword

The books in this series stem from the conviction that all those who are concerned with education should have a deep interest in the nature of children's learning. Teaching and policy decisions ultimately depend on an understanding of individual personalities accumulated through experience, observation and research. Too often in recent years decisions on the management of education have had little to do with the realities of children's lives, and too often the interest shown in the performance of teachers, or in the content of the curriculum, has not been balanced by an interest in how children respond to either. The books in this series are based on the conviction that children are not fundamentally different from adults, and that we understand ourselves better by our insight into the nature of children.

The books are designed to appeal to *all* those who are interested in education and who take it as axiomatic that anyone concerned with human nature, culture or the future of civilization is interested in education – in the individual process of learning, as well as what can be done to help it. While each book draws on recent findings in research and is aware of the latest developments in policy, each is written in a style that is clear, readable and free from the jargon that has undermined much scholarly writing, especially in such a relatively new field of study.

Although the audience to be addressed includes all those concerned with education, the most important section of the audience is made up of professional teachers, the teachers who continue to learn and grow and who need both support and stimulation. Teachers are very busy people, whose energies are taken up in coping with difficult circumstances. They deserve material that is stimulating, useful and free of jargon and that is in tune with the practical realities of classrooms.

Each book is based on the principle that the study of education is a discipline in its own right. There was a time when the study of the principles of learning and the individual's response to his or her environment was a collection of parts of other disciplines –

history, philosophy, linguistics, sociology and psychology. That time is assumed to be over and the books address those who are interested in the study of children and how they respond to their environment.

Each book is written both to enlighten the readers and to offer practical help to develop their understanding. They therefore not only contain accounts of what we understand about children, but also illuminate these accounts by a series of examples, based on observation of practice. These examples are designed not as a series of rigid steps to be followed, but to show the realities on which the insights are based.

Most people, even educational researchers, agree that research on children's learning has been most disappointing, even when it has not been completely missing. Apart from the general lack of a 'scholarly' educational tradition, the inadequacies of such study come about because of the fear of approaching such a complex area as children's inner lives. Instead of answering curiosity with observation, much educational research has attempted to reduce the problem to simplistic solutions, by isolating a particular hypothesis and trying to improve it, or by trying to focus on what is easy and 'empirical'. These books try to clarify the real complexities of the problem, and are willing to be speculative.

The real disappointment with educational research, however, is that it is very rarely read or used. The people most at home with children are often unaware that helpful insights can be offered to them. The study of children and the understanding that comes from self-knowledge are too important to be left to obscurity. In the broad sense real 'research' is carried out by all those engaged in the task of teaching or bringing up children.

All the books share a conviction that the inner worlds of children repay close attention, and that much subsequent behaviour and attitudes depend upon the early years. They also share the conviction that children's natures are not markedly different from those of adults, even if they are more honest about themselves. The process of learning is reviewed as the individual's close and idiosyncratic involvement in events, rather than the passive reception of, and processing of, information.

Cedric Cullingford

Preface and Acknowledgements

This book is different from the books that will follow in the same series. It tackles a huge and difficult subject in order to define the principles of learning that will be taken up in later volumes. Each chapter could be turned into a book in itself. This introductory volume does not, therefore, go into the practical implications of the principles it explores; that will be carried out by later volumes. Nor is this book a research monograph, although it is based on extensive research, on many interviews with children, observations of them in the classroom, and the experience of other teachers and researchers in the same field.

If this book is not a research monograph, nor yet is it an introductory textbook that summarizes the literature. There are many textbooks on child development, most of which are very similar to each other, rearranging the same content in different ways, but there are very few books on learning, very few that concentrate on *how* people respond to information and what goes on inside their heads. In this way this is an educational book, not a psychological one. It is more concerned with exploring the inner lives of children than with measuring their performance. It is also concerned with exploring the nature of human learning, which is as applicable to adults as to children. It is in children that we see learning demonstrated most clearly, but virtually all that is said about children applies to all of us.

The book is designed so that the learning is understood in a holistic way. There are certain themes, such as play and stories, that keep recurring because they are always relevant, whatever the age. Each of the four major themes, on children's abilities, their responses to the environment, their inner worlds and their relationships to others, is concerned not only with young children but with the essential principles that are relevant for all ages. The book is only developmental up to a point and does not give precise accounts of what happens at different ages because of the concern with the major characteristics of learning.

This causes a problem in tone. There is no need to fix different principles of learning at different ages; if the principles are right they will hold good under the surface differences of growth and maturity. But a phrase like '(all) children' might seem to suggest more generalization than is intended. The book is concerned with the individual as well as the whole child. The evidence from which it is derived is not limited to particular ages any more than the principles of learning are confined to particular ages. But the principles should be recognizable in different ways in different children – the age factor is only one difference. If there had not been the modern problem that 'he' no longer means all 'mankind', I would have preferred to use something other than 'children' and 'they', but I felt that the continual use of 'he/she' and 'his/hers' would not work. I have used the conventional 'he' for the child (and for babies, although they are in some texts referred to as 'it') and I have used the even more conventional 'she' for a teacher.

The individual child described here is not an ideal. The emerging view of the world that is depicted is not confined to the articulate and well fed. The many children with special educational needs and those who are undernourished, undervalued and abused are at least as important as the rest, and are just as much the subject of the book. They are not a special and separate category. It is sometimes surprising to discover how often an individual child's difficulties in learning stem from a specific physical or emotional cause. It is out of the belief that we do not make anything like the proper use of children's capabilities that this book emerged.

I have learned from many more people than I could ever name. Many more people have taught me than they themselves would acknowledge. I owe a special debt to the many teachers I have worked with, as well as to the children on whom any book of this kind is based. In a subject of such complexity there have been many decisions to make; what to leave out, how to simplify, how to sum up and how to organize. The final choices are mine, but I owe special thanks to David and Linda Winkley, and to Nichola.

C.C.
Brighton, 1990

Introduction:
Learning and Development

The Vanity of Teaching often tempts a man to forget he is a blockhead.
George Savile, 1st Lord Halifax

The most popular educational issue of our time is the question of *what* children should learn. It is an issue that demonstrates the conflicting aims of education. Should education be essentially for the development of the individual, to enable him or her to lead a fulfilled life, or should education, supported by the State, be designed to help meet the requirements of society? Should education be seen as a manifestation of the development of the individual or a means of giving the individual the necessary knowledge and skills for employment? The underlying dichotomy of education is rarely seen as clearly as this in debates about the curriculum. The social and the individual needs overlap, and can sometimes be assumed to be the same. The terms with which people debate education are rarely so clearly expressed as a choice between different purposes. But one enduring reason why the purposes of education, in terms of the curriculum, are never clearly articulated or debated is that what children learn depends on *how* they learn.

While it is tempting to think of measurable goals in education – standard criteria for knowledge of mathematics, science, language and history, all measured against what should be achieved at particular ages – we know that the long-lasting outcomes of education are more complex than the acquisition of measurable knowledge, and depend on the individual's attitude towards learning and his ability to apply what is learned to new material. In secondary schools it is rather more easy to concentrate on what is measurable in terms of required knowledge, but in primary schools the difficulties of trying to define a 'core' curriculum stem

1

from the fact that children's learning cannot be explained simply in terms of particular goals.

The different ways in which children learn, and their different attitudes to learning, lie at the heart of any education system. The curriculum can only be properly understood through knowledge of the different ways children acquire information, organize it, assess it and value it. The distinction between knowing things and thinking about them is important and we must doubt the common assumption that the ability to think is a matter of inherited genetics about which nothing can be done. Learning to think must itself be learned. While nearly all children have the capacity to learn, not all make, or are enabled to make, equal use of it. Mastery over different aspects of the curriculum clearly depends on opportunities to learn, and on the circumstances in which learning takes place. An understanding of how people learn would make a more fundamental change to the education system as a whole than any decision on what should be contained in the national curriculum, for understanding how people learn forces a reassessment of the purpose of learning, the curriculum and the way it is communicated.

Learning is not, however, a popular subject. Far more attention has been paid to child development. One reason for this is that learning is obviously individual and difficult to measure. It is so fundamental to every human being that it does not lend itself easily to evaluation or to observation; it gives no easy access to analysis. Development is, on the contrary, comparatively easily measured. Physical growth, differences in the manifestations of language and the accumulation of knowledge are all clearly observed to take place. The results of such a process are clear, and the changes perfectly visible. But *why* people develop differently, and the ways in which they acquire their sense of value and morality, are more complex indications of the interplay between individuals' biological development and the circumstances in which they are placed. At the heart of all development is the fact of learning itself, a process that has no ending, does not result in a visible outcome, but affects everything else. It is this process, not that of development, which concerns this book.

To study and understand learning is to enter that no-man's-land between thinking, as a capacity, and development, as a process of change. Learning is both constant and changeable; it depends on moods and on general attitudes; it changes according to emotions and yet is a constant base on which other matters depend. The difficulty with understanding the process of learning is that it functions at a variety of levels. The difference between intense concentration on a task and a mind wandering over various associations, as in daydreaming, is clear; both are different types of learning. Although it is far easier to measure the performance of the brain when reading and remembering a series of nonsense syllables over a short time than it is to test the information derived from an evening's viewing of a series of television programmes, the more 'normal' state of learning is the latter. Many people do not concentrate their minds at all, let alone for any extended period of time; the most influential learning is very rarely derived from circumstances such as the close analysis of a text. The distinction between the capacity to learn and the actual performance of learning is crucial. Children can apply their minds wonderfully when they wish to. If you ask them to look at a television programme because you are going to test their memory of it afterwards, you will find them giving detailed information of the kind that they would not think of providing after watching the same programme without those conditions. What children *can* do and what they normally do are quite distinct. Furthermore, they apply different levels of response to the same material at different times.

Children's learning processes are as complex as the definition of truth. When children are asked, for example, about the messages of advertisements they show that they are able to analyse them at a variety of levels.[1] Children of six, as well as children of twelve, are aware of the different kinds of truth and half-truth manifested by advertisements. They know that one response to the truth of the advertisement is that if the product depicted exists and can be bought in the shops then that is true enough. This pragmatism is the level of truth supported by the Advertising Standards Authority, to whom truth is anything that is not legally false.[2] But children also know that to say that a 'White Horse can go anywhere' is nonsense; that the fantasies depicted on advertisements are nothing more than that. They are aware, in fact, of Kant's distinction between analytic and synthetic truth, between those

3

things which are always true and those which could be true.[3] But they also know about the designs that advertisers have on them, and about the gap between the product as depicted in an advertisement and its everyday reality. They also know that some of the implied promises, that possession of a product boosts virility or attraction, are nothing but make-believe.

As children grow older they are more inclined to concentrate on the social morality of advertisements. In their teens they become annoyed with the abuse of general truth for the purposes of the hard sell, even when they enjoy the way that advertisements are presented. Younger children accept the fact that the advertisement has a level of pragmatism in presenting the product. At all ages children know about the complexity of truth, but are inclined to answer questions about the distinctions between types of truth according to their age. Younger children first express the mechanistic level of truth before mentioning their knowledge that advertisements have designs on them. Older children answer in the reverse order. Children's underlying awareness remains the same; but the use they make of their awareness changes. Many of the misunderstandings about children have derived from taking their first answer to a particular question at face value, and assuming that a statement expressing their interest is one that demonstrates their capacities.

When one considers how difficult are the questions that children ask and how insistently they demand answers, it is surprising how few people ask children questions in return. Perhaps the concentration on the wares of the teacher and the belief that what is taught is the same as what is learned has led people to assume that it is not worth asking children questions. Perhaps there is a shared assumption that children will answer questions as guardedly and ambiguously, and occasionally as falsely, as adults, especially about a subject like birth or death. But a great deal can be learned about children from using the most significant asset of human beings: language.[4] It is a pity that such a method of enquiry should have been so little used. We know that children *can*, and do, give answers as designed to deceive as answers given by adults, but it is more obvious when they do so. We know when they are exploring other people's reactions, when they are trying to shock, when they are trying to impress and when they are concentrating not on giving an answer but on saying anything that will stop the questioner insisting on an answer.[5] But if they are less skilled at deflecting questions, so they are better at revealing the extent to which they are thinking about the great questions that are the subject of learning.[6]

Two facts about learning emerge from the accumulation of research evidence and observation. Both upset part of the common mythology about learning. The first fact is that children are intelligent learners from an early age.[7] Even before birth, as new techniques are constantly revealing, the baby is already responding as a human being. Just after birth the baby is able to copy, to follow actions, to see consequences. To survive, children need to learn fast not only to have some measure of control over their physical needs, but also to make sense of the world, to find some inner equilibrium that makes the relationship between them and their environment sensible and full of meaning. The achievement of this personal sense of order demands a feat of thinking that is as difficult, as cerebral, as any other during the rest of their lives. To be able to perceive, to categorize, to guess, to make distinctions, to generalize, to draw inferences, understand concepts, tease out ambiguities; all these describe the earliest responses of a child to the world as well as they do the erudition of a scholar. Learning in that sense is, and remains, a complex and emotional act.

The second fact about learning that emerges from research is that not all adults are especially 'clever'. They do not constantly apply their minds to tasks, without any break in concentration and without the distractions of emotions or tiredness, whether reading or watching television. One of the misunderstandings about learning is that children are limited in their rationality and that cleverness only arrives with maturity. It is natural to assume, from the perspective of one's own point of view, that all wisdom has been accumulated in oneself, but misleading to suggest that children do not have the ability to think deeply. Knowing that there are great changes that all of us undergo throughout our lives and knowing that the academic demands on the undergraduate are so much higher than those on a two-year-old should not mislead us into thinking that children are incapable of thought. Nor should it mislead us into assuming that wisdom is automatic, a result of maturity itself. Thinking is not a purely cerebral process. It is not a feat constantly practised. The rule of emotions, of inner needs or prejudices, of self-deception and illogicality is strong in adults and remains so. The use of information to support a chosen point of view, the dislike of changing one's mind and the resentment that anyone should ask us to apply the mind are all characteristics of the normal adult. Many adult pleasures, from soap operas on television to detective stories and pop music, are characterized by *not* making intellectual demands on the recipient.[8] In fact we do not see why we should become mentally deeply engaged in magazines or romances. But it shows a use of the mind that, when seen in children, in their own pleasures, tends to be put down to 'childishness', as if play or stories could not be at all intellectually challenging, and as if only children act irrationally or self-indulgently. Of the great changes that mark the development of maturity there can be no doubt. The goal of learning is wisdom and self-knowledge, but the process of learning takes place all the time, and rarely so intensely as in the earliest, formative years.

The use that children make of their minds in trying to make sense of the world they are in is often more constant and demanding than in adults. While they might appear idiosyncratic in their interpretation of events when dealing with only part of the evidence, children are still capable of making distinctions of a kind normally associated with maturity. Even perception is a conceptual analysis of implicit definitions, rather than the automatic recording of what is seen.[9] The intellectual act of understanding distinctions between shape and size, between depth and purpose, is that of creating categories, and is a rational ability to apply the mind. Children are practical theorists and can think about thinking, and the act of thinking, when very young.[10] They understand an abstract word like 'word' very well by the age of five.[11] They apply their awareness of practical spatial distinctions to their understanding of individual points of view.[12] Even the difficulties children seem to have with the difference between appearance and reality show their ability to apply rational judgements to a problem. They try to judge what is real even if they are particularly conscious of the attractions of appearance.[13] They are easily influenced by distractions and yet, at the age of three, are able to understand the distinction between reality and appearance.[14] At the ages of four and five children demonstrate their understanding of the distinction between the animate and inanimate.[15] Children are also able to make sensible judgements about procedural justice by the age of five.[16] Even as difficult a concept as that of death is understood in terms of its irreversibility and universality between the ages of five and seven.[17] Children feel the need to develop their own insights into the world very early.

The problem with the common assumption about child development, suggesting the continual improvement from a piece of unformed clay to something as refined as bone china, is that it presupposes that people learn all that they are taught; that the human being is, as far as the educational system is concerned, a result of the 'delivery' of the curriculum. It is very hard not to be influenced by the accepted view of learning as an outcome of the more understandable fact of teaching. This is partly why so little attention is paid to learning. It is far more difficult to analyse the response, the inner world, of human beings than the performance and knowledge of the teacher. We naturally take on the vanity of the teacher: we analyse the stimuli, see what is offered through the different media of communication and assume almost automatically that the delivery, the product, equals the response. Such vanity is not just personal. It implies that education is a system of delivery formed by the content of what teachers try to convey. It is plain to the individual that what is learned depends on him, uniquely. But with that human capacity for holding two conflicting opinions at the same time, we tend to assume that *other* people are the results of teaching, the products of those who have designs on them. The rules that govern 'us' are quite different from those that govern 'them'.

Creating a relationship between one's own point of view and that of other people implies subtle social attitudes and social skills of which children are clearly capable. By the time they have reached school, children demonstrate their ability not only to influence each other in different ways, but also to influence or undermine the teachers. Both in their own groups – 'gangs' and 'attention seekers' – and in their testing of the teacher's style of reactions – 'jokers' and 'teasers'[18] – they test out the responsiveness of others. While teachers clearly influence the performance of children, the idea of the self-fulfilling prophecy, by which children achieve what they are expected to, is made more difficult because the teachers are themselves influenced by what children expect them to expect.[19] Children are aware of others, their points of view and their behaviour long before they reach school. Their moral development depends on it. Children's understanding of adults deepens with age; they observe closely the distinctions between rules and ritual, between rules and principles.[20] They learn the concept of fairness by their careful scrutiny of other people, and they learn that particular strategies of behaviour succeed when they connect them to other strategies that achieve the same result. The earliest exchanges with other people and the earliest analyses of what they see are an important influence on learning both then and later. Whether at home or in nursery schools, children seek and need warm personal relationships which demand thought, judgement and articulacy.[21] Their language depends to some extent on what they feel is necessary for the circumstances. They do not always display what they are capable of and can surprise their parents when, at two years old, instead of simple verbal signals like 'more', they suddenly display the ability to use complex sentences when they have something particular to say, such as 'I don't like having Jennifer around', or 'I want to go to school one day'.

Some mistaken assumptions about learning are the result of a lack of interest. Other assumptions about learning are a result of the influence of particular theories. Like individual learners, societies can cling to a set of given concepts even in the face of overwhelming evidence, and only gradually admit to change. Certain theories of child development have, through the attractions of what seem like empirical evidence and rigid methodology, gained a strong hold on approaches to the understanding of children. Within an orthodoxy of a semi-scientific kind all new insights are only allowable or academically respectable if they are a refinement of the same tradition. Anyone who challenges the tradition is at once accused of not following the correct methods of research, and of therefore being empirically unsound. The most common orthodoxy about learning is the idea that it is a matter of information processing: that the mind analyses, organizes, stores and remembers material at one, testable, level. While this is the function of the mind that can be most readily measured, it is not the only part of it. Learning includes more than demonstrations of concentrated ratiocination.

The idea of learning as a question of imitation is not only simple and popular, it has also led to a great deal of research in testing out the hypothesis, by trying to affect children's behaviour by providing them with set stimuli.[22] But the idea runs counter to what we know of ourselves and observe in others. Children are too self-conscious merely to copy one single action; the way they observe and make what they observe their own is shown in the way they cling to their own sense of the orthodox and the way they can be deeply embarrassed by their parents when their parents seem to break the rules or behave in an unorthodox way.

One of the most rigid of orthodoxies about child development, in its use as a basis for research and for understanding children, has been that of Piaget's theory of development. One can hardly blame Piaget for his biological point of view or his interest in scientific thinking[23] when he suggests that development occurs through an invariable hierarchy of stages, or that the completion of one stage is a prerequisite for the next. Although his experiments are based on very few children they still remain interesting. But the uses to which Piaget's theories have been put illustrate the worst aspects of intellectual orthodoxy. Many a thesis and many a book have been encumbered with the need to refer back to Piaget, to show that new findings *will* fit into the given framework. This has meant that some of the most exciting findings, as well as the most significant parts, of the research have been ignored since Piaget had already provided the academic gospel. And the gospel spread far more widely than Piaget ever intended.[24] Piaget's theory separates the two processes of development and learning, making one general and the other specific. While the question remains whether one *can* split the two, and whether learning is always specific, his own intention to look on maturity, heredity and environment as subordinated to the regulatory mechanism of growth has usually been ignored, even in its own terms.[25] There are a number of examples of how some of the Piagetian assumptions are undermined[26] – for example, in some of Bruner's work on Piaget's experiments, which showed that there were *other* interpretations that showed that children were *not* as limited as they were supposed to be – but it is the rigidity of the classifications that has caused most problems. If, after all, Piaget were right, there would be little need to re-examine the experience of children, or to reflect on the ways in which they are taught.[27]

There are a number of explanations about how children learn to improve their ability to organize material.[28] One possible (if discredited) view is that young children are passive receivers of information and that with age they gradually learn how to organize their learning. A second view is that young children actively organize the environment and learn to do so more efficiently as they get older. This view is more commonly held. But the third view is closer to observation and recent research.[29] This is that the improvement of the young child's acquisition of information is a result of his learning to adapt to common ways of categorizing information, replacing his own idiosyncratic means of organizing it with more conventional ones, understood more readily by others. Because it is difficult to gauge the activity of the brain when it is not articulate, and because it is hard to measure the variety of associations that make up thinking, it does not follow that little learning is taking place. The great changes that children go through are the result of learning from the moment they are born. Changes are a sign of adaptability, of attempts to make sense of their environment.

The main interest in theories of development lies in the ways in which people display the ability to grow up into civilized human beings, but these theories also suggest that people do not always fulfil this promise. In Plato's *Republic* the stages of man's development are stages in moral understanding, the first being the optimistic love of clear answers and solutions, a desire for security and an interest in binary opposites (good and bad), the second being excitement with the outer world, with a love of facts and the idea of adventure, the third being the craving for general moral truth and for ordered schemes to which the world should conform, and the last being the ironic stage, realizing the imperfect nature of the world and forgiving even oneself as well as others.[30] In such developmental terms some people never achieve more than a hardening into the second or third stages. In such terms the uses of learning are as important as learning itself.

The problem with dealing with learning as simple development is that people might pass through phases but might equally return to earlier ones. Thus, when Bowlby talks about the need for the infant to establish a relationship with a clearly defined person, and cites the mother, he leaves out the fact that such a relationship remains important in different ways, and that 'bonding' to the parent is only one sign of it.[31] The differences between the constant and present attention and the ability to maintain an awareness of the relationship in her absence are clear enough, but we need to understand more about the long-lasting needs for such relationships that transcend the immediate presence. The needs of children at particular ages are important because they have a wider significance and reveal universal needs rather than passing ones. Even Gesell's meticulous observations of children's development reiterated certain states that are always there in some form or another.[32] The tension between equilibrium and disequilibrium is observed in different guises at different stages in the norms that Gesell sets out. Parents observe the difficulties their children go through at particular ages, but all the time the troubled and optimistic forces go hand in hand, and every stage contains inward looking and outward looking tendencies. Both instincts are there, but one might dominate the other for a time. In the balance of self-centredness and disinterestedness the five-year-old is a preliminary version of the adult.[32] Interest in collecting different things goes through various guises, from collecting drawings, Christmas cards, postcards or dolls, to collecting stamps or cars, but all are part of the same manifestation of learning, in the accumulation of facts and the instinct to possess.

When we observe the different phases of learning that people go through, we see both a definite progression and the possibility that some never reach the later stages. The need to acquire some framework in which to understand the world is true of all people; and all accumulate a mass of information. But some never seem to go beyond seeing the world in very biased simplified terms; others never seem even to achieve that. Such a sense of development, however, is characteristic of all learning, of learning a new subject or new facts and new ideas. The first, necessary, attempts to fit information into a simplified personal framework are followed by the realization that the mass of disorganized facts is too complex for any simple order. This is followed by a sense of lucidity, as order is brought to bear on the complex material. Only when there is a real grasp of the new material is there a sense of its simplicities and its ambiguities, its formal generalization and its connection to a variety of other subjects.

Some principles of learning remain both constant and universal. Osgood [33] suggested that there are shared semantic networks that people all over the world define through synonyms and antonyms, a system of meaning through the concepts of evaluation, potency and activity.[34] We can accept the differences that languages suggest, the metaphors for understanding that provide a way of perceiving the world, without assuming that learning is fundamentally different according to circumstances. The developmental aspects of learning are *always* apparent; and it is the process of learning, in all its activity, that makes development interesting. The desire for order and the desire for exploration, the need for security and the need for guessing, the realization that there is a whole world to explore and the perception that the way the world is communicated is perpetually limiting, are all principles of learning that grow and change, but do not disappear. Learning is an active process, a constant engagement with the environment and with other people. It depends on all kinds of relationships, including the relationship with oneself. It can develop or decay. It is necessary but never automatic. To understand how children learn is to understand something about the excitement and curiosity of being human.

REFERENCES AND NOTES

1 Cullingford, C. *Children and Television*. Aldershot: Gower, 1984, Chap. 14, pp. 119–132.

2 Advertising Standards Authority *British Code of Advertising Practice*. London, 1976.

3 Kant, I. *Kritik der Reinen Vernunft*, Riga, 1781. Analytic truth is that which is always true, like 'mothers are female'; synthetic truth refers to what could be, like 'old people are physically inactive'. Quine, however, points out that there is no fixed borderline, i.e. 'chairs have legs'.

4 J.L. Austin remarked that even in the worst examples of misuse words are still 'accurate' for more than 90 per cent of the time.

5 Davies, B. *Life in the Classroom and Playground: The Accounts of Primary School Children*. London: Routledge & Kegan Paul, 1982.

6 Much of the original material in this book is based on children's answers

to a variety of questions, as well as on observation. There is, however, no
space here to tabulate all the answers that they gave, nor all the circumstances in which children were observed.

7 See, for example, Murray, L. and Trevarthen, C. 'The infant's role in
mother–infant communications'. *Journal of Child Language*, **13** (1), 15–29,
1986; and Kuzmak, S. and Gelman, R. 'Young children's understanding
of random phenomena'. *Child Development*, **57**, 559–556, 1986.

8 See for example, Taylor, L. and Mullan, B. *Uninvited Guests: The Intimate
Secrets of Television and Radio*. London: Chatto and Windus, 1986. The
children tended to say 'don't know', rather than answer the question –
until they felt confident.

9 Geert, P. van *The Development of Perception, Cognition and Language*. London:
Routledge and Kegan Paul, 1983.

10 Davies, B. 'Children through their own eyes'. *Oxford Review of Education*,
10 (3), 275–292, 1984.

11 Bowey, J.A., Tunmer, W.E. and Pratt, C. 'Development of children's
understanding of the metalinguistic term *word*'. *Journal of Educational
Psychology*, **73** (3), 500–512, 1984.

12 Loveland, K.A. 'Learning about points of view: spatial perspective the
acquisition of "I/you"'. *Journal of Child Language*. **11** (3), 535–556, 1984.

13 Taylor, M. and Flavell, J.H. 'Seeing and believing: children's understanding of the distinction between appearance and reality'. *Child Development*, **55** (5), 1710–1720, 1984.

14 Flavell, J.H., Flavell, E.L. and Green, F.L. 'Development of the appearance–reality distinction'. *Cognitive Psychology*, **5**, 95–120, 1983.

15 Richards, D.D. and Siegler, R.S. 'The effects of task requirements on
children's life judgements'. *Child Development*, **55** (5), 1687–1696, 1984.

16 Gold, L.J., Darley, J.M. and Hilton, J.L. 'Children's perceptions of
procedural justice'. *Child Development*, **55** (5), 1752–1759, 1984.

17 Speece, M.W. and Brent, S.B. 'Children's understanding of death: a
review of three components of a death concept'. *Child Development*, **55** (5),
1671–1686, 1984.

18 Pollard, A. *The Social World of the Primary School*. London: Holt, Rinehart
and Winston, 1985; and Sluckin, A. *Growing up in the Playground*. London:
Routledge and Kegan Paul, 1981.

19 Brophy, J.E. 'Research on the self-fulfilling prophecy and teacher expectations'. *Journal of Educational Psychology*, **75** (5), 631–661, 1983.

20 Siegal, M. *Fairness in Children: A Social-cognitive Approach to the Study of Moral
Development*. London: Academic Press, 1982. In a very careful summary he
overturns many of the standard Piagetian notions.

21 Whether at home – Tizard, B. and Hughes, M. *Young Children Learning*.
London: Fontana, 1984 – or in pre-school, as in G. Wells's study in
Bristol, or in other programmes – such as the High/Scope Educational
Research Foundation work started by Weikart (Weikart, D., Berrueta-

Clement, J., Schweinhart, L., Barnett, S., Epstein, Λ. and Weikart, D. *Changed Lives*. Michigan: High/Scope Press, Ypsilanti, 1984) – the same essential findings emerge.

22 For the theories of disinhibition, imitation and desensitization applied to television violence, sometimes with a 5 per cent correlation between the stimulus and the response, in laboratory conditions, and attempts to isolate a variable and test it, see Rowland, W.D. Jr. *The Politics of TV Violence: Policy Uses of Communication Research*. Beverly Hills: Sage, 1983; and Cullingford, C. *Children and Television*, Aldershot: Gower, 1984.

23 See Rotman, B. *Jean Piaget: Psychologist of the Real*. Brighton: Harvester Press, 1977; and Brown, G. and Desforges, C.W. 'Piagetian psychology and education: time for revision'. *British Journal of Educational Psychology*, **47** (1), 7–17, 1977.

24 Bryant, P.E. 'Piaget, teachers and psychologists'. *Oxford Review of Education*, **10** (3), 251–259, 1984. He also questions why teachers, of all people, have allowed Piagetian ideas to become an educational orthodoxy.

25 Piatellie-Palmarini, M. *Language and Learning: The Debate between Jean Piaget and Noam Chomsky*. London: Routledge and Kegan Paul, 1980.

26 For example, Donaldson, M. *Children's Minds*. London: Fontana/Croom Helm, 1978.

27 But see Furth, H.G. and Wachs, H. *Thinking Goes to School: Piaget's Theory in Practice*. New York: Oxford University Press, 1974.

28 Nelson, K.J. 'The organisation of free recall by young children'. *Journal of Experimental Child Psychology*, **8** (2), 284–295, 1969.

29 Egan, K. *Education and Psychology: Plato, Piaget and Scientific Psychology*. New York: Teachers College Press, 1983.

30 Cornford, F.M. (ed.) Plato's *The Republic*, book 6, 509–511; 'Eckasia; pistis; dianoia and noesis'. Oxford: Oxford University Press, 1937.

31 Bowlby, J. *Child Care and the Growth of Love*. Harmondsworth: Penguin, 1964.

32 Gesell, Λ., Ilg, F. and Ames, L.B. *The Child from Five to Ten*. New York: Harper and Row, 1946; new edition 1977.

33 Osgood, C.E., Suei, G.J. and Tannenbaum, P.H. *The Measurement of Meaning*. Urbana: University of Illinois Press, 1957.

34 Compare to Whorf's linguistic relativism where culture is shaped by the vocabulary available. The two points of view actually cohere.

CHAPTER 1
The First Stages of Learning

> The *great* snare of the psychologist is the *confusion of his own standpoint with that of the mental fact* about which he is making his report.
>
> William James, *The Principles of Psychology*, Vol. 1

Advances in scientific knowledge have given us significant insights into the functioning of the human mind. We know how the brain is constructed and how brain cells grow and decay. We understand the nervous system and know how to replace parts of the body as well as how to repair them. But the more we know about the human organism the more such knowledge contrasts with how little we know about how and why the mind develops as it does. We know about our bodies. We know how to dissect. We can trace the patterns of the brain. But we know comparatively little about what takes place inside the mind. As we develop the power to manipulate cells through biotechnology, and analyse ever more intricate and microscopic parts, from cells to particles and from particles to quarks, the sense of the miraculous, of the unknown, is in no way diminished. The age-old questions remain. What makes individuals different from each other; what gives human beings the ability to think, and what is the connection between language and thought? We still derive as much from self-knowledge and through speculation as we do from science. Close observation has increased the sense of the unknown by making us reconsider general assumptions about the development of learning.

The remarkable increases in biological knowledge have revealed some of the most significant facts in our understanding of the inner worlds of human beings. The study of the organism has clarified the fact that growth is responsive, dependent in part on engagement with the environment and not merely a simple vegetable matter of cells increasing and dividing. The sense of wonder at the development of human beings begins at the point where we recognize that in the most inner region of life, beyond the structures of cells, there is a clear, if mute, consciousness. From the first moments of growth the human organism is not merely a dependent nervous system but a creature that is reacting to and engaged with, as well as relying on, the security of its surroundings. All measurements and observations of babies, and of life in the womb, show how personal and specific is the individual response to sound or movement.[1]

The relationship between the inside and the outside of the womb is a close one. The obvious shock of the baby's sudden entry into the world and the transfer from one form of breathing to another mark a great change. But many of the new sensations, of air, temperature, sight and sound, are developments of what had already been taking place inside the warm spaces of the womb. There are differences between premature or late babies which continue throughout the first year of life. Such differences can be shown through the testing of visual recognition.[2] The baby's ability to discriminate between shapes depends as much on the age from conception as on the amount of time from birth. All the work that was carried out on the conditioned reflex by Pavlov and others is really concerned with these early, most basic responses. Every refinement of the idea of 'conditioning', the influence of the environment on the individual, makes the concept less and less a simple matter of automatic reflex. From the earliest notions of 'imprinting' – the fact that a lamb will follow the first moving object it sees on the assumption that it is its mother – through to the complexities of memory, the study of the simplest form of learning reveals how varied such 'conditioning' is. Pavlov's notions of the conditioned reflex include four different levels.[3] These are the 'impellant', when a baby copies a gesture like clapping hands, the 'inhibitory', when the baby continues an action it has started, the 'regulatory', when the child makes an action according to a signal, and finally 'self-regulation'. The work of Skinner and other behaviourists, far from proving an automatic reaction to external stimuli, actually shows how individually and idiosyncratically people respond.[4] The notion of 'operant' conditioning recognizes the individual's power to determine his reactions.

Advances in technology give us the means to monitor the inside of the body and to measure minute changes. It is through the identification of electrical charges in the brain (EEGs) that we know that each individual has a different brain pattern, even more distinctive than fingerprints.[5] Sometimes these brain patterns are called alpha waves; they show the activity of the mind behind physical expression or consciousness. These patterns are clearly recordable in three-month-old babies and are at their maximum, in terms of frequency, by the age of ten.[6] They reveal not only distinctions between people but also clear patterns of response between different types of people, between those who have more tactile perceptions and those with a gift for visual imagery. Different kinds of consciousness are shown in the study of the two hemispheres of the brain, in which the ancient dichotomies, between the intellectual and the sensuous, the explicit and the tacit, the verbal and the spatial, the rational and the intuitive, are already apparent.[7] The left side of the brain is more concerned with logic and analysis, with linear, sequential arguments. The right hemisphere is associated with synthesis, with the visual rather than the verbal, with recognition and with imagery.[8]

The richness of activity in the brain is shown through the universality of dreaming, when for two hours each night the mind continues to function, to associate and connect ideas. Even if dreams are not a form of 'unlearning' they are closely connected to the realities of wakeful experience.[9] Very young babies appear to dream; they already have a store of active ideas that might seem shapeless because of the impossibility of explaining them but are a distinct feature of their perception of the world. At a level of consciousness that can be observed in infants, one can see the complex mixture of capacities that marks each one as an individual. Children come into the world already thinking and responding. They are by no means the helpless, unthinking creatures that they might sometimes seem to be.

To the baby the world is massively confusing. The sounds, smells, touches and sights seem like a series of meaningless impressions. Only a few sensations, like the sound of the human voice, stand out with any distinction. The first condition of learning is to know which part of the confusing complexity needs to be singled out from the rest. To the baby the difficulty is knowing what particular part of the detailed world to select for attention. Imagine, for a moment, all the different impressions babies receive when they first enter the world of sight. There are different shapes, moving and still, as well as bright lights, different colours and objects varying in clarity according to distance, the sudden closeness of a face and the intervening emptiness of space. The information is too complex to comprehend until a child gradually learns to discriminate between one object and another. If we listen for a moment to the world about us, wherever we are, we become aware of all the sounds that we habitually ignore when we are concentrating on a book; the sound of the wind in the trees, the aeroplane droning overhead, the fly on the window pane, the radio next door, the ticking of the clock, the shuffling of feet in the library, or the distant whispered conversation. They are there all the time, but we learn to ignore them until a sound that makes sense to us – a name or a bell – rouses us from our auditory privacy. To a baby every sound is equal in meaning until he perceives some as more significant than others.

The first activities that babies undertake are the mental ones of trying to make perceptual sense of a confusing world. It is especially difficult for them because the different senses are linked, and the imagery of one sense is aroused by the sensations of another, rather as when the taste of sweets is influenced by their colour. Children begin with difficulty in discriminating between shapes or sounds, not only in terms of their outlines but also in terms of colour or loudness. Perception is a process of analysis: the ability to synthesize experience and reconstruct meaning from it.

Perception depends not on what is seen but on how we interpret it. We can chose to look at a Neckar cube (Figure 1) in one of two

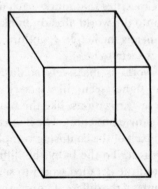

Figure 1

ways, seeing the front either at the top left hand side or at the bottom right, and we can shift our perception at will. Our perception depends so much on our experience that we find it very difficult to see the two horizontal lines of Figure 2 as being the

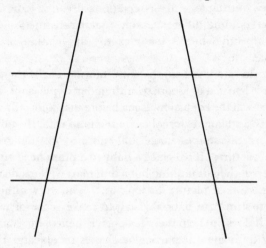

Figure 2

same length. We find it difficult to overcome our knowledge of perspective, having seen train lines narrow into the distance, and cannot easily unlearn our experience. The very first refinements to thinking take place as babies discriminate between perceptual clues and as they perceive the significance of what is seen. The need to categorize is already revealed in their perception, both of things that move and of things that stay still.

It was once assumed that new-born babies were unable to see. But we know that adaptation to their visual surroundings takes place from the moment they open their eyes, even before they learn the skill of focusing on particular objects. Their curiosity in inspecting the face of the parent holding them is intense and sustained. Their first visual responses might be unselective but they are nevertheless attempts to make sense of what they see. Even in adult perception there are ambiguities: the emergence of a figure from a background is not seen at a particular instant that can be measured but depends on the analysis made by the observer, as in a film where a picture is gradually brought into focus.[10] To a baby the world consists of such moments, working out the significant from the general background. Perception is a matter of making sense of the rules of discrimination. It can be 'synthetic', putting together associations already made, or 'analytic', understanding differences and making distinctions. Perception is subjective but it includes the application of previous experience.

The world of a child throbs with information of the kind that adults have learned to ignore. Children derive pleasure, as well as difficulty, from the confusion. Long before they know the words for the objects, and long before they understand what the objects are, even before the shapes make any sense at all, children enjoy looking at pictures. If we place a baby in a pram he is much more likely to cry if there is nothing but a dull matt wall inside the pram than if there is a picture to look at.[11] The very difficulties of perception stimulate babies to try to make sense of what they perceive; it does not help them to deprive them of the complexities by trying to single out particular shapes or objects. The more stimulation a baby receives, the better, and there are few means at our disposal for deliberately concentrating on certain shapes, colours or sounds. Although we often assume that primary colours are easier to perceive than others, even they need three dimensions to be distinguished from each other: line, saturation and lightness. For a baby the first obvious discriminations are between black and white.[12] Some colours are of greater salience than others, a colour like red being a particular attraction. But colours that seem like 'solid' representations are very difficult to discriminate from the perception of contours, since objects stand out from each other through the different gradients of brightness, one of the facets of colour. Light and shade can imply both differences in the actual surfaces, as in a painting, and differences between one shape or distance and another, as in the differences between shadow or depth.

If the complexities of perception are difficult to explain it is partly because language has taught us more about classification, about symbols and types, than about the ambiguities of things that cannot be 'placed'. Language helps us to simplify our perceptions by enabling us to make generalizations. We understand that a 'chair' is still a chair however varied its manifestations. The word does not refer to a single object but to a group or class of objects, and thus helps us to categorize the world into manageable proportions. Even before a child possesses language he has to learn to perceive the similarities and distinctions of his surroundings. He learns to detect, to recognize and to discriminate and by doing so learns the relationship between himself and other parts of his world, and the relationship of parts of the world to each other.

Even before the perceived world is simplified into meaning, the chaos of what is experienced is itself fascinating. The more varied the stimuli the more attention they attract. Babies spend more time looking at pictures that are complex than at more simple ones, even if they are specially designed for them.[13] Irregularity of material or shape and incongruity fascinate like a puzzle. Before the time when perception depends on expectations of what we *wish* to perceive, before we control what we see by our anticipations and previous knowledge, the visual world is relished for its inchoate complexity. The most difficult things to see are those that move and yet it is movement itself that first stimulates the brain, for only the more sophisticated animals can perceive meaning in the absence of movement.[14] While babies notice the distractions of movement they also learn to perceive the uses of movement. Their understanding of the visual world is not based only on the dimensions of shape but on the actions about it, the use to which the visual units are put.[15] Objects are understood by the circumstances in which they are seen. It is through the repetition of certain experiences that a picture of the world is built up. Infants find their own ways of making sense of what they see, and can find themselves in difficulties by the very sophistication with which they come to guess at what are consistent rules.

The use of other perceptual clues than analysis of general shape can be seen in infants' reactions to faces. They are helped in their recognition of faces by movement, by changes in expression and particularly by contrasts in movement.[16] But their interest in activity is matched by their ability to imitate adult gestures, such as opening and closing the mouth or sticking out the tongue.[17] It is more difficult for them to discriminate between static objects since they notice the edges of objects before they see the image as a whole, and look for any visual stimulations such as movement to

21

react to before they learn that a smile is a signal of an expectation of their reaction.

Babies make sense of the visual world not only by classifying shapes into meaning, but also by learning to make sense of the functions of shape. They learn the distinctive uses and features of faces, of apples, of trees, and also learn the various representations of objects. They learn to see the distinction between the picture of a dog and the real thing, just as they learn that an Alsatian and a Pekinese are both 'dog; that a cuddly toy and a wooden creature on wheels are also referred to in the same way. By the time that 'dog' has a distinct meaning the baby will have learned the nature of objects, of movement and response, of the meaning of the size and change of shapes. He will know that an object getting larger implies that it is getting closer, and wince at a ball coming towards him. He will know that to crawl over what looks like a ledge should be avoided, whatever the temptation of the other side, and even if he feels the glass that is there to protect him. In one famous experiment a child is placed on a 'visual cliff', a device which through the use of glass is actually safe but appears to consist of a sheer drop. Even the parent cannot tempt the child to cross it.[18] As

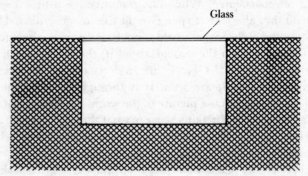

Glass

Figure 3

we learn to recognize those characteristics that define particular objects we also learn to impose our own sense of order and meaning on what we see. We construct the world through our perception of it.

The difficulties that babies face lie in their interpretation of what they see. Babies are apt to find significance and fascination in shapes or shadows which to us, later, are mere backgrounds to, or at the edge of, the matter that concerns us. Babies slowly learn to recognize the significance of distance and the visual clues, like edges, that mark out an object in the foreground from its background. Their fascination with complicated shapes is the fascination of learning to interpret, as they gradually learn to make increasingly sophisticated distinctions between light and shade and between different textures. The more we have stored in our minds the less what is newly perceived seems to impinge on what is already there. Clear memories for a selection of significant personal experiences or for important facts means that an hour during the day in the middle of last week becomes rather hazy as an experience, and we are not able to bring to mind even a few of the sensations, or the visual memories of that hour. This is not just because of the difficulties of remembering, but because, even at the time, our minds concentrated on the tasks we were performing rather than on the sensations of heat and light or the familiar place in which we spent that hour. When the world is new, everything that is perceived makes a similar impression. It might not be understood, it might not be placed in a familiar context, but it accumulates to build up the information from which babies create their own impressions of the world. Preceding the capacity to make sense of an item and store it in the memory, there is the moment when new information is immediately perceived and recorded.

The subtleties and ambiguities in the visual world are matched by those in the world of sounds, and are equally complicated for those unaccustomed to account for them. The almost permanent background noises, the almost untraceable sounds that pervade the air, with varying strength and direction, gradually fade from significance. Each sound gradually becomes sorted out by attachment to its source. The baby learns to associate sound with meaning, like the sound of the mother's heartbeat, as well as the distinction between sounds that refer to things and sounds that are made by things. And while visual perception is immediate, and visual memory complex, auditory perception depends even more on the ability to pick out a particular sound from the rest. It also depends on sequences. Babies respond to all sound differences, even though they soon learn that some, like the sound of voices, are more significant than others.[19] Before they appreciate the complexities of meaning they learn that human voices, especially those of the parents, are significant. They very quickly learn not only to be aware of the differences between sounds but also to choose which sounds to listen to. Anyone listening to two sounds at once automatically chooses to concentrate on only one of them.[20] If one sound (the voice of someone talking to us, for example) is not obviously more significant than another, the first sound that is heard remains the one on which the ears concentrate, despite other subsequent sounds, which are treated like mere interruptions.[21] But once the interruption interferes with the first sound in such a way that the mind becomes conscious of it, then it is difficult to revert to the previously perfect concentration on the earlier sound.[22]

When babies listen to the sound of the voice it is the tone, the distinctive timbre, that is most important to them; the voice is heard not as a projection of language but as a consistent type of sound. We are so used to language that we do not realize how many different sounds create the words we hear. But what we hear depends on our knowledge of the segments that make up language: we know a 'd' exists, although it cannot be recorded acoustically by itself, since it can only be heard together with a vowel following it.[23] The 'd' in 'di' or 'du' seems to us to be the same conventional phoneme but is actually a different kind of sound. To babies, as to adults first hearing a foreign language, all words seem to be part of a continuous sound without beginnings or ends. Gradually they learn to perceive the significance of some sounds and some types of sound and extract increasingly significant familiarities from the rest.

In all the accounts of perceptual learning there is agreement about the fact that children are immediately and actively engaged in coming to terms with their surroundings, in making meaning out of the mass of details. Perception is never possible without some means of organizing what is received. However babies learn to perceive, whether we describe it in terms of learning probable cues,[24] through subconscious inference, through an active constructive process or through a series of hypotheses,[25] they are not merely passive recipients of information. Nor can their perception be differentiated from their thinking abilities. It is sometimes assumed that perception and intellectual processes are distinct from each other; they are usually described separately. But for babies the two processes cohere and depend on each other. There are a number of ways in which babies learn how to perceive what is significant, through their improving sense of discrimination, by associating particular responses and through the detection of patterns and distinctive features. Learning comes about through the perception of similarities and differences, at first learning to discriminate and then learning to categorize. The process is not just a matter of increasing refinement and awareness of different visual factors but also a matter of knowing what to ignore and what information to discard.

One of the most distinctive features of the early development of babies is their responsiveness to the sensations around them, both to the sounds and to the sights. The body responds to all changes in the environment; it is not just a 'product' of the environment but is fully engaged with it.[26] A baby concentrates all his resources on the perception of new stimulation, not in passive reception but with curiosity. He attunes his senses to the world. The fact that the baby is not articulate, that he does not immediately know which parts of the rich environment to ignore, does not mean that he is insensible or incapable. The richness of sensations far surpasses the ability to isolate those elements that are significant.

Many of the developments of the mind take place at a level of the subconscious; and they begin early. Whether children are responding deliberately, carefully, attentively or sequentially, they are all 'constructing' their idea of the world.[27] They are learning to discriminate, are looking for distinctive features, are learning to grade what they see and hear and feel. They begin to learn to make distinctions when the differences are obvious, and gradually learn to fit new features into those already familiar. In all these developments they are helped, often unawares, by their parents. But for the most part they are helping themselves.

NOTES AND REFERENCES

1 See Carmichael, L. 'Onset and early development of behaviour'. In Mussen, P.H. (ed.) *Carmichael's Manual of Child Psychology*. New York: Wiley, 1970.

2 Rose, S.A. 'Differential rates of visual information processing in full-term and pre-term infants'. *Child Development*, **45** (5), 1189–1198, 1983.

3 Pavlov, I.P. *Conditioned Reflexes: An Investigation of the Physiological Activity of the Cerebral Cortex*. London: Oxford University Press, 1927. See also Luria, A.R. *Cognitive Development: Its Cultural and Social Foundations*. Cambridge, MA: Harvard University Press, 1976.

4 Skinner, B.F. *Verbal Behaviour*. Englewood Cliffs, NJ: Prentice-Hall, 1957.

5 Shute, H. 'Underlying factors in reading success and failure'. *Aston Educational Enquiry Monograph No. 3*. Birmingham: Aston University, 1976.

6 Ellingson, R.J. 'The study of brain electrical activity in infants.' In Lipsitt, L.P. and Spiker, C.C. *Advances in Child Development and Behavior* Vol. 3. New York: Academic Press, 1967.

7 See the work of Polanyi, M. *The Tacit Dimension*. London: Routledge and Kegan Paul, 1967.

8 Ornstein, R.E. *The Psychology of Consciousness*, 2nd edition. New York: Harcourt Brace Jovanovich, 1977.

9 Crick, F. and Mitchison, G. 'The function of dream sleep'. *Nature*, 111–114, 14 July 1983.

10 Vernon, M.D. *The Psychology of Perception*. Harmondsworth: Penguin, 1962.

11 Kagan, J., Kearsley, R. and Zelazo, P.C. *Infancy: Its Place in Human Development*. Cambridge, MA: Harvard University Press, 1978.

12 Bornstein, M.H., Kessen, W. and Weiskopf, S. 'The categories of hue in infancy'. *Science*, **191**, 201–202, 1976.

13 See McCall, R.B. and Kagan, J. 'Attention in the infant: effects of complexity, contour, perimeter and familiarity'. *Child Development*, **38**, 939–952, 1967.

14 Berlyne, D.E. 'The influence of complexity and novelty in visual figures in orienting responses. *Journal of Experimental Psychology*, **55**, 289–296, 1958.

15 Gregory, R.L. *Eye and Brain: The Psychology of Seeing*. London: Weidenfeld and Nicholson, 1966; and Gregory, R.L. *The Intelligent Eye*. London: Weidenfeld and Nicholson, 1970.

16 Nelson, C.A. and Horowitz, F.D. 'The perception of facial expressions and stimulus motion by two and five-month old infants using holographic stimuli'. *Child Development*, **54** (4), 868–877, 1983.

17 Meltzoff, A.M. and Moore, M.K. 'Newborn infants imitate adult facial gestures'. *Child Development*, **54** (3), 702–709, 1983.

18 Gibson, E.J. *Principles of Perceptual Learning and Development*. Englewood Cliffs, NJ: Prentice-Hall, 1969.

19 Condon, W.S. and Sanders, L.W. 'Neonate movement is synchronised with adult speech: interactional participation and language acquisition'. *Science*, **183**, 99–101, 1974.

20 Broadbent, D.E. *Perception and Communication*. Oxford: Pergamon, 1958.

21 Lindsey, P.H. and Norman, D.A. *An Introduction to Psychology*. New York: Academic Press, 1972.

22 Bruner, J.S. *Beyond the Information Given: Studies in the Psychology of Knowing*. London: G. Allen and Unwin, 1974.

23 Macginitie, W.H. 'Children's understanding of linguistic units'. In Samuels, S.J. (ed.), *What Research Has to Say about Reading Instruction*. Newark, NJ: International Reading Association, 1978.

24 Brunswick, W.E. *Perception and the Representative Design of Psychological Experiments*. Berkeley: University of California Press, 1956.

25 Bruner, J.S. *The Process of Education*. Cambridge, MA: Harvard University Press, 1960.

26 Sokolov, Y.N. *Perception and the Conditioned Reflex*. Oxford: Pergamon, 1963.

27 Neisser, U. *Cognitive Psychology*. New York: Appleton-Century-Crofts, 1967.

CHAPTER 2
Making Sense of Information

Could the young but realize how soon they will become mere walking
bundles of habits, they would give more heed to their conduct while in the
plastic state. We are spinning our own fates, good or evil, and never to be
undone.

William James, *The Principles of Psychology*, Vol. 1

The world is crowded with sights and sounds, with images and
with associations, most of which we deliberately ignore. No one
likes to be over-loaded with information, whatever form it is
presented in, whether it comes on screens or whether it derives
from the restless imagination of a sleepless night. For the most part
we control what we perceive by concentrating on the particular,
and march straight to the point. When we observe young children,
however, we see how much more intense is every sensation they
derive from what they do, we see how every time they walk they
demonstrate elements of adventure, as they meander on the way
noticing something new and momentarily important. They do not
walk with almost mechanical precision towards the task they have
in mind, like adults, but stop on the way to inspect something or
try out a new way of walking or test the sensations of their legs.
They are demonstrating physically the variety of excitements that
babies experience in perception. They are still expressing their
exploration of the physical and mental experiences available in the
world.

Infants have little choice but to be amazed by all the sensations
that bombard them, but they are not completely helpless in a mass
of information. The first engagement of the infant with his surroundings is the response of a human being naturally equipped
with the power of organizing what is perceived. The infant is
'shaped' but not 'constricted' by the circumstances he is in[1] since
the stimulation of objects seen and heard causes more than merely
automatic reactions. The infant immediately attempts to make
sense of what is seen, heard and felt, even if he does not know how.
The relationship between the cognitive power of infants' percep-

tual judgements and the information presented to them is such a close one that it is impossible to separate their capacity to organize from the quality of information to which they respond.[2]

The ability to make sense of the environment is not a purely ratiocinative one. Infant thought processes are complicated by associative reactions, by guesses as well as logic, through experiment, analogies and mistakes. These are abilities that are unrecordable in terms of intelligence measurement.[3] Freud's analysis of what takes place in these subconscious levels of thinking reminds us of the importance of such explorations and their power to influence what happens later.[4] The concepts of fixation and regression are especially helpful in explaining how thought can be driven by forces beyond the purely 'rational'. The idea of 'fixating' on a particular personal concern to the exclusion of everything else, so that even everyday reality is transformed, has reverberations for all learning. The possibility of regressing, of returning to earlier modes of thought and understanding, is a continual fact of learning.

The fact that children remember and interpret what they observe from an early age is demonstrated in the way in which they will surprise us years later, in their more articulate days, with details they can only have experienced before their ability to communicate. Sometimes such interpreted memories can be disturbing, as revealed by children suffering from psychiatric problems through the suppression of fears and memories. We sometimes see demonstrated the power of misinterpretation in children's reactions to television. A silent movie that ends with the classic slapstick of custard pies being thrown across tables on to people's faces can look to a one-and-a-half-year-old like a horror movie of faces suddenly changing shape and colour. The need to interpret as well as observe has all kinds of unforeseen bad effects, as well as good ones.

Even the behaviourist tradition, which suggests that the important influence of the environment is a measurable commodity, explores 'drives' as well as 'habits'. Human beings not only possess the ability to add, through experience, to known associations, as if they were a template on which each new layer of sensation makes an impression, but are also creatures of strong urges.[5] While these strong drives, or fixations, might emerge from the early influences of their surroundings, they are not merely impressions of their surroundings, and like all emotions and all subconscious processes, remain powerful.

Infants learn how to make shapes out of the dense confusion of impressions.[6] They categorize what is observed and gradually learn to see the world as a series of expected clues, where all the details fall into place. They learn to see similarities and differences in objects from cars to animals through their shape, their size or their sound.[7] They learn how various objects relate to each other, and how to relate to each one in turn.[8] While defining objects in terms of shape or size is one form of discrimination, understanding the way that they function, especially in relation to themselves, is another.[9] A cup is still a cup, whatever its size, and is used in a particular way. A horse, whether in a picture, cartoon or photograph, consists of a variety of colours and sizes, but tends to be defined in certain stances that reflect the movement of actual life.

Categories rarely have well defined boundaries[10] until the accepted conventions of language are learned; the distinctions between a Pekinese and an Alsation and between a picture and a wildly energetic puppy are subsumed within the category of 'dog', and the word 'cat' covers not only the Persian or tabby varieties, but also an even larger family of wild animals. These conventions are not just a matter of nomenclature. If we understand the difficulties of discriminating between different pictures of the same object we will see how hard it is to relate exactly what it is that makes one different from another. To understand the distinctiveness of categories infants need to presuppose, to guess, to select certain elements to encode and to choose what details to look out for. They have to guess which elements to exclude from their analysis.[11] The difficulty they face is not being able to analyse automatically the distinction between the details and the whole. They do not automatically know how to isolate the general structure from the shapes that make it up.[12] Infants gradually adjust to their unfamiliar surroundings by their realization of the permanence of some things, through their reappearance. They also learn through 'habituation', their orientating reaction to stimuli, the relationship between their own movements and sense of direction and their surroundings. At first their reactions to events are more immediate and clear than they later become when they reflect on them, for they learn to recognize and tune in to what is familiar. At the age of one to one-and-a-half, for example, some infants are better at reproducing the sounds of words than they are later, when they try to work out *how* to pronounce sounds with which to communicate.

The first distinctive features that children notice are the differences between the individuality of the unique, such as faces or the tone of a voice, and the general familiarity of shapes, such as apples or trees as well as people. It is sometimes supposed that they learn the representations of things, such as words, pictures and letters, later in their development.[13] But very young children do not at first know the difference between real objects and their representations; the picture on the inside of the pram is as full of meanings as any landscape. They slowly learn about the invariable *within* events; faces in different perspectives, or an object looking different but remaining itself whether it is approaching or receding.[14] The dimensions of shapes and the connections between shapes are complexities to infants who need to acquire enough knowledge of the environment to make it manipulable. Children have to learn how many sides an object has, and visual concepts such as 'top' and 'bottom' or 'front' and 'back'. Some features of space are more difficult than others. How many sides, for example, has a ball or an animal? We can reduce every object to four sides, a top and bottom by our knowledge of the terms, but before we have acquired such words there is no such simple logic to complex shapes. Concepts such as 'deep' and 'shallow' or 'thin' and 'thick' are learned later than 'high' and 'low' or 'big' and 'small', reflecting experience and the order in which babies learn to categorize what they perceive.[15]

Infants actively organize what they receive from the stimuli around them, and acquire more efficient ways of doing so through experience. We know that the increasing mastery of the environment comes about not only because of the need to learn how to categorize information, but because of the ability to adapt an idiosyncratic way of seeing the world to a way that is more in tune with the conventions of perception and communication. Infants' capacity to *adapt* lies in their gradual realization that some of the information they receive – in sights and sounds – is less important than others. All individuals have to find their personal associations and their own recollections. There is nothing abstract about this learning. Infants learn by 'analogy', by seeing the conditions that cause similar events, rather than by 'homology', knowing the origins of a particular behaviour.

Observation of the world is a form of interaction with it, but young children like to test their interaction actively in a variety of ways. This is what is meant by 'play'. Play is not only something pleasurable or distracting, but is a means by which children learn more about themselves, more about their manipulative and oral skills, and more about the categories of object, shape, size and colour. Play is a means of mastering, of trying to control and organize. It is itself an early sign that children are actively engaged in learning.[16] This is why children are willing to repeat, and keep on repeating, a similar pattern of events, building up a tower of bricks only to knock it down again.

Play is not just the physical exploration of objects but also a sign of the imagination. While the ability to extend already achieved skills to new limits is one level of play, the exploration of what is *not* yet known is another: a kind of experiment of imagination.[17] Sometimes such imagination – the connection with ideas beyond the task in hand – includes a means of coming to terms with experiences, with re-living events, either traumatic or exciting.[18] Children play to experiment with their surroundings, at first in simple manipulative gestures and later to find out the difference between the real and the fantastic. Play consists of a series of accidents and mistakes as well as a deliberate building up of a task. Children playing ostensibly with bricks or patterns are to some extent already playing with ideas. Children learn what is 'normal' by testing normal events in play; discovering some natural laws we take for granted, such as balance.[19]

Play is also a form of practice demonstrated in infants' systematic imitation of sounds already belonging to their oral experience, or of movements they have already seen and made.[20] Some of the imitations are deliberate, some accidental, but they are all means by which infants create an understanding of the relationship between themselves and their surroundings. Whether play is more concerned with mastery of the body and its manipulative skills or with more imaginative extensions of ideas, it combines both individual and social abilities. Games have many uses, and continue to be important throughout life,[21] but they are especially significant in the early years when they are used directly as a means of understanding.

Play is the most obvious example of children's responses to their environment. They do not play just with building blocks or teddy bears, but with ideas. They play not only with their hands, gradually mastering the delicate skills of balance, but also with sounds, making words as much a toy as their bricks or dolls. Play is an active form of learning, an exploration of all the characteristics that define the world. Some of the play infants undertake is a fairly close version of what they observe in different contexts. They like to tidy some things away, putting a series of cards into a box or building blocks back on to the carriage where they belong. Children's play is systematic, their own version of what they observe and internalize.[22] Play is a child's means of practising the way in which the adult interprets the world – with set tasks and conventional gestures. The child hugging his teddy bear is a form of imitation of the affection he gives and receives.

Play can be interpreted broadly as a means of assimilating observed behaviour by practising the different levels at which adults manipulate their world.[23] Play is both a means of extending the mastery of the body and a way of exploring relationships with others. Play includes the active and the passive, constructional and functional games, and listening to stories and make-believe. Games are both a method of practising and a projection of shared symbols. Play is not arbitrary behaviour but has a sense of purpose; it is a natural part of human behaviour. It is only when our culture divides activities into those that are done without pleasure for a long-term goal, such as working for money, and those that are done for their own sake, for pleasure, that 'play' is associated with a less serious purpose. For young children there are no such divisions. There is no need temporarily to pursue the painful for the sake of an imposed circumstance; nor is there any pain in using their bodies or their brains. The 'work' of exploring the world, of understanding it, is undertaken with great energy, but it is done without a single purpose or the sustained concentration of the mind on one thing at a time. Play combines all the elements that are part of understanding the world. It remains important in individual lives, although, as we become older, so it tends to be more hidden from view, less obviously apparent.[24] For children play is a serious activity, since it allows experiments not only in techniques of thinking and organizing, but also in the understanding and negotiating of rules. Children of four employ rules in play, especially in the absence of teachers. Children of eight tend to bend the rules as they play, but later become almost deferential in their employment of rules, keeping a careful watch on others.

Children's play shows their developing ability to organize their manipulative skills and co-ordinate thought and action. Many of these manipulative gestures might seem wasted, since children have not learned to narrow their concentration so much that unnecessary gestures are excluded. To a learning child the distinction between distraction and the task in hand is not rigid. The experiments with sensations are a means of understanding contrasts. Children understand perceptual contrasts better than they can express them. They learn how to depend on selections of experience. Infants of eighteen months are far better at locating hidden objects, for example, in a natural setting (e.g. under a pillow) when there is a reason for finding them (if they are looking for a toy). Children of 24 months use landmarks (like pieces of furniture) as clues to locate objects.[25]

Children's sense of logic is a necessary condition for their understanding. They classify objects into concepts by testing hypotheses about the relevant facts on which to build up their own classifications.[26] They learn how to perceive the relevant and consistent connection in a mass of material, how to understand, in the linguistic analogy, how a 'mug', which is an object that encompasses a variety of sizes, colours and shapes (as well as more than one meaning), can in some distinct way be separated from a 'cup', which can appear in just as bewildering a variety of shapes, colours and sizes. Discrimination between different clues and attention to the relevant factors is partly a matter of learning what to ignore – such as the shapes on the surface or the different textures. It is also the ability to make analogies, seeing the logic of connections between figures, different shapes, sizes and colours. The connection between a cut apple and a knife, or between wet paper and a bowl of water, demands the capacity to judge relations, to understand the logic of consequences.

A child begins to use inductive logic (seeing the connection between parts of the same fruit, or between the cut paper and a knife) long before he is able to express such reasoning in analytical terms. The first movements of reasoning have a practical dimension but are nevertheless a form of inductive logic. When young children are asked to sort pictures into groups and asked to recall what they have seen afterwards they show the tendency to think in terms of taxonomies, on the basis of categories, such as 'vehicles' or 'animals', rather than in terms of complementary relations, such as 'things a cowboy uses' or 'things to be found on a farm'.[27] But all have a strong sense of the need to understand *some* form of classification that contains a logical basis.

Children's thinking processes develop through choice of which segments of information are most important. Like adults they have to store information in manageable amounts, in organized clusters of interrelated information like cells.[28] The difficulty for children, given a lack of experience of blotting out detail, and given the wealth of fresh material, is to choose *which* cells of information they need to construct. They process information into coherent units by a series of personal associations.[29] Some kind of association between one memory and another, between one experience and another, needs to be made, not as an automatic reaction to stimuli but as an active way of organizing ideas and reflections. It is the inner associations that are made by children that show the flexibility of their thinking process.[30] When Gagné sums up the 'vast amount of experimental evidence' that shows the importance of 'satisfaction to the learner', he is referring not only to the immediate rewards of food and praise, but to the inner satisfactions that children gain in their mastery of understanding.[31] The real rewards are rooted in their mastery over meaning, in mental as well as physical command.

Children's growing understanding of their environment shows even in the mistakes they make, in creating categories of their own invention, just as they apply a grammatical rule they have learned, like the past tense 'ed', to inappropriate words, such as 'hitted'. All people are forced to share a universal set of categories, partly through the use of language, but children have to discover their *own* way of coding their perceptions. The juxtaposition of one interpretation with another causes a *mismatch* not often noted since it is not often expressed. There was a time when it was thought that children could only classify objects in the conventional sense when they were eight,[32] but their ability to classify ideas develops by the age of three, when they can classify objects, for example, according to either their shape or their colour[33]. This is, after all, an extension of what they have learned through perception. Children need to be able to have a sense of categories to perceive the relationships between one object and another and between objects and words. Even their early drawings show a sense of convention, of creating general symbols to mark out types of objects, as well as showing a degree of subconscious self-perception in their relationships to others.[34] However, such manifest categorizations are underlined by the needs of the perception.

To understand the ways in which language functions, children need to perceive which boundaries of sound create the phonemes that make up a language.[35] Categorical perception is also the essence of understanding language. Children's difficulties with experience are partly caused by them not having yet developed the kind of language that can deal with the problems. Language is not only an aid to thinking but also a means of avoiding overload. Language can help to sort out the concepts that are the perceptions of experience so that the concepts can be dealt with, labelled, stored and kept for later attention. Language provides the categories of control and meaning. It is only as children develop language that certain concepts, such as those of quantity or time, make sense. Until they command a language they experience concepts but do not define them. They might understand them but they cannot communicate their understanding. The view that children first understand the concrete and then the abstract is rather misleading. Words help limit definitions; and while the objects to which children apply their minds, such as coloured bricks and beakers, are 'concrete' enough, the concepts they are employing before the limiting power of language comes to their aid are vaguer and more abstract than any verbal category. Language itself derives from a series of conventions based on classifications of sound and meaning. It has been suggested that the 'segmentation of nature is an aspect of grammar. We cut up and organise the spread and flow of events as we do, largely because, through our mother tongue, we are parties to an agreement to do so, not because nature itself is segmented in exactly that way for all to see'[36].

The sense that words give the world meaning by their dependence on a fixed interpretation of characteristics, from generalizations, such as 'tree', to the vaguely specific, like 'ash', and then to the definition of a particularly graceful ash tree in the middle of a field on a farm in the Lake District, is a strong one. The power of language lies not only in the ability to define but also in the power to initiate action through meaning.[37] Children use words as definitions and as games, as the means of initiating action and as the means of sharing reactions, all at the same time. The variety of choice with which children are presented shows in the different levels of associative meanings, for which they possess a representational 'code' stored for use, a referential meaning, which is an association between verbal meaning and imaginative representation of the same object, and also a series of choices of associative meanings. The mental 'code' does not at first dominate all the other possible associations that an object can have. While children need to understand the defined characteristics of different categories, they not only learn greater exactness of definitions, but also learn which associations to discard.

Much learning can be interpreted as a way of narrowing down a range of possibilities, of learning how to concentrate on a particular task. Against such learning, creativity is often likened to a way of doing the opposite, by opening up a fuller and more unusual range of associations. Indeed, one of the most influential theories of creativity has suggested that it consists of the ability to conjure up remote associations, when three different words, such as 'rat', 'blue' and 'cottage', would be joined in their conventional attribution with a word they all relate to: 'cheese'.[38] But these associations are not so much 'remote' or personal as the result of the ability to understand conventions, to know about cottage cheese, or other particular phrases dependent on a shared culture – as in the unconventional use of particular words, such as 'party line' or 'electric chair'. Children's own range of associations is less easily defined, partly because they relish 'misinterpretations' and partly because they are seeking out their own way of approaching the environment.

Chukovsky suggested that, far from being unable to categorize properly, a child is an 'unacknowledged genius of classification, systemization and co-ordination of things'.[39] This is why children love puzzles and mental games, why they love to see set conventions overturned (provided they do not remain broken) and standard views re-interpreted and changed in jokes and stories. Their sense of the normal is made manifest in their excitement in having it upset. Children cling to a clear and certain view of the world, feeling utterly abandoned by what they take to be 'unfair'. At the same time, from the safety of clearly interpreted rules and conventions, they love to explore alternatives. Children's testing of conventional categories, and their need for them, derives from their subconscious realization of how arbitrary and fluid these interpretations can be. Adults take conventions for granted. Children do not. They are therefore jealous for a convention once it is established in their minds. The excitement of turning conventions upside down stems from their strong sense of what is established as conventionally normal.

Children's sense of exploration continues to develop as fast as it does in their drawings. In drawings or paintings they are caught up in the process of interpretation rather than producing an object designed to be recognizable to an adult.[40] The realism of children is not visual but intellectual, their own interpretation of what they know. The relationship between their own drawings and the pictures that they enjoy and interpret is a complex one.[41] They easily recognize the symbols that denote an object like a teddy bear in its presentation as a cartoon or photograph, in colour or black-and-white. But they also explore their own interpretations within that conventional framework. Their acceptance of the general categories of the world does not mean that they are not interpreting it in their own way. There is always a sense in which their need for what is reliable and for order is fostered by their knowledge of the difficulties of their own interpretation.

Young children have their *own* way of seeing the world, which does not always cohere with what they subsequently learn. But this does not imply that they are so caught up with themselves that they are not able to see the world 'as it is'. The world *is*: the child perceives it, but the way the child perceives it is richer, more complex and more difficult than our later more controlled responses. It is also hard to communicate understanding until what one has to communicate is unambiguous enough to have one level of meaning and precise enough for a simple interpretation. It is just as likely for the adult or teacher to be 'egocentric' in their point of view when they are trying so hard to understand what they see and hear.[42] Children see the world differently from adults, not more stupidly. The assumption that children live in an 'unconscious' state, unaware of themselves or the world outside, is undermined by all the evidence that has accumulated over the past few years.[43] Perhaps the frustration of not being able to manipulate young children's responses has led many people to suggest that children are limited in their intelligence. Certainly the desire to put babies through a series of experimental tests as a way of discovering their abilities at different ages is undermined by the difficulties they have in fitting in with the experiments. But when we think of their alternative interests – in new sounds, in the distinctions of tone or in the weight of emotional expectation – we can see why the very fact that children make difficult subjects for experiments says something positive about their abilities, rather than negative.[44]

NOTES AND REFERENCES

1 In terms used by J.S. Bruner in a number of publications.
2 Gibson, E.J. *Principles of Perceptual Learning and Development*. New York: Prentice-Hall, 1969.
3 Wells, B.W.D. *Personality and Heredity*. Harlow: Longman, 1980.
4 Freud, S. *An Outline of Psycho-analysis*. London: Hogarth Press, 1964.
5 Hull, C.L., Felsinger, J.M., Gladstone, A.I. and Yamaguchi, H.G. 'A proposed quantification of habit strength'. *Psychological Review*, **54** (5), 237–254, 1947.
6 Schlesinger, I.M. 'Production of utterances and language acquisition'. In Slobin, D.I. (ed.), *The Ontogenesis of Grammar: A Theoretical Symposium*. New York: Academic Press, pp. 63–101, 1971.
7 Clark, E.V. 'Some aspects of the conceptual basis for first language acquisition'. In Schiefelbusch, R.L. and Lloyd, L.L. (eds), *Language Perspectives: Acquisition, Retardation and Intervention*. Baltimore: University Park Press, pp. 105–128, 1974.
8 Sugarman, S. *Children's Early Thought: Developments in Classification*. Cambridge: Cambridge University Press, 1983.
9 Nelson, K. *Structure and Strategy in Learning to Talk*. Monographs of the

Society for Research in Child Development, No. 38. Chicago: Chicago University Press, 1973.

10 Rosch, E.H. 'On the internal structure of perceptual and semantic categories'. In Moore, T.E. (ed.), *Cognitive Development and the Acquisition of Language*, New York: Academic Press, 1973.

11 Bates, E. *Language and Context: The Acquisition of Pragmatics*. New York: Academic Press, 1976.

12 Vernon, M.D. *The Psychology of Perception*. Harmondsworth: Penguin, 1972.

13 Gibson, E.J. 'The development of perception as an adaptive process'. *American Scientist*, **58** 103–107, 1970.

14 See Gregory, R.L. *The Intelligent Eye*. London: Weidenfeld and Nicholson, 1970.

15 See Neisser, U. *Cognition and Reality*. New York: Appleton-Century-Crofts, 1976.

16 Bruner, J.S. 'Organisation of early skilled action'. *Child Development*, **44**, 1–11, 1973.

17 Piaget, J. *Plays, Dreams and Imitation in Childhood*. London: Routledge and Kegan Paul, 1962.

18 Chukovsky, K. *From Two to Five*. Berkeley: University of California Press, 1963.

19 Piaget, 1962, op. cit.

20 Caillois, R. *Man, Play and Games*. London: Thames and Hudson, 1962; and Huizinga, J. *Homo Ludens: A Study of the Play Element in Culture*. London: Routledge and Kegan Paul, 1942.

21 So much so that Piaget, 1962, op. cit., likens it to an imitation.

22 Roberts, A. *Out to Play: The Middle Years of Childhood*. Aberdeen: Aberdeen University Press, 1980. Roberts suggests that adolescents go on playing but keep their games more private.

23 Vygotsky, L.S. *Language and Thought*. Cambridge, MA: Massachusetts Institute of Technology Press, 1973; Vygotsky, L.S. *Mind in Society*. Cambridge, MA: Harvard University Press, 1978; and Bruner, J.S. *Towards a Theory of Instruction*. Cambridge, MA: Harvard University Press, 1967.

24 Garvey, A. *Play*. London: Open Books, 1977.

25 Bower, T.G.R. *The Perceptual World of the Child*. London: Open Books, 1977.

26 Bruner, J.S., Goodnow, J.J. and Austin, G.A. *A Study of Thinking*. New York: Wiley, 1956.

27 Bjorklund, D.F. and Zaken-Greenberg, F. 'The effects of differences in classification style on pre-school children's memory'. *Child Development*, **52** (3), 888–894, 1981.

28 Miller, G.A., Galanter, E. and Pribram, K.H. *Plans and the Structure of Behaviour*, New York: Holt, Rinehart and Winston, 1960; Miller, G.A.

'The magical number seven, plus or minus two: some limits on our capacity for processing information'. *Psychological Review*, **63** (2) 81–97, 1956; Broadbent, D.E. 'The well-ordered mind'. *American Educational Research Journal*, **3** (4), 281–285, 1966.

29 Yntema, D.B. and Muesner, G.E. 'Remembering the present states of a number of variables'. *Journal of Experimental Psychology*, **60** (1), 18–22, 1960.

30 Gagné, R.M. *The Conditions of Learning*. New York: Holt, Reinhart and Winston, 1965.

31 Ibid., p. 76.

32 Mosker, F.A., and Hornsby, J.R., 'On asking questions', in Bruner, J.S., Olver, R.R., and Greenfield, P.M. (eds), *Studies in Cognitive Growth*. New York: Wiley, 1966.

33 Sugarman, S., 1983, op. cit.

34 See the significance of children's early drawings, in the way they construct a version of the world according to a balance between their own sense of exploration (including paint), their manipulation of symbols and their inner feelings.

35 A phoneme is a unit of sound which is recognizable as carrying a distinct and recognizable meaning in a particular language. |p| is one phoneme in English, but is divided into two in Bengali. In Cantonese there is no distinction between 'l' and 'r'.

36 Whorf, B.L. *Language, Thought and Reality*. Cambridge, MA: Massachusetts Institute of Technology, p. 240, 1956.

37 Austin, J.L. *How to Do Things with Words*. Oxford: Oxford University Press, 1962; and Searle, J.R. *Speech Acts*. Cambridge: Cambridge University Press, 1969.

38 Mednick, S.A. 'The associative basis of the creative process'. *Psychological Review*, **69** (3), 220–232, 1962.

39 Chukovsky, K. *From Two to Five*. Berkeley: University of California Press, p. 104, 1963.

40 Brittain, W.L. *Creativity, Art and the Young Child*. New York: Macmillan, 1979.

41 Compare the fact that children *like* the drawings that they could not create themselves.

42 Leontiev, A.A. 'The heuristic principle in the perception, emergence and assimilation of speech'. In Lenneberg, E.H. and Lenneberg, E. (eds), *Foundations of Language Development: A Multidisciplinary Approach*, Vol. 1. New York: Academic Press, pp. 43–58, 1975.

43 Karmiloff-Smith, A. and Inhelder, B. 'If you want to get ahead, get a theory'. *Cognition*, **3**, 195–212, 1975.

44 Unlike rats they do not make simple, manipulable subjects.

CHAPTER 3
Meanings and Relationships

Sensation ... differs from Perception only in the extreme simplicity of its objects or content.

William James, *The Principles of Psychology*, Vol. 2.

Learning can seem like an almost automatic process. As children become older and gain experience they begin to choose the way in which they will learn and the extent to which they will deliberately try to accumulate new information. They will learn whether to continue applying their minds or whether to rely on reflex. This is the popular distinction between learning as an everyday act, and learning as applied to the set tasks of school, between 'discovery' learning, solving everyday problems of living by experiment and observation, and 'reception' learning, the acquisition of a large body of information.[1] For children the relationship between the two is much closer than for an adult, because of the need to discover the meaning of what they perceive, and because the sense of purpose in learning remains strong.

Learning can seem automatic, and learning can be learned, with great diligence, but it is never a simple matter of addition or accretion. This is not because of different capabilities in different people. It is more a matter of whether the individual has learned *not* to learn. Unlearning, the discarding or ignoring of evidence, is one of the most powerful tools of the mind at any age. We see it in politicians seeking anecdotes to support a belief, we see it every day in those who will not recognize the consequences of their actions, but the seeds of subsequent uses or misuses of learning are sown in young children. The choice of reflecting on or ignoring experience can be made the moment children first enter into relationships, the moment they need to reflect on how others react to them.

Some information is acquired for its own sake but much information accumulates whether we like it or not. Differences between 'rote' learning, the almost mechanical memorizing of new material, and 'meaningful' learning are not distinct to young children. At first the child needs to use both 'representational' learning, the meanings of single symbols such as words, and 'propositional' learning, the understanding of composite ideas. This is why there has been so much argument about the capacity of children to take in more than one idea at a time. Whether the argument concludes that children can process and recall three items of information at once or seven items, children need to make judgements about what is learned, to choose which items contain meaning worth remembering.[2] Information is, of course, rarely presented to children in such a clear, distinct fashion as a limited number of new ideas. They need to know how to impose their own structure on the material that is presented to them.

No idea can be defined as a simple 'item'. Although it is possible to test the ability to remember a series of numbers or letters that have no particular significance in themselves, this has a tenuous connection with the grasp of a concept that can be applied to many different circumstances. And the most complex of all concepts is that of other people, in their coming and going, their cajoling and reacting. The thought processes of children are founded not just on discrimination but on the relationships between themselves and others.

Children's acquired habit of sorting out and categorizing the material presented to them reveals the close relationship between thinking and perception. The shift from perceptual, sometimes called 'ikonic', representation to symbolic or 'linguistic' representation is not a sudden one. Perceptual understanding continues alongside the use of language. Thought processes include a variety of levels: the enactive (for example, gestures), the ikonic (for example, fantasies) and the lexical (for example, the uses of language).[3] One particular process of the mind *can* be isolated, as in the concentration on a puzzle or a problem, but this happens when close attention is being paid to the task in hand. Intelligence and attention are closely related concepts because, in certain conditions, when the recall of information is tested, such intelligence is a trained response of the mind to concentrate on *one* thing and ignore all other distractions.[4]

If a listener hears two things at once he will choose to listen to only one of them. He will also concentrate on a particular piece of information, and learn to simplify the information he receives by processing it into a few clear concepts. Infants' distinctions between one sound and another are one of the first signs of their organization of information. Once they develop the ability to concentrate on the first piece of information they are presented with, they learn to avoid the distractions, from both within and without, that might prevent them continuing to pay attention. As a general rule the first and last items of any message are the best remembered.[5] The first item influences and helps to organize subsequent information, and, at least for one moment, does not have to compete for exclusive attention. The last item in a sequence is not interrupted by what follows and can receive more attention.

The more complicated the stimulus, the more attention is paid to it and the more time is spent in examination of it.[6] Babies express a natural demand for material that is rich and complex, out of which their minds can choose what they find interesting, as if there were not so much a desire for abundance for its own sake as a relief in having enough material to make part of it redundant. The eye, looking at a landscape, never takes all of it in, unless in deliberate indifference ('seen one, seen them all'), but shows an interest in the variety of the material to be seen, in picking out the salient features. It is easier for the eye to find new material and to respond to new stimulation than to concentrate closely on one thing for a length of time. This is partly because it is easier to select information on the basis of physical cues than it is on the basis of semantic ones.[7] After a period of concentration the overtaxed brain uses a defence mechanism in which a slow ductility wave takes over. Hence the trance-like look. The mind is not able to perform with all its powers of concentration for very long, even if this is the easiest part of the mind to understand and explore, and the one to which the most attention has been paid.

The need to select information comes about because whatever is presented to us will be either too little or too much. We all know what it is like to be overloaded with information until the brain hurts. Children become exhausted every day through their response to new information; their tiredness is not just physical. Children also need to learn how much to respond to in their relationships. They can suffer from overload or from being ignored. They can be given the wrong kind of information, or a false impression can remain uncorrected. This is why parents can worry so much about their inability to organize the experiences of their children.[8] There is no controlling the inner lives of children, and yet their future depends on all these fragile experiences.

Concentration on items of information is a sign of the ability to ignore or discard unnecessary information; it is a process of exclusion as well as of understanding. Once a particular hint or clue is followed it is very hard to change tack; the mind assumes that what follows is a natural extension of the first hint. Lip-readers need to guess part of what a person is saying since they receive only part of the relevant information. Once they make an incorrect guess about what is being communicated to them it is very hard for them to follow what is subsequently being expressed, however good they are at lip-reading. To some extent we all anticipate what we think other people are saying, guessing what comes next and even, in some cases, trying to finish their sentences with what is already familiar and predictable. The logical pattern of a sentence, however long, is easy to follow, but a sudden shift in meaning causes problems. When a sentence might continue in either of two directions the listener guesses which way it will go and assumes that what follows fits. 'The man put the straw ... on a pile ...' or 'the man put the straw . . . in the drink . . .' are unambiguous once you know what *kind* of straw is being referred to. The 'garden path' theory suggests that people assume only one reading of a sentence at a time, so that they can be suddenly surprised if there is an alternative interpretation to the ambiguity that they had not expected.[9] The processing of a sentence, therefore, includes enough guessing to predict its logical outcome. Young children, before they appreciate the difficulties of construction, prefer simple, logical structures in statements. They find it much easier to understand that 'A is before B', where the statement demonstrates its meaning in its structure, than to understand 'B is after A', where there is a dichotomy between meaning and structure. As they begin to understand the coherence of what is perceived they expect a greater analogy between the coherence of fact and the coherence of its expression.

Children have a natural taste for logic, and can understand

clear analogies. This is why they respond to learning the names of letters. The more formally they are taught, by parents, for example, the better their achievement. There has been a mythology about parents dangerously forcing their children by making them learn the letters of the alphabet, by taking on the tone of 'come on', as if this would upset children's subsequent abilities to learn.[10] But all the accumulated evidence of the past few years shows that parents, helping their children formally, make a great difference to children's attainment.[11] The stress is on the formal, not because this is a better approach, but because of children's abilities to be logical, to grasp what they are expected to learn.

Parents make a more important contribution to their children's attainment than through formal learning. The expectations that they have and the sharing of interests, their curiosity and their patience, together with a steadiness of purpose, all make a difference to the child's belief in his abilities. For children are continuously observing as well as experimenting, wanting to be given a clear framework in which to operate. They also learn very fast from observing how adults react to other children, as well as to themselves. There is a significant relationship between the behaviour of children at the age of four and at the age of eight.[12] Those who have more friendly and positive social interactions with others are happier and more competent than those who have to do without.

Children are acute observers and will soon anticipate adult reactions to their behaviour, expecting consistency and being disappointed if it is not there. But they observe not only external behaviour but internal, psychological *reasons* for behaviour, well before they go to school.[13] They understand not only logic but also causality; not just the effects of events but also the personal reasons for behaviour. They understand random phenomena far earlier than used to be supposed.[14] But if children understand psychological causes, they also understand other people's feelings, knowing motivations and causes of pride and embarrassment by the age of five.[15] And we know that at the age of three children are aware of the distinction between truth and falsehood – the central point about relationships.[16]

The picture that emerges of young children's thinking reveals the ability to categorize and to discriminate about relationships, not just cognitive ability but also emotional insight. And at the same time we see children develop their moral insights, at first quite pragmatically but, even at the age of four, understanding the implications of guilt.[17] This ability to understand complex relationships lies at the heart of learning, whether the relationships are with other people or with more abstract and less emotionally demanding material. We should not underestimate, therefore, children's abilities to learn from each other and from teachers, as well as from parents. Pre-school children become aware of their own learning through dialogue with others, when they can relate their learning through experience to learning by being told information.[18] Two of the important factors of learning in school already play an important part in children's lives well before they go to school. The two factors are teachers (which includes parents) responding to children through praise, criticism and discipline, and children working together co-operating on a task.[19]

Children explore a range of possibilities before they accept the 'static' nature of their surroundings. They gradually learn that most things are *not* alive, that not all things that move are responsive. They learn that *some* things are formed by outside agents rather than existing naturally. They gradually sort out the relationship between things and people, the difference between the parents' choice of when to fetch a book and the parents' automatic response to the sound of the telephone. They learn to connect separate ideas, such as the voice of the adult and the artificial voice on the telephone, and they discover the connections not only between actions but also between different parts of the same thing, like the parts of a car or different articles of clothing and their wearers.

Children learn to make some connections through applying rules in their own way. At first they learn about phenomena, such as balance, through natural experiment; later they begin to apply rules, sometimes making mistakes. When, for example, a set of blocks with weights in them, some at one end and some in the middle, is given to some children, the youngest balance them well, without thinking about it; the older ones begin to apply their own rules, often without success.[20] Children enjoy solving puzzles for their own sake and can learn complex sequences. They match new information about the world, like balance, against an inner standard, against what they have already learned, constantly guessing and predicting what will happen, and sometimes having to go through to the end when it seems to us obvious what will happen – knocking a plate off the edge of a table or spilling some milk. When we observe children's *own* experiments instead of experimenting with them we see how they learn from their mistakes.[21]

The world is made coherent to us by a series of conventional signs we all share. Infants' inner coherence is a different matter. They try to match their own view to that presented to them, deriving an idea of wholeness, of internal coherence, from the information they receive. From the beginning children are not driven only by the primary desires of hunger and self-preservation in the Freudian sense. They begin through relationships outside themselves, with parents, and with objects they touch and see. They learn different types of knowing: 'figurative' knowing – how to imitate a world of objectives and events (demonstrated when a child imagines a toy block in its absence) – and 'operative' knowing – how to manipulate the external world (demonstrated when a child imagines the block placed somewhere else before putting it there).[22]

For young children there is always a tension between their interaction with the environment and their understanding of it, between their sense of language as reference and language as doing. Even before they use words for objects children need to understand the relationships between objects that look the same, or taste, sound and feel the same, and the relationships between objects that function in the same way, regardless of what they look like, especially when they function in relation to the child, such as showing a tendency to fall over when pushed.[23] Children are concerned both with references, with interpreting and classifying the world around them, and with their expressive relationships with the world. Their interpretation will not always match what they see exactly, so that when they begin to use words they will make mistakes that reveal inexact categorization: the over-extension of one concept and the over-discrimination between others.[24]

Before children begin to sort out their sense of the world through using language they are already aware of many of the functions of language, through the expression of demands and through the

references towards objects. They possess a sense of representations of particular properties of the world, seeing that certain
things have functions that remain fairly constant. They possess a
sense of the conceptual as well as a sense of the sensory or
pictorial.[25] Their imaging is, therefore, a kind of organizing, not
an alternative coding system to language but a way of locating the
memory for an object or events. The very difficulty of making
objective distinctions between their own experience and the condition of the environment makes imaging the more important.

Imaging includes personal recollections and recreations, as well
as creating a picture of the world. It is the continuing way of
reconciling the interpretation of what is seen with what can be
defined as seen, a visual means of expressing an uncommunicated
concept. Imaging is inward representation, and continues to be
important even when we are accustomed to the definitions of
language. Children begin to develop the use of language through a
growing sense of the connectedness of events in the world outside
them. They do not learn through the routines of habit or instinct
but through the understanding of two connected but contrary
facts: the objective unchangeability of the world outside and the
possibility of changing certain things on demand. Far from being
so subsumed by their own inner worlds that they wait for events to
take place, they learn how they can manipulate and order their
sense of the environment and their sense of how it responds to
them. It is at first difficult – and this remains true of all learning –
to make a distinction between memory and fantasy, between
perceptual images and imaginative images. Since perception
depends so much on the nature of our engagement with what we
see and hear, we have to learn to image as well as perceive. Each
categorization of the world, symbolized by the fact that language
can subsume all objects of a particular type in one word, is a form
of imaging. Many images enter the mind; when they are unbidden
they come from the inability to *repress* them. For imaging is not just
a stage towards language but a constant and important part of the
relationship of the mind and the world outside. There are, after all,
many different types of imaging: Horowitz analyses 23 major
kinds, from thought images, dreams and flashbacks to illusions,
déjà vu, after images and body images.[26] The various experiences of
imaging that blend into each other seem particularly strong in

childhood, since imaging is both a form of perception and a way of trying to make an internal representation of what is perceived. Every picture of the world is a form of symbol, even before we use the symbolic pattern of words.[27] We can to some extent choose whether to remember what we have seen in either images or words and rely on imaging for memory.[28] Familiarity with the object that is imaged makes for greater clarity of imaging so that imaging is very closely related to ordinary perception.[29]

Awareness of perceptive relationships is the first sign of the development of language. The basis for linguistic expression is the realization that certain events have meaning and the learning of a set of functions with 'potential for meaning'.[30] Children understand more than they can say. A child of about thirteen months can begin to understand the nomenclature of a variety of objects without bothering to communicate the fact and without using all the sounds that he has at his disposal. It is possible to develop the means of communicating in a sophisticated way without language: both 'functional' words ('gone', 'up') and 'substantive' words ('chair', 'mamma') can be subsumed within the use of a term like 'da' when the clues of expression or need are quickly taken up and answered. There is always a gap between comprehension and production. When babies appear to be inarticulate they are not necessarily unknowing. After all, a child crying with arms outstretched to his father is communicating effectively enough.[31]

NOTES AND REFERENCES

1 Both Ausubel, D.P. *Educational Psychology: A Cognitive View*. New York: Holt, Rinehart and Winston, 1968; and Gagné, R.M. *The Conditions of Learning*. New York: Holt, Rinehart and Winston, 1965, make central distinctions between 'reception' and 'discovery' learning and 'rote' and 'meaningful' learning.

2 Broadbent, D.E. *Perception and Communication*. Oxford: Pergamon, 1958; and Miller, G.A. 'The magical number seven, plus or minus two: some limits on our capacity for processing information'. *Psychological Review*, **63** (2), 81–97, 1956.

3 Horowitz, M.J. *Image Formation and Cognition*. New York: Appleton-Century-Crofts, 1978.

4 Stankov, L. 'Attention and intelligence'. *Journal of Educational Psychology*, **75** (4) 471–490, 1983.

5 Work often duplicated since Ebbinghaus, H. *Grundzüge der Psychologie*. Leipzig: Veit, 1902, on the principles of primacy and recency.

6 Berlyne, D.E. 'The influence of complexity and novelty in visual figures on orientating responses'. *Journal of Experimental Psychology*, **55**, 289–296, 1958.

7 Darwin, C., Turvey, M. and Crowder, R. 'An auditory analogue of the Sperling partial report procedure: evidence of brief auditory storage'. *Cognitive Psychology*, **3**, 255–267, 1972.

8 Bettelheim, B. *A Good Enough Parent*. London: Thames and Hudson, 1987.

9 Clark, H. and Clark, E.V. *Psychology and Language*. New York: Harcourt Brace Jovanovich, 1977.

10 Bettelheim, B., 1987, op. cit.

11 Tizard, B. *et al. Young Children and School in the Inner City*. London: Erlbaum, 1988.

12 Vandell, D., Henderson, K. and Wilson, K. 'A longitudinal study of children with day-care experiences of varying quality'. *Child Development*, **59** (5), 1286–1292, 1988.

13 Miller, P. and Aloise, P. 'Young children's understanding of the psychological causes of behaviour: a review'. *Child Development*, **60**, (2), 257–285, 1989.

14 Kuzmak, S. and Gelman, R. 'Young children's understanding of random phenomena'. *Child Development*, **57** (3), 559–566, 1986.

15 Seidner, L., Stipek, D.J. and Feshbach, N. 'A developmental analysis of elementary school-aged children's concepts of pride and embarrassment'. *Child Development*, **59** (2), 367–377, 1988.

16 Gopnik, A. and Astington, Y.W. 'Children's understanding of representational change and its relation to the understanding of fake belief and the appearance/reality distinction. *Child Development*, **59** (1), 26–37, 1988.

17 Nunner-Winkler, G. and Sodian, B. 'Children's understanding of moral emotions'. *Child Development*, **59** (5), 1323–1338, 1988.

18 Pramling, I. 'Developing children's thinking about their own learning'. *British Journal of Educational Psychology*, **58** (3), 266–278, 1988.

19 Blatchford, P., Burke, J., Farquhar, C., Plewis, I. and Tizard, B. 'Associations between pre-scchool reading related skills and later reading achievement'. *British Educational Research Journal*, **13** (1), 15–24, 1987.

20 Papousek, H. 'Individual variability in learned responses in human infants'. In Robinson, R.J. (ed.), *Brain and Early Behaviour*. London: Academic Press, 1969.

21 Bates, E. *The Emergence of Symbols: Cognition and Communication in Infancy*. New York: Academic Press, 1979.

22 Bowerman, M. 'Semantic factors in the acquisition of rules for word use and sentence construction'. In Morehead, D.M. and Morehead, A.G. (eds), *Normal and Deficient Child Language*, Baltimore: University Park Press, 1976.

23 Clark, E.V. 'What's in a word? On the child's acquisitions of semantics in his first language'. In Moore, T.E.(ed.), *Cognitive Development and the Acquisition of Language*. New York: Wiley, 1973; Nelson, E. 'Concept, word and sentence: interrelations in acquisition and development'. *Psychological Review*, **81**, 267–285, 1974; and Clark, E.V. 'Some aspects of the conceptual basis for first language acquisition'. *Papers and Reports on Child Language Development*, **7**, Stanford University, pp. 23–51, 1974.

24 Pylyskyn, Z.W. 'What the mind's eye tells the mind's brain: a critique of mental imagery'. *Psychological Bulletin*, **80**, 1–24, 1973.

25 Paivio, A. 'On the functional significance of imagery'. *Psychological Bulletin*, **78**, 385, 1970.

26 Horowitz, M.J. *Image Formation and Cognition*. New York: Appleton-Century-Crofts, 1978. This book defines images categorized by vividness, by context, by interaction with perceptions and by content.

27 Some of the most interesting discussions about this ancient philosophical/psychological problem are to be found in the work of Wittgenstein.

28 Tversky, B. 'Pictorial and verbal encoding is a short term memory task'. *Perceptual Psychologies*, **6**, (225), 220–243, 1969. See also Paivio, A. 'On the functional significance of imagery'. *Psychological Bulletin*, **78**, 385, 1970; and Paivio, A. *Imagery and Verbal Processes*. New York: Holt, Rinehart and Winston, 1971.

29 See Sheehah, P.W. 'The functional similarity of imaging to perceiving: individual differences in vividness of imagery'. *Perception and Motor Skills*, **23**, 1011–1033, 1966.

30 McShane, J. *Learning to Talk*. Cambridge: Cambridge University Press, 1980; and Halliday, M.A.K. *Learning How to Mean – Explorations in the Development of Language*. London: E. Arnold, 1975.

31 Lock, A. 'The emergence of language'. In Lock, A. (ed.), *Action, Gesture and Symbol: The Emergence of Language*. London: Academic Press, pp. 3–18, 1978.

CHAPTER 4
The Development of Language

> So much of the actual knowledge is of the relations of things – even our
> simplest sensations in adult life are habitually referred to classes as we take
> them in.
>
> William James, *The Principles of Psychology*, Vol. 2.

'I have to use words when I'm talking to you.' We are so accustomed to language that we tend to think of all thought and even perception in terms of language, in the terms with which we communicate. We forget that thought takes many forms; that we go on thinking even when we are inarticulate. We find it difficult to understand what it was like before we had the use of language, just as we find it hard to explore states of mind that do not reveal themselves in precise terms. And yet the incipient forms of language, the categorization of experience under general headings, the ability to make things happen and to express what is felt are all already established in babies before they make their first recognizable attempts at communication.[1] Language pervades every other experience before it is manifest, and dominates experience once it is possessed. But it also continues to have an ambiguous relationship with other modes of thought; it is never as free and precise as it might seem. While language gives power to control ideas and gives command over surroundings, it is also controllable in itself, driven by forces that dominate as well as help. Language remains capable of obscuring as well as explaining. It can be used to lie and to mislead, to cover truth with a cliché as easily as it can be used for the expression of the most subtle thought.[2]

The relationship between language and thought has always fascinated philosophers, although the development of linguistics and experimental psychology has, ironically, sometimes led to a tendency to ignore the complex nature of the relationship.[3] The nature of language and thought is an ancient field of debate precisely because it is a problem. It gives an insight into the inner workings of the mind that is outside the interest of those who prefer to study only the production of language. The tradition that words are a kind of equivalent to the real world, reflecting and arranging what is seen through a series of images, is a helpful insight into some of the rudiments of language.[4] Words have often been thought of as the images of things.[5] To William James words are sensory images awakened. Internal imaging is not only the perceptual memory of what is seen – to remember the house we used to live in we immediately picture it – but also a way of perceiving things. We create images in our mind continually. For mnemonics, for memory games or for remembering a series of numbers we can use imaging deliberately but for the most part it is a subconscious activity. For young babies the distinction between the deliberate and the subconscious is less precise. For them imaging, the placing of an idea of consistency around a chosen group of objects, is an essential means of coming to terms with the environment. Images and verbal coding systems are closely linked as means of symbolic representation, which is the way in which human beings show themselves capable of thought.[6]

The relationship between imaging and language is so close that it is often impossible to disentangle. Bruner made a helpful distinction when he talked of the difference between the 'enactive', a psycho-motor reaction, automatic and purely perceptual; the 'ikonic', the ability to see and create images; and the 'symbolic', the use of words.[7] Language is, in this definition, a specialized form of symbolic system. There are other forms of symbol, but language is the most sophisticated. Both imaging and the use of language depend upon the ability not merely to reproduce, but to anticipate.[8] Images are both immediate and deferred, reacting to what is seen and creating the idea of what is seen. Imaging is the entry into other material and not just the reception of other material. Images (or 'ikons') are essential for representing and effectively thinking about the features of the world.[9] The traditional view that images, on the one hand, are specialized for the representation of concrete objects and events and that language, on the other hand, is useful for concepts and abstract ideas, is actually an oversimplification. 'Images', that sense of a symbolic representation of reality, are most easily expressed in visual terms but are not necessarily purely visual. Information contained in a sentence is represented in terms of a set of interconnected concepts. Some of the terms used become the points around which the other ideas form. Words that form images easily are the easiest to learn but after a word is recognized the associations with that word and past experience build up a sense of its meaning that causes a patterning of symbols.[10] Underlying the development of language, therefore, is a seam of imagery, of non-verbal symbolism, of a set of personal concepts.

Infants develop the use of language out of a means of communication already established; they know how to understand as well as to express before they make such understanding linguistically abstract. The very first uses of language are interactions with other people or the naming of objects. Given the capacity to symbolize, to categorize and to communicate, young children make every effort to learn language; they are not templates upon which language is automatically stamped. They find their own idiosyncratic means of accumulating information, and by a series of guesses and the association of the same term with varying contexts build up a vocabulary, and, more importantly, an awareness of what language is for – as reference and as expression. New concepts and new words are learned in terms of what is already known. Language can be said to emerge from children, just as easily as it can be said that they acquire it, for they 'discover' language through their own re-invention as well as their perception of what is given to them.[11] Children are not 'inventing' language or demonstrating their innate capacity for language out of context.[12] They are aware of the functions of language before they have any chance to bring spoken vocabulary into the open. What 'emerges' is their knowledge of the act of language, or the 'speech act'.[13] They acquire the verbal means of making actions plain and demonstrate their growing awareness of the functions of people and objects. Language, like imagery, is *used* before it can be seen to be some kind of taxonomy of linguistic forms.[14]

Children's early use of language is obviously different from that of adults; it is also clearly independent of adult forms, in structure and meaning.[15] Children are more aware than adults of the sounds of words, of rhythm and tone, and make use of clues that seem to the adult no longer as relevant as the more formal features of language. Children's use of language is also almost painfully systematic, since they work out how certain words or classes of words can be used, making mistakes that are more logical than the arbitrary conventions of everyday use. Children do not learn language in exactly the same way as an adult learns a second language, although we can remind ourselves of the difficulties they experience by trying to make sense of a language we have never heard before.[16] Instead of a ready map of the concepts of language, or simple labels, children need to find new and difficult concepts that underlie language. They are trying, through the functions of language, to understand the nature of intelligent action, how plans succeed or fail, and how to repeat the action so that the same thing will happen again. Some of the earliest linguistic gestures that children make are those of direct action, in suggestions or commands like 'give' or 'I want'.[17] A 'sentence' summed up in the word 'there' and a gesture is more than a primitive label of what is seen; it is an expression of some form of relationship with what is seen, as are phrases such as 'all gone' and 'more'. Much of children's knowledge of language is tacit rather than explicit; it is a form of subconscious knowledge, like knowing which way a ball will bounce rather than the rules of advanced mathematics.[18]

All that we know about the development of the complex structures of language, from the use of single words to convey meaning to what is known as 'telegraphic' speech, such as 'daddy come', or 'baby wet', makes it clear that children in their use of language demonstrate their understanding of the concept of a sentence. Experiments with different structures, with all the complexities of syntax, actually show the main guiding principle of a complete unit of meaning, of an idea that needs a sentence for its articulation.[19] In the formulation of sentences children do not employ a set of rules but try out hypotheses that seem to offer hope of being right; every gesture is, in a sense, an implied sentence. Children learn how to express their needs and their demands of others in such a way that language is the inevitable outcome before it becomes the guiding principle.[20] They search for links between their concepts and the linguistic forms in which these can be expressed.[21] The semantic concepts that they wish to express are as powerful as an idea, for, like any rare ideas, they are attempts to go to the heart of things, to understand the meaning of their surroundings. When children develop the word 'why?' they have already developed the desire to explore the answers that they were seeking from the moment they first experimented through their hands with inanimate objects.

The learning of language is therefore clearly established before it adopts even a rudimentary verbal form. The response to tone of voice and the insight into the consistent function of certain objects are among the necessary prerequisites for the development of language. But once words are formed there are a number of additional concepts that need to be understood. The idea of a generalization – that a 'dog' can be of all shapes and sizes, depicted in a picture or seen in living fact – and the idea of word order are both essentials of language. Children's response to language is active. They notice that not all features of speech are significant for vocal communication. They know that the meaning of what is said goes beyond an immediate reference. They understand that there is no limit to the number of meanings that can be expressed. One word or sentence can be used for different objects and different conditions: 'I like' or 'I want' are not always used with the same intensity but simple expressions of a variety of concepts. Words can also be used in different metaphorical ways, like 'cold' in 'cold water' (physical) or in 'cold people' (psychological). Children of three naturally appreciate the physical more easily than the psychological.[22] Before they use and understand a term such as 'cold' the distinction between the two different functions of words is not yet made. The metaphorical and descriptive are as closely allied in children's minds when first meeting language as they later become to those who rely on set phrases like 'sitting ducks' or 'calling the shots'.

Infants begin to gauge the meanings of words when they know two things about them. They must learn that words have meaning, that they are connected to the existence of objects or that they denote some type of action. And they must learn that the sound of a voice does not consist only of a particular tone but also of meaningful phonemes – those sounds that are distinctive units of meaning. When we hear a foreign language it sounds to us as if the people are speaking very quickly, for we cannot separate one word from another. When infants listen to words they do not know the distinction of one sound from another, but they begin to hear that the people around them use certain types of sound. They hear that there are verbal patterns that consistently return. Thus their making a sound like 'ma' or 'da' is the first indication of their realization that speech includes distinct phonemes. They notice that there is a range of sounds that are often repeated, and they learn to detect the consistencies of sound.[23]

Babies are always quick to attend to language, at first because of the tone of the parent's voice, and then because they become attuned to the significance of sounds connected to actions. A cry soon turns to a demand, just as the soothing tone of the parental voice turns into a particular pattern of intonation. Infants can tell the difference between sounds very early and, just as they imitate the expressions of adults, so they begin to practise, in babbling, the sounds that make up speech, from the obvious ones like 'da', 'pa' etc., to those particular phonemes used by the language or languages that surround them, and the variations that occur in the degree of voicing and aspiration. Infants also show an early propensity for learning the rules of languages, even when these rules are not always consistent. In first sounding words they tend to prefer voiced consonants, 'b', 'd' and 'g', at the beginning of words and unvoiced consonants, 'p' and 'k', at the end.[24] The first uses of language at around nine months are often related to states of feelings: 'da, da', for example, is often associated with pleasure, 'ma, ma, ma' with need and 'na, na, na' with dissatisfaction. They also have a tendency to parody a tone of voice, as in a recognizable if odd equivalent to a phrase such as 'what is it?'. Young children are also capable of understanding a far greater range of tonal expressions than they can possibly use themselves.

The pronounceability of verbal material is a fundamental attribute of its early use. Children naturally isolate particular speech sounds that can be picked out, rather as we notice the general characteristics of a foreign language in a recognizable version of it, long before we know the meaning. This ability to pick up the important phonological clues is what gives Jakobsen's argument about children's acquisition of speech its value.[25] He suggests that children's language consists of the learning of a set of distinctive oppositions, selected from the essential oppositions of sound that underlie all the languages in the world, between 'voiced' or 'unvoiced', 'vocalic' or 'non-vocalic', between all the choices of sound that we can make with our lips and tongue. Jakobsen argues that children perceive a predictable series of contrasts in language, and that at first they need to simplify their perception of these contrasts until they understand the ground rules.[26] This ability to pick out particular sounds is best understood in relation to the understanding of language as function, as having a use, so that this understanding of the pattern of phonemes and blends of phonemes – 'pa', 'da', 'ma' – is allied to a set of propositions, actions or demands. As children understand the use of sounds so they no longer merely copy, often surprisingly well, the sounds repeated to them, but generate their own versions, often more distant from the sound of adult speech than their earliest efforts.[27] They create a set of common phonological processes of their own.[28] This explains why there are particular features of children's speech: the deletion of unstressed syllables, such as saying 'nana' for 'banana'; the reduction of clusters, such as 'step' to 'dep' and 'floor' to 'for'; the devoicing of final consonants, such as 'bed' to 'bet', 'big' to 'bik'; the progressive vowel assimilation, such as 'apple' into 'aba'; and the fronting of palatals, such as 'shoe' into 'su' or 'juice' into 'dzus'. The language of 'wawa' for 'flower', 'plss' for 'please' or 'da' for 'there' has a logic of its own. It is their own version of the given phonetic system, a kind of 'pidgin' English that shows an idiosyncratic adjustment to the problems of internalizing the sounds of speech. The distinctions that children use in their speech always relate to segments in adult words although they do not always sound as if they do. Children know their own limitations of pronunciation. However hard the parent insists that the word is 'tractor', they can only say 'tata'. But the child expects the adult to accept that two pronunciations can mean the same thing. We are all used to differences of dialect. To a young child every person's voice and pronunciation are different – as they indeed are.[29]

Infants appreciate language, and understand some words long before they can pronounce them. When an adult asks whether a child would like a 'drink', which the child calls 'dok', the child understands perfectly well that there are two different versions of the same word. They accept the gap between their own uses of words and those of adults just as they appreciate pictures that are far more advanced than and different from the kind they are capable of producing themselves.[30] They prefer and need information presented to them at a more complex level than they can manipulate themselves. There has always been a temptation to make a marked contrast between 'pre-linguistic' babbling, when the sounds that a baby makes do not appear to carry meaning, and the learning of actual words. But the two periods overlap. At all times the child's phonological system has a structure of its own, but a structure that shows consistent correspondence with the adult system. At first (they must begin somewhere) children hear the most obvious contrasts of sound and then slowly learn to detect more and more differences in meaningful sound.[31] Around the structure of the main framework of constrasting sounds the child then attaches the seemingly less significant variations.

The need to make almost crude general patterns arises because of the variety of what a child hears. Adults are no longer aware of the problem. We hear what someone intends us to hear or what we intend to hear. To a young child every voice is so different it is as if each individual speaks a wholly different language. Infants actually vary the frequency of their voice according to that of the person talking to them.[32] Six-week-old babies, for example, are able to discriminate sounds according to the place of articulation in consonants and tongue heights in vowels.[33] The fact that children's perception of the adult form of a word may be inaccurate actually shows that they are generating their own versions of what they hear.[34] They do not merely imitate. The process by which they make rules of what to reproduce in what they hear, from deletion ('tring' for 'string') and substitution ('bie' for 'pie') to general assimilation of sounds, shows that they understand more than they are capable of articulating.[35] Adults can be insensitive to the fact that children have difficulties in producing sounds[36] but children perceive speech and understand the nature of speech very early.

Children's acquisition of language is a sophisticated operation, governed by individual insight and dependent on the discovery of rules. Children learn to construct meaning by guessing the significant sound patterns and through their understanding of the context in which meaning occurs.[37] While it seems somewhat simplistic to explain everything by saying that infants possess a native language acquisition 'device',[38] their ability to respond to the purpose of language as they would to the significance of any other action means that they learn to understand the structure of sounds, and hence the later grammars of language[39]. By the age of three months the sounds that babies make are clearly related to the sounds they hear spoken around them.

Infants learn to isolate the sounds that are significant from an enormous mass of material. They learn to discover rules, like those of gravity, hardness or the manipulation of their bodies, through concentration on the significant, on what remains consistent in an expanse of the accidental. They also learn to understand some of the consistent functions of language: the fact that words refer to objects and the fact that words can make things happen. This realization that language consists of the means for expressing needs and is a way of labelling things, as well as fulfilling other more complex functions, marks out the early use of language observed in infants. Sometimes children specialize in learning words for objects; sometimes they are more concerned with the exploration of social gestures like 'want', 'please' and 'go away'.[40] While they perceive the uses of language, they also learn to attach components of meaning to the language that they hear; they begin to guess what a word signifies. Often children will learn to identify the meaning of a word with just part of its semantic components: they attach some meaning to a word and go on thinking about the word consistently in that way.[41]

Children either over-extend or under-extend words – as when they call all four-legged creatures 'dog' or when they see no analogy between a real dog and a toy dog, or when 'car' refers either to anything on wheels or only to the vehicle they habitually sit in and not to any others. Children are attempting to match their guesses to meaning and their own meaning to the conventional uses of words. It is through the awareness of context and by the elimination of particular clues and properties that they focus attention on the curious conventions of language. We see how difficult this task is. The word 'tree', often repeated, can be used to refer to the alder, the beech, the dead elm, the bay, to a picture by Renoir, to a cartoon, to a part of a jigsaw or to a representation on a plate. 'Tree', the children hear again and again, 'tree'. And then, it seems arbitrarily, the shape of the leaves and trunk is pointed out as a 'hedge' or 'bush', or a small part picked out as a 'branch' or 'trunk' or 'leaf', or the shape is seen in the larger context of a 'wood' or 'copse' or 'forest'. How does the child attach a consistent sound and a meaning? The interchangeability of words and the fact that each picture can be described in accurate detail or overall generalization force children to guess for themselves what is being referred to. It is not surprising that children have difficulty in attaching exact meanings to the terms we use. It is not surprising that they have a tendency to simplify and over-generalize, so that there is a mismatch between what a child means and what an adult infers.[42]

The variations children reveal in their development of language actually demonstrate the processes through which they have to go to unravel the information that is presented to them. Some children begin to structure their understanding around the references for things; others through actions. There are several types of meaning that children can choose among, from general nominals (i.e. objects) and specific nominals (i.e. people), to modifiers ('big', 'red') and function words ('where?').[43] They show different ways of interpreting and classifying the world around them, through either the observation of categories or more direct involvement through language as an action. It is often assumed that language is learned through the association of a word and an object, but the anomalies of this view can best be expressed by pointing out that children have to learn a series of abstractions as well as responses. They know the word 'colour' as well as the specific qualities it refers to. What kind of meaning is evoked by 'Christmas'? The reference points of children remain important, but these references are not made only in the presence of a salient object, but also in the linking of a consistent action or gesture, static or moving, and whatever is referred to.[44] While some meanings are learned with regard to just *one* object, children's tendency to over-generalize shows that they soon learn to group things together, to create a sense of language that goes beyond mere labelling.[45]

Children's mistakes demonstrate that their understanding of language precedes their actual use of it. Their command of syntax is not just a matter of learning the structure of sentences but a demonstration of their grasp of the essentials of meaning.[46] Studies of children who have difficulty in producing sounds give evidence for the primacy of the comprehension of language over the expression.[47] When handicaps occur the comprehension of words returns long before the expression. And yet children develop, through their awareness of meaning, a very sophisticated idea of syntax, of the order of words and of the use of morphemes like 'ed', which denotes non-present time.[48] This ability to make use of interchangeable parts derives from their need to structure meaning. They first learn the morpheme 'ed' for words for activities that *can* be finished, are quickly over, such as 'jumped' or 'dropped', rather than for activities that have no such definite ending, like 'talked' and 'walked'. Some children learn to try out new words in structures they already use; other children try out known words in new structures as types of experiment.[49] The rate of development varies greatly between different children, as does the way in which children acquire their sense of syntax.[50] The ability to put words into the right order, with the descriptive word preceding the noun, as in 'a red flower' or 'that my nana', is acquired very early, showing that the grasp of syntax as an essential means of conveying sense develops alongside vocabulary.[51] Children very rarely put words in the wrong order – they do not tend to make mistakes like 'wake up her'. Their awareness of the order of syllables within a word is paralleled by their sense of the order of words that make up a sentence. Children develop their awareness of rules, even if some are exaggerated or some of the exceptions are missed. This understanding develops through the logic of experience, learning firstly about plurals, then about possessives and then about verb endings.[52]

The mistakes children make with syntax are the result of their tendency to apply certain rules *too* rigorously. They appear to have an instinctive grasp of the necessity to understand grammatical structure for the sake of formulating generalizations and creating new categories that they can apply to what they experience. They try to find the inherent semantic relations that govern all juxtapositions of words.[53] They make an analysis of the relationships between parts of the sentence so that they can use word order like a gesture that continues, such as pointing a finger at the object about which they are concerned.[54] Their tendency to over-generalize rules is shown in the use of words like 'comed' or 'goed' in place of 'came' and 'went', or in 'he hitted me' in place of 'hit'. Their logic is as fallible as the curiosities of the English language. Indeed children of two and three years old who have *not* worked out the rules that govern syntax are more likely to express correctly the grammatical curiosity of a strong ending like 'sang' instead of the consistent but incorrect weak ending 'singed'. Children of four will have worked out the generalizations of grammar and will apply them despite the fact that they do not hear an adult using words like 'singed' or 'hitted'.[55]

When children learn the different parts of speech they do so in a logical manner. When encountering pronouns, for example, they are inclined to begin by using proper names. They then go on to use the pronoun 'it', followed by 'my' or 'mine'. It is logical to see the object itself before developing the idea of possession. They use singular pronouns like 'he' before plurals like 'they'.[56] As young children make use of language they show a surprisingly early proficiency with plurals, possessive nouns and past tenses.[57] All the testing of children's syntactical abilities through their use of specially invented words, such as 'bung', 'sib' or 'wug', has demonstrated the pragmatic way in which children approach the problem of syntax and their ability to generalize their discoveries.[58] Underlying these demonstrations of syntax is, of course, the sense of meaning, even if they cannot express it. The holophrase – in which words mean something more than is obvious – is something we all use. 'Tea?' 'Coffee', can be a conversation of great complexity. For example, 'Tea?' = He: 'Even while I think you are wrong and don't deserve any consideration from me I'll show my magnanimity. I wonder if you would like me to make you a cup of tea and bring it to you as a gesture of reconciliation.' 'Coffee' = She: 'Thank goodness you've stopped feeling sorry for yourself rather than taking your own pomposity so seriously that you won't talk. I'm most grateful for your asking, darling, and will accept the gesture, but I'd rather prefer a cup of coffee if you don't mind making it.' While we would not suppose that every holophrase was similarly charged we should not suppose that words used by children are not capable of conveying extended meanings. There are times when it is difficult for them to know how little they have conveyed. It is sometimes suggested that children acquire two grammars, one for comprehension and one for production, but the potential weight of every utterance is such that there is always a sense in which the capacity is greater than the performance.

The fact that children use one-word utterances and then two-word utterances – open and pivot words – is not significant in itself.[59] The significant stages of acquisition are the rules of semantics and modulations of meaning.[60] Children use the structures of language in their own way. To describe only the surface of two-word sentences is to miss the place of meaning in every demonstration of language.[61] While it is possible to show the general order of language development and the 'normal' age at which each grammatical usage is acquired,[62] the real excitement with children's language is the use they make of it in their own way. Their grasp of instructions through gesture and intonation is early, as is their understanding of mood. The capacity to use more than one word shows that a rudimentary sentence has replaced the gesture, that they are able to manipulate their environment more successfully. The naming of parts, including themselves, refines their sense of relationships. Even the first sounds that children use, with meaning, show their need to communicate not just a sense of their pleasure or discomfort, but their awareness of commentary on other events.[63]

The ability of young children to make use of language and to comprehend the rules that govern the use of language should not suggest that the learning of language is a deliberate cerebral activity. Learning develops from instinct and from need and seems *more* like a series of accidents than a deliberate campaign. Much of their learning derives from the ability to associate a number of different things. Young children, despite their more limited vocabulary, have many more associations for words than adults.[64] The younger the child, the more varied are the associations, for meaning comes about through what can be called 'collocations', habitual associations of words in the context of sentences. The learning of words is not a deliberate semantic network[65] but an understanding that elements in a sentence can carry a unique meaning and that two things can be associated with meaning in a similar way.[66] Children's realization of the meaning of words can be accidental or the result of distinct needs and interests but is always developed through the juxtaposition of sound with meaning.[67] There is a surprising orderliness in the associations of four-year-olds who seem to be struggling to possess a semantic memory, an associated network of concepts.[68]

The clearest demonstration of children's energy in learning is their command of language. This is not a matter of learning nonsense syllables or labels, but of learning ideas. It is a matter of learning to generalize as well as to be particular. Children's rate of learning suggests the impossibility of any demonstrable capacity to teach them. By the time a child enters nursery school he has a vocabulary of between eight and fourteen thousand words (there is an increase of up to eight words a day between the ages of one to six). The 'normal' child of six knows, according to Templin, thirteen thousand words.[69] By the time he is seven, he knows twenty-one thousand six hundred; at eight, twenty-eight thousand. This is an increase of twenty-one new words every day. When new words are introduced children quickly pick them up and use them. They understand the context and the concepts. They do not merely receive and 'store' new information but make use of it. Thus their learning is a means not only of receiving new information but also of understanding its context: discriminating between different uses of words and between different morphologies. The language that children remember so rapidly is the active material that connects them with their environment. Nothing could be less like the standard test of memory. And nothing could show a greater contrast than the capacity to use language, the knowledge of vocabulary, and the actual use of language by adults in everyday circumstances.

NOTES AND REFERENCES

1 It is possible to discover through experiment something of infants' response to and recognition of different stimuli, and yet little work is done on what ideas children have when they express what they think of what they see.

2 The most obvious examples are the languages of political propaganda.

3 Deese, J. *The Structure of Associations in Language and Thought.* Baltimore: Johns Hopkins Press, 1965.

4 Wittgenstein, L. *Tractatus Logico-Philosophicus.* London: Routledge and Kegan Paul, 1961.

5 The beginning of the tradition of Greek philosophy.

6 Paivio, A. *Imagery and Verbal Processes.* New York: Holt, Rinehart and Winston, 1971.

7 Bruner, J.S. *On Knowing: Essays for the Left Hand.* London: Belknap Press, 1976.

8 See Piaget, J. and Inhelder, B. *Mental Imagery in the Child*. London: Routledge and Kegan Paul, 1971.

9 The term 'ikons' is particularly used by Bruner.

10 Tulving, E. and Madigan, S.A. 'Memory and verbal learning'. In Mussen, P.H. and Rosenzweig, M.R. (eds), *Annual Review of Psychology*, **21**, Palo Alto, CA: Annual Reviews Inc., 1970.

11 Lock, A. (ed.) *Action, Gesture and Symbol: The Emergence of Language*. London: Academic Press, 1978; and Chomsky, N. *Language and Mind*. New York: Harcourt Brace Jovanovich, 1968.

12 Tyler, S.A. *The Said and the Unsaid: Mind, Meaning and Culture*. London: Academic Press, 1978.

13 As Austin and Searle (see Chapter 2, note 38) would put it.

14 Fodor, J.A. *The Language of Thought*. Brighton: Harvester Press, 1976.

15 Shvachkin, N. 'The development of phonemic speech perception in early childhood'. In Ferguson, C.A. and Slobin, D. (eds), *Studies of Child Language Development*. New York: Holt, Rinehart and Winston, 1973.

16 Gopnik, A. 'Words and plans: early language and the development of intelligent action'. *Journal of Child Language*, **9** (2), 303–318, 1982.

17 Rodgon, M.M. *Single Word Usage, Cognitive Development and the Beginnings of Combinatorial Speech: A Study of Ten English-speaking Children*. Cambridge: Cambridge University Press, 1976.

18 Polanyi, M. *The Tacit Dimension*. London: Routledge and Kegan Paul, 1967.

19 McNeill, D. *The Acquisition of Language: The Study of Developmental Psycholinguistics*. New York: Harper and Row, 1970.

20 Lenneberg, E.H. and Lenneberg, E. (eds) *Foundations of Language Development: A Multidisciplinary Approach*, 2 vols. New York: Academic Press, 1975.

21 Bowerman, M. 'Semantic factors in the acquisition of rules of word use and sentence construction'. In Morehead, D.M. and Morehead, A.E. *Normal and Deficient Child Language*. Baltimore: University Park Press, 1976.

22 Asch, S.E. and Nerlove, H. 'The development of double-function terms in children: an exploratory investigation'. In Kaplan, B. and Warner, S. (eds), *Perspectives in Psychological Theory*. New York: International Universities Press, 1960.

23 Foss, D.J. and Hakes, D.T. *Psycholinguistics*. New York: Prentice-Hall, 1978.

24 Jakobsen, R. *Child Language, Aphasia and Phonological Universals*. Hague: Mouton, 1968.

25 Ibid.

26 Atkinson, M. *Explanations in the Study of Child Language Development*. Cambridge: Cambridge University Press, 1982; and Stampe, D. 'A dissertation on natural phonology'. PhD Thesis, University of Chicago, 1972.

27 Piaget, J. *Language and Thought in the Child*. London: Routledge and Kegan Paul, 1926.

28 Ingram, D. 'Current issues in child phonology'. In Morehead, D.M. and Morehead, A.E. (eds), *Normal and Deficient Child Language*. Baltimore: University Park Press, pp. 3–27, 1976.

29 Hence the use of voice detectors: the 'ideolect' in the pattern of speech sounds unique to each individual.

30 Booth, A. 'Drawing status and picture preferences in primary school children'. *Educational Studies*, **1** (1), 63–76, 1975.

31 Moskowitz, A.I. 'The two-year old stage in the acquisition of English phonology'. *Language*, **46**, 426–441, 1970; and Waterson, N. 'Child phonology: a prosodic view'. *Journal of Linguistics*, **7**, 179–211, 1971.

32 Lieberman, P. *Intonation, Perception and Language*. Cambridge, MA: Massachusetts Institute of Technology Press, 1967.

33 Eimas, P.D., Siqueland, E.R., Jusczyk, P. and Vigorito, J. 'Speech perception in infants'. *Science*, **171**, 303–306, 1971.

34 Garnica, O.K. 'The development of phonemic speech perception'. In Moore, T.E. (ed.), *Cognition and the Acquisition of Language*. New York: Academic Press, 1973.

35 de Villiers, J.G. and de Villiers, P.A. *Language Acquisition*. Cambridge, MA: Harvard University Press, 1978.

36 Gilbert, J.H.V. 'Individual variation in some phonetic aspects of language acquisition'. In Fillmore, C.J., Kempler, D. and Wang, W. (eds), *Individual Differences in Language Ability and Language Behaviour*. New York: Academic Press, pp. 229–241, 1979.

37 Francis, H. *Language in Childhood: Form and Function in Language Learning*. London: Paul Elek, 1975.

38 To quote Chomsky's phrase.

39 Miller, G.A. and Isard, S. 'Some perceptual consequences of linguistic rules'. *Journal of Verbal Learning and Verbal Behaviour*, **2**, 217–228, 1963.

40 Nelson, K. 'Structure and strategy in learning to talk'. *Monographs of the Society for Research in Child Development*, **36**, 1 & 2.

41 Clark, E.V. 'Some aspects of the conceptual basis for first language acquisition'. In Schiefelbusch, R.L. and Lloyd, L.L. (eds) *Language Perspectives: Acquisition, Retardation and Intervention*. Baltimore: University Park Press, pp. 105–126, 1974.

42 Clark, E.V. 'What's in a word? On the child's acquisition of semantics in his first language'. In Moore, T.E. (ed.), *Cognitive Development and the Acquisition of Language*. New York: Academic Press, 1973; and Clark, E.V. 'Knowledge, context and strategy in the acquisition of meaning'. In Daton, D. (ed.), *Proceedings of the 26th Annual Georgetown University Round Table: Developmental Linguistics: Theory, Applications*. Washington DC, 1975.

43 Nelson, K., 1973, op. cit.

44 Macnamara, J. *Names for Things: A Study of Human Learning*. Cambridge, MA: Massachusetts Institute of Technology Press, 1982.

45 Cruttenden, A. *Language in Infancy and Childhood*. Manchester: Manchester University Press, 1979.

46 Brown, R. *A First Language*. London: George Allen and Unwin, 1973; and Brown, R. and McNeill, D. 'The "tip of the tongue" phenomenon'. *Journal of Verbal Learning and Verbal Behaviour*, **5**, 325–335, 1966.

47 Lenneberg, E.H. *Biological Foundations of Language*. New York: John Wiley, 1967; and Fourcin, A.J. 'Language development in the absence of expressive speech'. In Lenneberg, E.H. and Lenneberg, E. (eds), *Foundations of Language Development: A Multidisciplinary Approach*. New York: Academic Press, pp. 263–268, 1975.

48 A morpheme is the smallest unit of meaning. The plural 's', for example, is a morpheme.

49 Bloom, L. 'An integrated perspective on language development'. *Papers and Reports on Child Language Development*, **12**, 1–22, 1976.

50 Ramer, A.L.H. 'Syntactic styles in emerging language'. *Journal of Child Language*, **3**, 49–62, 1976.

51 Bellugi, V. and Brown, R. 'The acquisition of language'. *Monographs of the Society for Research in Child Development*, Serial No. 92, **29** (1), 1964.

52 Jakobsen, R., 1968, op. cit.; and Cazden, C.B. *Child Language and Education*. New York: Holt, Rinehart and Winston, 1972.

53 Bloom, L., 1976, op. cit.

54 Brown, R., Cazden, C.B. and Bellugi, V. 'The children's grammar from I to III'. In Hill, J.P. (ed.), *1967 Minnesota Symposium on Child Psychology*. Minneapolis: University of Minnesota Press, 1969.

55 Ervin-Tripp, S. and Mitchell-Kernan, C. *Child Discourse*. New York: Academic Press, 1977.

56 Cruttenden, A., 1979, op. cit.

57 Berko, J. 'The child's learning of English morphology'. *Word*, **14**, 150–177, 1958.

58 Brown, R. 'The development of 'wh' questions in child speech'. *Journal of Verbal Learning and Verbal Behaviour*, **7**, 227–290, 1968; and Ervin-Tripp, S. and Mitchell-Kernan, C., 1977, op. cit.

59 Braine, M.D.S. 'The ontogeny of English phrase structure'. *Language*, **39**, 1–13, 1963.

60 Brown, R., 1973, op. cit.

61 Deese, J. *Thought into Speech: The Psychology of a Language*. Englewood Cliffs, NJ: Prentice-Hall, 1984.

62 Gesell, A., Ilg, F. and Ames, L.B. *The Child from Five to Ten*. New York: Harper and Row, 1977.

63 Leopold, W.F. *Speech Development of a Bilingual Child*. Evanston, IL: Northwestern University Press, 1949.

64 Entwhistle, D.R. *Word Associations of Young Children*. Baltimore: Johns Hopkins Press, 1966.

65 Kiss, G.R. 'Steps towards a model of word selection'. In Meltzer, B. and Michie, M.C. (eds), *Machine Intelligence 4*. Edinburgh: University Press, pp. 315–336, 1969.

66 Deese, J. *The Structure of Associations in Language and Thought*. Baltimore: Johns Hopkins Press, 1965.

67 Collins, A.M. and Quillian, M.R. 'Retrieval time for semantic memory'. *Journal of Verbal Learning and Verbal Behaviour*, **8**, 240–247, 1969. See also Collins, A.M. and Quillian, M.R. 'Facilitating retrieval from semantic memory: the effect on repeating part of an inference'. *Acta Psychologica*, **133**, 304–314, 1970.

68 Quillian, M.R. 'Word concepts: a theory and simulation of some basic semantic capabilities'. *Behavioural Science*, **12**, 410–430, 1967; and Collins, A.M. and Loftus, E.F. 'A spreading excitation theory of semantic processing'. *Psychological Review*, **82**, 407–428, 1975.

69 Templin, M.C. *Certain Language Skills in Children: Their Development and Interrelationships*. Minneapolis: University of Minnesota Press, 1957; and Miller, G.A. *Spontaneous Apprentices: Children and Language*. New York: Seabury Press, 1977.

CHAPTER 5
Relationships with Others

There are two kinds of knowledge – knowledge of and knowledge about.
William James, *The Principles of Psychology*, Vol. 1.

To learn language is to learn about relationships with other people. Language arises out of the need and the desire to communicate. When children first realize that they can cajole or command a response from people around them, and when they share their knowledge of the naming of things, they use language in a social way and as a means of placing and categorizing information. To learn language is to gain the capacity to take someone else's position, to understand what words mean to other people. The inner drive that teaches children to ignore the distracting and the incidental for the sake of the more significant facets of perception also fosters a steady concern for relationships with other people. We are gregarious creatures by nature, and even if we sometimes deny ourselves the pleasure of being with other people, we remain intensely conscious of them. The awareness of other people, even when painful, when driven by envy or fear, is constantly important to adults and immediately so to young children, aware of the people who move around them, who approach them and who handle them.

When children first begin to comprehend language they do so through tone of voice, through the use of language in maintaining a relationship. The parent's soothing or sudden impatience, inadvertently revealed, are quickly perceived by a baby. He realizes that the words contain an emotional meaning. He understands the use of tone, the distinctions between commands and comforting, between being informed and being manipulated.[1] Tone of voice makes the distinction between making an expressive statement or making a reference to other things. The speaker can be primarily concerned with demanding a response or with sharing knowledge.

71

This distinction in tone and use of language demonstrates verbal behaviour as an act of speaking or listening rather than a display of knowledge in the abstract. For language and gesture are closely related. Both are extensions of actions to and for other people.[2] A baby raising his arms demanding to be picked up gives a clear expression of his intention; coupled with the sound of the voice this is one of the earliest indications that there is a deliberate move towards other people, not merely unleashing a sense of distress or discomfort in crying but making a clear statement and hoping for a reaction. The earliest sounds are thought to be the rudiments of language, as they too are gestures implying action.[3]

Speech is always a form of activity, even if the communication is with oneself. The practising of sound by children in their cots is a demonstration of the readiness to make use of the sounds as well as an activity in itself. Speech is a sophisticated form of action, concerned not only with the description of an action but also with the analysis of it. The use of language gives children the power to organize ideas that cannot be achieved in an abstract way. Words extend the powers of organization by making more complex ideas possible.[4] The organization of ideas is necessary because there is someone else with whom to communicate, someone else who will listen and attempt to understand. The mastery over abstract ideas derives from the shared experience of communication even when such communication is practised in isolation, as when a baby talks while playing alone. The definition of colour or shape would mean nothing, would not *need* to mean anything, without another's presence. Speech is governed by the purpose of communicating ideas, and is a sign of a kind of 'optimism' that such contacts can be made. Speech fulfils a need for children by helping them communicate their sense of their surroundings.[5] Without the fostering of relationships the capacity for language that they possess in the abstract – the distinction between categories of perception or the development of motor abilities – would soon fall away.

The first important relationship for a baby is, of course, with his parents. But this relationship is not just a matter of his need to be fed and kept warm. It is more than pure dependency. The way in which parent and baby communicate to each other is important from the beginning, not only emotionally, so that both are relaxed with each other, but in terms of mutual understanding. The Freudian interest in young babies suggests that the very first attachments are driven entirely by hunger and self-preservation, and that only at the age of three do they show interest in essentially *human* objects.[6] All the accumulating evidence about babies shows that this is not so. Very young babies are aware of others *as* others and are soon aware of strangers as well as familiar people. They are curious about their parents in many more ways than through the act of feeding. The child's mental development itself depends on the way in which the parent responds to and organizes the child's experiences. At first the child learns how to establish a relationship with a particular person; then it needs her as a companion for other shared activities. The child remains aware of this relationship even when it does not depend on a parent's actual presence.[7] Young babies obviously need the emotional and intellectual support of their parents. This is not just a matter of frequency, of constantly demanding attention, but a matter of the parent's sensitivity to a child's needs.[8] The responsiveness of parents is more than an urge to keep babies quiet and content, it is an interest in them as personalities. The relationship needs to be mutually established by both parties. Children whose parents show a lack of interest gradually learn to ignore or disobey them and become unresponsive to their approaches.[9] Some children are themselves poor at eliciting a response or showing an interest in it. Children respond with attention to those who show interest.[10] Perhaps that is why grandparents and other relations can sometimes play a significant role.

The relationship between the parents and a baby has in many ways more emotional subtlety than relationships between adults. It is as if both instinctively realize its importance. Even the language used by mothers shows an awareness of the needs of children. They vary the way they talk and simplify their speech when they are trying to convey specific points about language. Mothers use little fantasy in speaking to one-year-old children, but talk to two-year-olds about imaginary objects a great deal.[11] Children will often show an ability to use the sounds of animals or other things, to share a comment rather than merely identify the object of interest. Children find that parents re-cast their sentences into a different form and relate the pattern of their own sentences to those of the parent; but each understands the difference. A child retains his own grammatical forms even when the adult constantly repeats the 'correct' version. The mutual understanding through speech is also an outcome of a mutual acceptance of each other: the desire and the will as well as the pleasure.

The development of a child's learning can always be seen in terms of demonstrable abilities – physical and verbal. But these are all centred upon the child's reactions to the circumstances, to other people as well as things. These reactions are a discriminating, sensitive insight into the type and quality of the information. Just as we find it difficult to express the power of relationships between people so it is hard to analyse the nature of these early responses to other people. When children first develop language in terms of their own involvement with roles, attitudes and wishes and in terms of the interpretation of their experience of the world around them, they are actually demonstrating what they have already learned about relationships. The use of language is a result of the insights already gained. Language refines the experience, and often dominates it, but it is also a symbol of the experience.

Descriptions of children's early development of gesture often make it sound as if the earliest signs were mechanical and as if the more extended physical manipulations were mere imitation without reason.[12] Response to other people is never a mindless repetition. An infant's ability to imitate the adult gesture before him is a way of communicating as well as a way of showing physical control. To do something that he sees and copies, like sticking out a tongue, is a complex task of intersensory co-ordination, but is also one that gives him pleasure.[13] Enjoyment of imitating gestures communicates a sense of humour, which is another level of communication. The gestures of babies – for example, clapping hands when an adult does – are not just the result of automatic reflexes. An important part of children's ability to communicate is the way they react to each other as well as to adults.

The need that children feel to communicate with someone who understands, and the challenge they receive from adults who insist, whether aware of this or not, on certain procedures of communication, are both shown up in the study of twins. Young children often understand each other better than parents do. They perceive nuance, tone and gesture, and accept imprecision and the lack of attention to obsessive detail. It is natural and proper for adults to insist on precision. When children have someone of their own age as a constant alternative to talk with, they tend to bother less with adults and their demands. Adults then find it difficult to break into their absorption, to make an alternative relationship. Twins talk far less than single children, not just because it is harder for parents to look after them but because they become used to 'talking' to each other, by-passing the normal methods of communication. Twins are consistently slower to talk, and often invent an almost private language. This is, in a sense, the alternative to the necessity of creating relationships with adults.[14]

The child's relationship with an adult is not just an emotional security but also a means of learning. The amount of language that he overhears, or the experiences that are presented to him, are not in themselves the central factor of the parents' role in children's learning. The most important point is the dialogue they have with the child and the expectations they have of him. The child's intellectual development depends on the quality of the early dialogue with adults, on their interest in him and on their receptivity to tone. The relationship is, of course, more than an intellectual one; but then real relationships always are. It has been recognized for many years that the child's emotional well-being depends on the earliest of relationships.[15] The security of the child's hold on the world and the certainty of self-esteem grow very rapidly, or diminish rapidly, according to the first years of the relationships. This is not a question of money or comfort but something far more subtle.

Understanding of the importance of the home has developed through exploration of children's needs and comparisons between children with foster parents and children in institutions, and the distinction is great. What is striking about the comparative studies is how they all indicate not only more advanced emotional attitudes in those from secure backgrounds but also increased intellectual ability. Children who are brought up in isolated circumstances, in an institution which does not provide close personal attention, suffer far more than emotional handicaps. The needs that children have for safety, love and esteem and for self-actualization are more than a matter of comfort. Their greatest need is for a relationship that is demanding, for people to show an adult interest in them. When child-minders, for example, provide some of the obvious physical needs for children, their lack of concern to do more can show clearly. Children with child-minders were found in one study to be quiet, detached and passive, contrasting with their normal behaviour at home.[16] But then what is provided at home can vary widely: at best parents (and other adults) provide the kinds of interests and motivations that affect children for the rest of their lives.

When we study symptoms of deprivation we see very clearly how important is the child's desire for demanding company. Children begin to turn in on themselves when they find a lack of response; having expressed anger and discontent at the lack of personal concern they tend to become increasingly passive, until they can turn in on themselves to such an extent that they begin to resent any subsequent offer of human warmth.[17] After the search for the parent the child will cry, and will want to cling to any available adult. But if there is no response from an adult the child then becomes quiet and unresponsive. He doesn't show any interest in objects and doesn't grasp anything offered. He becomes more and more passive and dejected, eating and sleeping badly. Even the routine needs of food and sleep are affected and are disjointed by the lack of personal contact. When a young child of three feels deserted he first imagines how happy he would be when his parent comes back. But when the parent fails to appear, the child becomes angry, and wants to wreak some form of revenge on those who cause the deprivation.[18] Afterwards he reveals bitterness and cynicism at the lack of response to him. Over a long period children deprived of close attention go into a decline, 'starving' for lack of emotional and intellectual stimulation. It is as if they had suffered from some kind of sensory deprivation. Without the real interest of an adult, without a close relationship, the child becomes, and remains, handicapped.

If we try to pick out any one thing that influences the subsequent development of people more deeply than any generalization about social structure, perhaps the most important is the earliest relationship that young children have with parents and other adults. The pervasive emotional tone and the subtlety of the interest shown by parents makes more of an impression on children's development than anything else.[19] This is a question not of particular techniques of child rearing – potty training, type of food, rules about whether a child will be ignored or not – but of the ability to create a relationship with another human being. The general emotional tone of the home and an understanding relationship can survive difficulties or traumas. In fact a single traumatic experience does not have a lasting effect in circumstances where the child feels secure. The connection between the earliest of children's experiences and their later intellectual achievement lies in their attitudes. Coming to terms with the complexities of the world depends on the encouragement to make guesses, without being afraid of being wrong.[20]

There have been a number of careful studies of young children that have tried to isolate the factors that make a difference to their subsequent abilities. In the Bristol research of 1972–82 a number of findings confirmed that children varied widely in their rates of development, but that the sequence of development was very similar, and that the class of the family background did not have a significant effect on a child's rate of development.[21] What was also clear, however, was that the early experience of conversation and of the sharing of ideas was of great importance.[22] Sometimes this early relationship is placed under the heading of 'literacy'. But 'literacy' in the broad sense consists of that extension of language and the exploration of ideas that children need. To read a story is to undergo an experience with a child. Looking at pictures, or the naming of trees, flowers or cars, and the desire to involve children in looking at books or magazines are all an extension of a real relationship, formed through the common use of language. The quality of the interest that parents show makes the great difference. In various studies on Mexican Americans, Laosa found that there was a causal link between parental attainment at school and the subsequent attainment of their children because of the quality of the interactions within the families.[23] The higher the expectation of parents, and the greater the belief in the ability of their children to show interest, the better their children's performance in school. Richman and his colleagues came to the conclusion that the *crucial* point in a child's growth, academic achievement and behavioural maturity is the relationship with an adult.[24] This research tried to explore all the possible factors that helped or prevented success in schools and, to the researcher's own surprise, this one factor emerged again and again. The relationship between the child and the adult depends not just on the interest that the parent shows but on the capacity the young child has for dealing with relationships. Either a sensitive parent *or* a sensitive child was able to make up for inadequacies in the other. When both were not good at striking up a relationship then behavioural and intellectual problems began to emerge.

Children's ability to organize their ideas, especially through language, depends on their relationship with adults. The subtle side of learning – confidence, optimism, interest, desire to learn, curiosity and, in the end, that degree of irony and self-knowledge on which real learning depends – arises from this ability. The surprising thing about young children is that they already show that they are good at it: not just showing their own will, or making demands for food, but demonstrating great curiosity and interest in other people's reactions. A good example of such almost disinterested concern for other people, such an understanding of relationships and of the bond between them, is babies' sense of humour.

NOTES AND REFERENCES

1 Skinner, B.F. *Verbal Behaviour*. Englewood Cliffs, NJ: Prentice-Hall, 1957.

2 Quine, M.V. *Word and Object*. Cambridge, MA: Massachusetts Institute of Technology Press, 1960; and Ryle, G. *The Concept of Mind*. London: Hutchinson, 1949.

3 Mead, M. *Letters from the Field, 1925–1975*. London: Harper and Row, 1977.

4 Bruner, J.S. *The Process of Education*. Cambridge, MA: Harvard University Press, 1960.

5 Vygotsky, L.S. *Thought and Language*. Cambridge, MA: Massachusetts Institute of Technology Press, 1962.

6 Freud, S. *The Ego and the Child*. London: Hogarth Press, 1962.

7 Bowlby, J. *Child Care and the Growth of Love*. Harmondsworth: Penguin, 1964.

8 Hogan, R. 'Moral conduct and moral character: a psychological perspective'. *Psychological Bulletins*, **79**, 217–232, 1973.

9 The worst effects on children come about when they do not know what kind of mood the parent will be in. Children find manic-depressive parents more difficult than depressed ones. Radke-Yarrow, M.,

Cummings, E.M., Kuczynski, N. and Chapman, M. 'Patterns of attachment in two and three year olds in normal families and families with parental depression'. *Child Development*, **56**, 884–893, 1985.

10 Stayton, D., Hogan, R. and Ainsworth, M.D.S. 'Infant obedience and maternal behaviour: the origins of socialisation reconsidered'. *Child Development*, **42**, 1057–1069, 1971.

11 Kavanaugh, R.D., Whittington, S. and Cerbone, M.J. 'Mothers' use of fantasy in speech to young children'. *Journal of Child Language*, **10** (1), 45–55, 1983.

12 Piaget, J. *The Child's Conception of the World*. London: Routledge and Kegan Paul, 1929.

13 Meltzoff, A.M. and Moore, M.K. 'Newborn infants imitate adult facial gestures'. *Child Development*, **54** (3), 702–709, 1983.

14 Compare Gorney, C. 'Twins with a language all their own'. In Mussen, P.H., Couger, J.J. and Kagan, J. *Readings in Child and Adolescent Psychology*. New York: Harper and Row, 49–51, 1980.

15 Maslow, A.H. *Motivation and Personality*. New York: Harper and Row, 1954.

16 Bryant, B., Harris, M. and Newton, D. *Children and Minders*. London: Grant McIntyre, 1980.

17 Spitz, R.A. 'The importance of the mother–child relationship during the first years of life: a synopsis in five sketches'. *Mental Health Today*, **7**, 7–13, 1948.

18 Bettelheim, B. *The Children of the Dream: Communal Child-rearing and the Implications for Society*. London: Paladin, 1971.

19 Berelson, B. and Steiner, G.A. (eds) *Human Behaviour: An Inventory of Scientific Findings*. New York: Harcourt Brace, 1964.

20 Turner, J. *Made for Life: Coping, Competence and Cognition*. London: Methuen, 1980.

21 Wells, G. *Language Development in the Pre-School Years. Languages at Home and School, Vol. 2*. Cambridge: Cambridge University Press, 1985.

22 These conclusions derive not just from the work of G. Wells but from Tizard and Hughes and others.

23 Laosa, L.M. 'School, occupation, culture and family: the impact of parental schooling on the parent–child relationship'. *Journal of Educational Psychology*, **74** (6), 791–827, 1982.

24 Richman, N., Stevenson, J. and Graham, P.J. *Pre-School to School: A Behavioural Study*. London: Academic Press, 1982.

CHAPTER 6
Experience and Remembering

For a state of mind to survive in memory it must have endured for a certain length of time.

William James, *The Principles of Psychology*, Vol. 1.

We learn from experience, but experience consists not only of a series of external events which happen to occur and happen to affect us, but also of a combination of these events and our response to them. We also learn from suffering, but again what happens to us is not as significant as the use we make of the experience. To demonstrate the weight that needs to be attached to the individual response rather than the external circumstances alone we only need to think of the timing of an important event in our lives: at one time it might have happened too soon for us to make use of it, at another it might have happened too late.

To a young child the weight of every experience is uniformly greater, and there is no such clear distinction between the sensation of an event and its meaning. The understanding of what we see depends increasingly on the reconstructions implied by our perception. The process of learning is the difference between realizing the potential of every sight and sound as significant in themselves, and recognizing how every sight and sound carry either particular significance or no significance to ourselves.[1] Our perception of what we see translates an abstract or imaginative version of reality into a form we can understand. What we see depends on the attention we pay to it. Some suggest that attention and intelligence are closely related concepts and that it is impossible to make a clear distinction between an approach to experience and what is gleaned from experience, especially as attention also deeply affects what we subsequently remember.[2]

For young children the choice of thinking or not thinking, of paying close attention or not, is not such a simple one. By the time we are conscious of the choice of using our minds, as in the work demanded by an approaching examination, we are well aware of the differences between taxing our brain and indulging in less cerebral pleasures. By then the distinction between mental labour and unmental pleasure is stark. But for young children the need to think out what is happening, to question perceived experience, is constant. They do not suddenly present a display of their thinking to us. They fumble with ideas because they find it hard to pick out those ideas that are significant from the masses of new ideas that are bombarding them as rapidly as their vocabulary develops. As they are trying to combine generalizations with the immediate they do not know which rule to apply or where to apply it. They do not know when to fixate on an idea and when to see a new concept as something to be ignored. They can suffer from overload of information and yet seem to be taking nothing in. They sometimes seem to cling to ideas to which they have already become accustomed rather than to change their thinking immediately in the light of new experience or to a new perspective. They do not simply add new information to the accumulating detritus of half-forgotten facts, but respond much more sharply to the present. The dependence on the immediacy of context means that the way they react to a new idea can contain a far wider range of response than a simple assimilation.[3] They can react against 'entry' into the problem of learning a new idea by being deflected by the way in which the problem is presented and choosing to be interested in the presentation rather than the idea.

When a baby uses the same gesture for a second time he demonstrates the other great ability to understand the world: the ability to employ memory. Some forms of memory are based on the associations of personal experience but other forms are functional.[4] Without memory, or without the use of it, there could be no means of categorizing or discriminating. In one sense, any response to new experience is the beginning of a form of memory, one end of a range of organizing abilities that extends from a habitual response to the ability to remember an answer, with references, in examinations. But the most important distinction usually made about memory is that between short-term and long-term memory, although it is a difficult distinction to maintain, given the complexity of the process of remembering.

Short-term memory can be likened to verbatim memory; the

immediate recall of information received. Long-term memory records the meaning of what has been experienced; it is the conscious processing of experience.[5] Short-term memory is often likened to a temporary storage space for material that will later be 'placed' in a new form in the long-term store. The awareness that we take in much more information than we subsequently recall has led to many attempts to explain *why* some information is 'processed' and some is not. The difficulty is that memory is a matter of filtering part of what is received. Remembering includes reconstruction, new associations and nostalgia, as well as implying forgetting some things. The reasons for the recalling or the forgetting of an incident are very different from those which underlie the recall of a fact.[6] The difference between short-term and long-term memory is a distinction between understanding the means by which material is remembered and understanding the reaction to material to be remembered.[7] The mind of the infant is complex because the personal unforced incidents are as important as the 'academic' analysis of fact. There are, after all, many ways of processing information, including associations as well as meanings.[8]

When children first discover the processes of memory they learn that the use of memory depends on propositions, on information understood in a particular way. Meaning needs to be understood in a definite form before there is any chance of deliberate storage, or even of accidental connections of a kind that provokes recall. Anderson and Bower suggested that propositions themselves are units of memory.[9] It is clear that children focus far more easily on those things they find easiest to understand, and which have far clearer meaning – for example, active rather than passive sentences.[10] Any fact to be remembered easily needs to fit within a general framework, becoming a part of an already established understanding.[11] Most facts represented in memory form part of a network of propositions.[12] Thus memory is itself an active means of organizing material and not merely a storehouse into which the information of the perceived world is placed. Memory is 'involved' on some occasions rather than others, through a stimulus, attribute or association with a different context. This is what Tulving calls a 'retrieval cue'.[13] It suggests that a complete distinction between short-term and long-term memory is not always that helpful.[14] The 'rehearsal' of information that is to be remembered is not a mechanical reaction, but a discriminating application of perception.[15]

There are some things we would never remember if we did not choose to do so; and others we *only* remember if we do not choose to do so. It is because memory is so pervasive and undeliberate that children absorb so much, not because all events leave a trace which is then recalled when attention is directed at it, but because there are so many ways of paying attention to information.[16] Memory depends on how the child encodes material[17] as well as how he perceives it.[18] Some items actually impede the ability to recall them, because of the characteristics of the way they are expressed or because of the depth of the experience itself.[19]

The simplest truth about memory for facts is that it depends on a desire to learn. When young children are learning to adjust to, and analyse, their environment, they are not deliberately coding facts, or items which can be useful. The whole world is too much a fact in itself for them to know which parts of it are significant. But their desire to make sense of it, to discriminate, to make associations between particular objects or events, is strong. This comes about because they cannot *help* responding to what is outside them and internalizing it, recreating it in their own minds.

Remembering develops out of babies' perception. Their analysis of experience depends on the associations they make, putting together the past and the present. It can be said that there are three types of remembering rather than two, not only the long-term, from which familiar material can be recalled, and the short-term, which is the process through which information passes before it is stored, but also the sensory. Sensory memory is like a tap on the arm, or what we see when we open our eyes just for a second; it soon fades. Short-term memory is the way that we interpret what someone has just said when we were not really listening; realizing that we are expected to answer we can 'tune-in' to what we have just heard or else we will ignore it and forget it completely. These distinctions are helpful in any analysis of memory, but for young children no such obvious distinctions exist. The visual information that they receive cannot be consciously 'stored' until they know what they can analyse; but they recognize what is familiar none the less.

The *recognition* of what is perceived is more important than the recall. The images that are taken in, and quickly forgotten, accumulate in the mind until they begin to make sense. Infants see much more than makes sense to them, just as adults taking part in experiments see much more than they can report.[20] These unbidden images are sometimes referred to as 'ikons': the repeated sensations lead to memory.[21] Babies encode what they see and hear rapidly and as rapidly forget, since they have no means to analyse and recall it: the impressions are made, and create an active response. The difficulty is that such an activity cannot be expressed, and does not lend itself to the kinds of experiments that can so easily be carried out on long-term memory.

But even the work of those who are concerned with older subjects shows how important is the initial stage of sensory memory.[22] Every item that is remembered needs first to be perceived before it is analysed in what Tulving calls the 'ecphoric' process.[23] While babies are learning to perceive their environment and building up their sense of the world they are doing so not as a deliberate process but as a need to sort out what confronts them. Tulving makes the distinction between our memory of events from our own lives and our memory of facts that we have acquired about the world; between 'episodic' and 'semantic' memory, between that moment in the restaurant under the moonlight, and the knowledge that ostriches do not fly.[24] Such a distinction is of great importance to those who are trying to clarify the processes of memory. But for infants personal perception and the analysis of meaning are one and the same.[25] The processes that young children undergo are not purely semantic, depending on their ability to define their ideas, but are dependent on their personal associations.

One of the characteristics of the mind is that memory is never perfectly organized, although a limited amount of material of any type can be memorized completely. The associations made in the mind are on a variety of levels. The mind predicts what it will receive as well as structuring it, so it is aware that there is far more material stored in memory than it can actually recall. We can remember that we know the name, and we can have a feeling about the name, without being able to recall it.[26] (Sometimes we cannot recall it until we stop trying to remember it.) We are as aware of our organization of memory as of what we remember. While we discard, almost immediately, vast quantities of material we half perceive, or perceive without analysis, we make a structure out of what we consciously wish to remember and an image of the context in which such events took place, as if we could only remember the place in which we were thinking.

Some memories, like a familiar landscape, are surprising both for what we know about them and for what we don't know. At the level of immediate recall we know how few details can be conjured up; but when we recognize the landscape again there will be any number of details that connect with what was earlier experienced. Although frequency in itself does not cause learning, there is a relationship between frequency and the learning of meaningful material. The familiar is after all often repeated: not inspected as such but seen again and again. Although the learning of concepts seems to free us from control by specific stimuli, familiar material becomes a particular part of our concepts.[27] Concepts are generally not easily, or completely, forgotten, since they are what the mind chooses to make of material that it has learned. But there are also many other details that the mind chooses to recognize that form part of the pattern of perception.

The propensity for the brain to remember what it takes to be the significant details pervades those things learned consciously and those things that are perceived in passing. In writing down and remembering what they have been told, people recall the salient parts according to the semantics, whatever the structure of the sentence given them or the style of presentation.[28] When asked to recall what they can of a passage, people tend to remember better all those things that they agree with rather than those things with which they feel in conflict.[29] When new words are presented, it is almost automatic for people to try to find a connection with words heard before. They will find some association of sound or meaning that makes them feel that something new is, in fact, familiar.[30] It is as though the desire to construct what is remembered creates two levels of control over new material: an imposed structure and a natural one through which impressions are formed more subjectively. Memory is not passive; nor is it automatic, any more than learning is just a deliberate activity of the will.

'Transfer', the application of what is learned from one circumstance to another, includes all these different levels of learning. Forgotten material can be relearned more easily than it was learned the first time, having already made some impression, never utterly wiped out from the mind. 'Transfer' comes about partly from recognition of half-familiar material and partly from all the associations with other similar material. Transfer is not just the application of a general principle to a new circumstance but an ability to make a connection between new material and material already learned, between what is already known and what needs to be known. It can take place as if it were a technique using relevant clues to find an appropriate style of analysis, and can also be a subconscious awareness of familiar actions. 'Much of what has been called transfer of training can be fruitfully considered a case of applying learned coding systems to new events.'[31]

When the mind is applied to immediate events it balances pre-set hypotheses, habits or 'sets' into which new material must fit, and a new response which is created by the material. As in the case of phonological and semantic clues, there is a degree of overlap as well as balance between sensory perception and organization. It is clear that much more is perceived than is remembered and that material that is remembered over a long period is given a new shape.[32] What the mind retains is influenced by sensory perception, by other clues than those of classification.

Memory involves analysis of material at a number of different levels. Associations in the mind can be as easily created by the chance of a word or an image as by the processing of information. Remembering is a mixture of associations and the deliberate rehearsal of ideas. Those items that are most closely analysed are most likely to be remembered; it is therefore often judgements about information that are better remembered than the information itself. Above all, memory needs to serve a purpose: a fact will be better remembered if it supports an argument or is part of a consistent interest. It is possible to remember facts for a short time for the purpose of an exam, but most of the material will soon be forgotten.

Memory is served best if it is organized around a series of structures; in examination conditions, around arguments or points of view. The peculiarities of exam techniques explain something else about memory. It is impossible to memorize everything that has been read and learned, but a gradual process of reduction into main points, clustered round central arguments, and then further simplified and reduced until the whole is of a manageable amount, means that out of the deliberate remembering of particular points comes the retention of many other pieces of information. Just as lengthy notes are reduced to short ones, and then further refined into file cards, and *then* remembered, so the memory, in a less deliberate way, organizes itself.

The problem with the concept of memory as a 'store' is that it fails to lay due emphasis on the organizing powers of the mind, and on the fact that both consciously and subconsciously the mind controls what it receives and makes internal discriminations. It is not just one vast vat into which information is poured, not, to use the favourite modern analogy, a mainframe computer into which hordes of information can be keyed. Memorizing is not therefore a matter of storage but an active strategy of attention; it is a function of depth of processing or level of analysis.[33] When people listen to a discourse and are then asked questions about it, they create their own version of the passage rather than reproducing the words in which it was presented. Tulving's distinction between episodic and semantic memory, between the encoding of events and the way in which the material is interpreted, is useful but it must be reiterated that the two have a close relationship: what is remembered depends on the way in which the material is approached.[34] Obviously there are many items that are perceived but not 'recorded', but the memory nevertheless organizes and encodes what is perceived. The way in which material is processed shows in the way the mind can record and retain the words of a long sentence before analysing the meaning.[35]

Memory is fascinating because it is such a potent mixture of deliberate application, which can be trained, and chance associations and judgements; controlled experiences and chance glimpses of experience, as in a scene on television. The ability to organize material, to see the crucial point of it, is at the heart of remembering as it is of perception. We tend to admire those who have practised their memory so that they can recite scenes of a play or long poems or can recall the names of all the cup finalists for the past 100 years, but such a use of remembering is distinct from knowing how to use what is remembered, and understanding its significance.[36] Subconscious connections of ideas and associations that are not carefully constructed are by definition those that do not allow themselves to be tested over the short- or long-term, and that are not the result of deliberate application to material in set conditions. But it is the brain's activity in encoding material that matters, and there is a great difference between memory of a set task, like a train of nonsense syllables, and recall of personal associations.

The more we know about memory the more we realize the importance of associations and categorical relationships, the subjective organization of material and the way in which long-term retention depends on the way in which the material is encoded.[37] Dynamic memory, a mind responding, adapting and changing, is far closer to the true model of the mind than is the brain as a passive receiver of information. The reminding of previous events, categorization and generalization are dynamic memories that do not merely accumulate new information but that re-organize themselves according to the experience.[38] Learning how to remember is akin to learning how to categorize, how to see the connections between words and objects and between similar experiences.

Memory is not just storage of material. Memory depends on many more connections than those that are dependent on immediate recall. As the pioneering work of Bartlett made clear, remembering is an activity which involves not only attention but also different values and attitudes.[39] We choose what we want to remember, both consciously as a matter of attention and subconsciously through a series of personal associations and preferences. Memory involves not only facts or perceptions, but also ideas. Associations, as well as images, are involved in the storage of material from which recall derives.[40]

The way sensory memory feeds short-term memory, and the way that this leads to long-term storage, can only be understood in terms of the mind's ability to organize and to choose what it wishes. Too often accounts of tests of recall seem to lose sight of both that distinction and the fact that in all cases reactions are organized. Sometimes the very fact that the brain imposes its own attitudes towards what will be remembered suggests that the memory is not always the most perfect instrument. Sometimes pleasant memories are more easily recalled than unpleasant ones, but unpleasant memories can be less easy to ignore.[41] The mind can, as in cases of extreme stress, seek to suppress or deny memories that are particularly horrifying. But even in more everyday terms the mind chooses what to remember, and we all display a natural propensity for certain facts which interest us to linger in the mind without effort while information that we know we ought to remember slips away. It is as if the mind is not designed for the uses to which it is put.

Despite the organizing powers of the mind over the needs of facts, children's response to their environment is not dominated by pre-arranged assumptions about what will be experienced. They do not determinedly and subconsciously order what they see according to their expectations. Although their 'set', the mixture of memory and prejudice, is important, they are more likely to receive new impressions in a new way; more likely to re-order their previous arrangements of understanding according to a new experience. Their memory is a mixture of new additions and the substantiation of part impressions, of change according to the new and re-formulation of the old. This process of rearrangement, of strengthening particular ties and loosening and forgetting others, is typical of the way in which memory functions.

The sense of duality in memory – the ability to recall particular things at will, and the insistence of unbidden images coming to the mind – has long been recognized. We do not always remember to organize. Given the different layers of information that are perceived it is natural that the associations made in the mind will often seem fairly idiosyncratic. The forming of opinions is not always carried out with the rationality that anyone espousing a cause would like to think. The knowledge that people are not pure products of all the cultural information given them helps us to understand better the intricacies of human nature. We need to realize that children are actively engaged in discriminating between different segments of material presented to them. They take in a great deal; they forget less. They receive ideas and form ideas. They guess which material to concentrate upon. What would appear to be insignificant information might leave a deeper impression on them than the main point we are trying to make. The mind is always active, even if it is not always working to its fullest capacity.

The activity of the brain creates a tension between what is already remembered and what is new. All information is perceived according to the experience that has already been recorded and organized. The analogy with a computer, which is programmed to receive ever-increasing quantities of information all subject to a similar plan or code of connections, is a false one. Most of the associations that are made depend not on the information offered but on the inner, sometimes uncontrolled, relationship with what is already known.[42] The 'transfer' of information, the connection made between the use of one idea and another, depends upon correlations and combinations made by the active mind engaged in making its own order out of the chaos of possible material.[43] Bartlett's distinction between perception and memory, between reaction *by means of* organized psychological material and reaction *to* organized psychological material, is important.[44] There is no automatic connection between memory in the short-term and memory in the long-term.

William James was the first to draw attention to the difference between primary and secondary memory.[45] Primary memory is that currently in the consciousness, in the psychological present. Secondary memory is made up of items that are at some point absent from the consciousness, that are in the psychological past. Explanations given for forgetting included decay or interference from other items (reasons of time or space), or the difference between the short-term ability of the brain to retain information and its long-term and less detailed versions of the same information. The distinction between primary and secondary memory was re-introduced by Waugh and Norman, partly because of the accumulating evidence that showed associative connotations (traces) depended on whether the subject directed his attention to material or not.[46] 'Primary' material is subject to decay unless, through a deliberate act of rehearsal, the material is transferred to secondary memory.

We know, however, that many things painfully remembered and rehearsed before an exam are forgotten, and that the most surprising items, chance associations or connections are remembered. Children remember a great deal without knowing the secrets of categorical storage, although they are continuously refining their network of associations.[47] They constantly remember two different types of information. They recall events, one incident or date: 'I was given that book on my birthday'. They also learn how to process generalized knowledge: 'I am usually given a book on my birthday'. We all know the pain of trying to remember a name in our mind, chasing along the roads of the brain to catch up with what we are aware we know. We are less aware of the process by which that same name enters the mind when we least want it or need it. Sometimes trying not to remember facilitates remembering, just as trying too hard can make recall almost impossible.

The 'two store' model of memory has been influential in its explanation of short-term and long-term recall, but it has not explained the more complex range of associations of which the brain is capable. The shift of emphasis in research from the 'structure of the brain' to the way in which it actively functions is a recognition that the important parts of memory are those that cannot be tested through experimental verbal recall. The shift of emphasis from 'verbal learning' theories [48] to 'information process' theories has given way, in its turn, to a greater awareness of the way in which the mind reconstructs its own version of events it has experienced, and the way in which unusual connections almost re-invent memory. The instinct that suggested that memory is an important function in intelligence remains correct, but not in the way that popular television quiz shows would suggest. It is the creativity of the memory, the use that is made of memory, that is more powerful than any capacity to remember an array of dates, although the two naturally have a close relationship.

Our greater knowledge of the functioning of computers has ironically enough served to point out how different is the mobile, uncontrolled ability of the brain. Some years ago memory was analysed in terms of the organization and retention of material, with forgetting a matter of interference. More recently memory has been understood in terms of a computer model with storage capacity, search and retrieval of information, through buffers and codes. But now we cannot see memory in such terms: its function lies in the way in which the world is habitually seen, and it connects to language in which such observation is expressed.

For children even more than adults memory is closely linked to recognition. Other senses are involved; the mood of the occasion itself colours the memory, like the 'moist, rich smell of rotting leaves'. When a particular association is involved – 'Do you remember that summer evening at Danny's?' – the mind tends to recall a clear image, picking out particular details not as in a photograph as much as in a sequence of shots by a film camera. The general shape of a scene rather than particular details tends to be first recalled, but when we try to conjure up the details it is surprising how much can be recognized, how many things not deliberately learned are still retained. Bartlett pointed out how the unfamiliar may hold us while the familiar is readily accepted so that we can remember what something is without remembering where it is. He also showed that: 'Remembering is not the re-excitation of innumerable fixed, lifeless and fragmentary traces. It is an imaginative reconstruction, or construction, built out of the relation of our attitude towards a whole active mass of organised past reactions or experience'.[49]

The fact that remembering is subject to social pressure as well as nostalgia, to fear as well as determination and to invention as well as analysis, means that its place in the perception of the environment is central. It is part of the constructive process of building up an attitude to the world as well as knowledge of it.

NOTES AND REFERENCES

1 Berkeley and other eighteenth-century philosophers, realizing the logic of such a truth, went so far as to suggest that the only reality that can be substantiated is that of the individual's experience. Even the chair kicked by Dr Johnson was only philosophically 'real' in the imagination.

2 Stankov, L. 'Attention and intelligence'. *Journal of Educational Psychology*, **75** (4), 471–490, 1983.

3 Shands, H.C. 'The hunting of the self: towards a genetic affectology'. In Modgil, S. and Modgil, C. (eds) *Toward a Theory of Psychological Development*. Slough, Berks.: NFER, pp. 61–89, 1980.

4 Tulving, E. 'Ecphoric processes in recall and recognition'. In Brown, J. (ed.) *Recall and Recognition*. Chichester: Wiley, pp. 37–73, 1976.

5 Tulving, E. 'Episodic and semantic memory'. In Tulving, E. and Donald-

son, W. (eds) *Organization of Memory*. New York: Academic Press, pp. 381–403, 1972.

6 Waugh, N.C. and Norman, D.A. 'Primary memory'. *Psychological Review*, **72** (2), 89–104, 1965.

7 Compare Bartlett, F.C. *Remembering*. Cambridge: Cambridge University Press, 1932.

8 Craik, F.I.M. and Jacoby, L.L. 'A process view of short-term retention'. In Restle, F. (ed.) *Cognitive Theory*, Vol. 1. Potomac, Maryland: Erlbaum, 1975.

9 Anderson, J.R. and Bower, G.H. *Human Associative Memory*. Washington, DC: Winston and Sons, 1973.

10 Turner, E.A. and Rommetveit, R. 'The effects of focus of attention on storing and retrieving of active and passive voice sentences'. *Journal of Verbal Learning and Verbal Behaviour*, **7**, 543–548, 1968.

11 Bransford, J.D. and Johnson, M.K. 'Considerations and some problems of comprehension'. In Chase, W.G. (ed.) *Visual Information Processing*. New York: Academic Press, pp. 383–438, 1973.

12 Kintsch, W. *Memory and Cognition*. New York: Wiley, 1977.

13 Tulving, E. and Osler, S. 'Effectiveness of retrieval cues in memory for words'. *Journal of Experimental Psychology*, **77** (4), 593–601, 1968.

14 Craik, F.I.M. and Lockhart, R.S. 'Levels of processing: a frame-work for memory research'. *Journal of Verbal Learning and Verbal Behaviour*, **11** (6), 671–684, 1972.

15 Rundus, D. 'Analysis of rehearsal processes in free recall'. *Journal of Experimental Psychology*, **89** (1), 63–77, 1971.

16 Bruner, J.S. *The Process of Education*. Cambridge, MA: Harvard University Press, 1960.

17 Kintsch, W., 1977, op. cit.

18 For example, Atkinson, R.C. and Shiffrin, R.M. 'Human memory: a proposed system and its control processes'. In Spence, K.W. and Spence, J.T. (eds) *The Psychology of Learning and Motivation, Advances in Research and Theory*, Vol. 2. New York: Academic Press, pp. 89–195, 1968.

19 For example, 'proactive interference'.

20 Sperling, G. 'The information available in brief visual presentations'. *Psychological Monographs*, **74** (498), 1960.

21 Sperling, G. 'A model for visual memory tasks'. *Human Factors*, **5**, 19–31, 1963.

22 von Wright, J.M. 'Selection in visual immediate memory'. *Quarterly Journal of Experimental Psychology*, **20**, 62–68, 1968; Kintsch, W. 1977, op. cit.; and Darwin, C., Turvey, M. and Crowder, R. 'An auditory analogue of the Sperling partial report procedure: evidence for brief auditory storage'. *Cognitive Psychology*, **3**, 255–267, 1972.

23 Tulving, E. 'Ecphoric processes in recall and recognition'. In Brown, R. (ed.) *Children and Television*. London: Collier Macmillan, pp. 37–73, 1976.

24 Tulving, E., 1972, op. cit.

25 Craik, F.I.M. and Jacoby, L.L., 1975, op. cit.; and Kintsch, W. 'Models of free recall and recognition'. In Norman, D.A. (ed.) *Models for Human Memory*. New York: Academic Press, pp. 333–373, 1970.

26 Bartlett, F.C., 1932, op. cit.

27 Gagné, R.M. *The Conditions of Learning*. New York: Holt, Rinehart and Winston, 1965.

28 Jarvella, R.J. 'Syntactic processing of connected speech'. *Journal of Verbal Learning and Verbal Behaviour*, **10**, 409–416, 1971.

29 Bauer, R. 'Limits of persuasion'. *Harvard Business Review*, **36** (5), 105–110, 1958.

30 Gardiner, J.M. *Readings in Human Memory*. London: Methuen, 1976.

31 Bruner, J.S. *Beyond the Information Given: Studies in the Psychology of Knowing*. London: G. Allen and Unwin, p. 224, 1974.

32 Craik, F.I.M. and Lockhart, R.S., 1972, op. cit.

33 Craik, F.I.M. 'A "levels of analysis" view of memory'. In Pliner, P., Krames, L. and Alloway, T. (eds) *Communication and Affect*. New York: Academic Press, 1973.

34 Tulving, E. *Elements of Episodic Memory*. Oxford: Clarendon Press, 1983; and Tulving, E. 'Subjective organisation and effects of repetition in multi-trial pre-recall learning'. *Journal of Verbal Learning and Verbal Behaviour*, **5** (2), 193–197, 1966.

35 Underwood, G. *Attention and Memory*. Oxford: Pergamon, 1976.

36 Kelley, H.H. 'Attribution theory in social psychology'. In Levine, D. (ed.) *Nebraska Symposium on Motivation*. Lincoln: University of Nebraska Press, 1967.

37 Kintsch, W., 1977, op. cit.

38 Schank, R. and Abelson, R. *Scripts, Plans, Goals and Understanding*. London: Lawrence Erlbaum, 1977.

39 Bartlett, F.C., 1932, op. cit.

40 Anderson, J.R. and Bower, G.E., 1973, op. cit.

41 Berelson, B. and Steiner, G.A. (eds) *Human Behaviour: An Inventory of Scientific Findings*. New York: Harcourt Brace, 1964.

42 Underwood, B.M. and Schulz, R.W. *Meaningfulness and Verbal Learning*. Chicago: Lippincott, 1960.

43 Ausubel, D.P. *Educational Psychology: A Cognitive View*. New York: Holt, Rinehart and Winston, 1968.

44 Bartlett, F.C., 1932, op. cit.

45 James, W. *The Principles of Psychology*. New York: H. Holt, 1890.

46 Waugh, N.C. and Norman, D.A., 1965, op. cit.

47 Lockhart, R.S., Craik, F.I.M. and Jacoby, L. 'Depth of processing, recognition and recall'. In Brown, J. (ed.) *Recall and Recognition*. Chichester: Wiley, pp. 75–102, 1976; Craik, F.I.M. 'The fate of primary memory items in free recall'. *Journal of Verbal Learning and Verbal Behaviour*, **9**, 143–

148, 1970; Tulving, E., 1972, op. cit.; and Craik, F.I.M. and Jacoby, L.L., 1975, op. cit.

48 Atkinson, R.C., and Shiffrin, R.M., 1968, op. cit.

49 Bartlett, F.C., 1932, op. cit., p. 213.

CHAPTER 7
The Order of the Inner World

> All improvement in memory consists, then, in the improvement of one's
> habitual methods of recording facts.
> William James, *The Principles of Psychology*, Vol. 1.

Most of us assume that we all have fairly similar perceptions of the
world. We lead our lives on the assumption that there are general
truths universally acknowledged, and that it is only a philosophical trick to suggest that we do not all understand the same truth by
the same word, and in the same way. Now and again our assumptions are rudely knocked, say by a religious group, by another
nation or by a group of terrorists who, with similar tenacity to us,
hold on to a type of 'morality' that is beyond our own comprehension. But although bruised, our conventional morality reappears,
for our communications and relationships depend on such a sense
of uniform normality. When an adult undermines conventions it is
natural to assume this to be aberrant; when a child does so it is
conventional to assume that he has not reached the ability to think
conventionally, that he is still unformed in thought as well as
expression.

Children have powerful inner lives because of the constant need
to reassess their relationship with their surroundings. Sometimes
their own interpretations of the world do appear significantly
different from the conventional view. Sometimes children over-
simplify. Sometimes they see ambiguities when adults insist on
simplification. But their attempt to fit their own point of view into
the prevailing one is made more complex by the immediacy and
richness of their perceptions as well as by their unawareness of
implied conventions. Sometimes this very need to observe and
judge leads them to significant conclusions. This is not a romantic
view – children do not come 'trailing clouds of glory' – but they do
try to clarify the complexities of thought and attitude without
shying away from conclusions.

The inner worlds of adults are usually only explored in literature or, in terms of implied failure, in psychiatry. The conventional wisdom that assumes adults are rational beings, careful in
their thought, weighty in their judgement and objective in their
conclusions, is one that is constantly undermined in novels, poems
and plays but is rarely questioned by empirical approaches to
understanding human nature. The emotional power and the
needs of children to understand are, on the contrary, accepted as
the right of childhood, with an implied assumption that they will
grow out of it. But many of the essential attitudes and emotional
attachments that children acquire in childhood mark their failures
and successes for the rest of their lives. The needs of young
children to have their emotional worlds understood are as strong
as their needs in having knowledge delivered to them. Their
attempts to make coherence out of their experiences and to make
sense of their emotional forces are all implicit in their learning to
categorize, to make use of language and to form relationships with
others. The subjective is always very difficult to analyse but it is
not just a matter of self-indulgence; indeed, many of the most
powerful concepts arise from emotional associations, from a sense
of the subjective that is more subtle than logic.[1]

Children's emotional frames of mind should not be exclusively
associated with behavioural problems. They are part of a pattern
of characteristics, traits that are constantly playing on more stable
attitudes, so that when we try to correlate behaviour with attitudes
it is hard to separate one from the other. A pattern of instincts is
formed into more permanent structures, and 'drives' are stabilized
by more conscious sentiments.[2] Children's attitudes derive from
an interaction between inner and outer realities, between the
world as seen and the world as understood. This distinction
between the different levels of reality, between emotions and
fantasy, is one which is never wholly constant, either in adults or in
children. The tendency, or the temptation, to revert to day-
dreams, to let the mind wander away from the subject and explore
distant associations, is always with us.

Many of the insecurities and anxieties of the new-born child
remain as a memory on which other feelings are based.[3] Children
are bound by their previous experiences and base their attitudes to
new ones on what has happened before. Feelings that have been

experienced in the past are transferred into present relationships. They are full of images of a fantastic kind, even fantasies of their parents.[4] The way in which children see the world must contain exaggerations or over-simplifications of good and bad, since their judgements are based on the *emotions* of their experience. The way in which an opinion of the world is formed is never based on purely deductive logic. It is formed through as many cognitive illusions as perceptual illusions. Opinions are formed through available and readily accessible knowledge or experience; hence the singularity of the point of view, and the dislike of changing opinions even in the face of overwhelming logical evidence.

The difference between the way in which adults and children are driven by their inner needs lies only in the fact that in children such inner needs are more obvious. Children are less defensive. They are also less self-deceiving. And they are often encouraged to mix up fantasy worlds with real ones. In school there are times when they are supposed to 'stick to the facts' and other times when they are made to do the opposite and create 'imaginative' fictions. The world of reading books, of writing and drawing, is supposed to be at one level of reality; the world of news and 'topics' at another. 'The pink elephant may exist in one of the story worlds or the world of mathematics but never in the "real" life world of news, of Peter and Jane or in "proper" painting'.[5] But this mixture of the fantastic and the real lies at the heart of the human experience, encouraged as it is in childhood. Children engage in make-believe activities that are a parody of the adult world. They can emulate the concept of ownership when they play with toys, can attach the wildest stories to their paintings and give deliberately absurd answers to questions.[6]

One of the reasons for the singularity of children's points of view is what Chukovsky called their 'optimism'.[7] They struggle for happiness, believing it possible, hoping to understand the world as just and logical. They want to see the adult world make sense in terms of perfect justice and genuine fairness.[8] This is itself a type of fantasy, and shows the juxtaposition between hope and reality. Children impose their own sense of order on what they experience. This might be a type of fantasy, but it is only through the recognition of shared beliefs and the ability to categorize information, that they can make sense of their environment.

The balance between the need for an individual point of view and the understanding of a shared means of conveying a collective point of view has often been observed in children, but rarely completely understood. The fantasy elements of normal life, the power of associations and the influence of overheard remarks are just those matters most difficult to define and tabulate. When the inner and outer worlds are observed they are often discussed in terms that do not reveal at first what is being discovered. 'Imprinting' is contrasted with 'discrimination', the need for associations with the need for the classification of potential stimuli.[9] But two processes, of learning and of development, the one specific, resting in intelligence and observable, and the other general, are not in fact separable.[10] Cobb discusses the 'child's evolving ability to learn clearly, think and create meaning in his perceived world, in contrast to the ability to memorise and record other people's interpretations of that world'.[11] What makes the inner world of children so exciting is the close relationship, as well as the tension, between their inner drives and their grasp of the techniques of understanding.

While children are trying to comprehend the adult world they remain very conscious of their own. Their sense of distinctions in age is strong. To a six-year-old the thirteen-year-old looms as large as a hero. To the thirteen-year-old, someone of 22 is already old. Children do not particularly like the idea of maturity, and generally look on an earlier time in their life as the best.[12] They also exhibit from an early age the capacity to be nostalgic and affected, even sentimental, about those younger than themselves. They feel that they have it in their own power to be happy, forgetting their misery by playing or thinking of 'nice things'.[13] Their sense of their own time of life and their pleasure derives from a belief in the orderliness of their own perceptions. As a number of observers have noted there is a 'surprising' orderliness in 'even' four-year-olds' associations, and this orderliness increases.[14] The sense of the inner logic of the child's point of view, the desire to arrange the picture of the world in clear terms, is so strong that it has led to the desire to find a universal basis for such clarity. Osgood talked of the balance between 'evaluation', 'potency' and 'activity' as the dominant factors in children's and adult's manipulative powers of understanding,[15] just as Wundt put forward a similar triangle of inner and outer influences, in terms of 'strain', 'excitement' and 'pleasantness'.[16] In all such observations the tensions between the observed and the experienced are manifest in different ways, revealing how driven people are by their emotions, while trying to make a rational whole out of what is a unique set of attitudes in each person.

Children's sense of order is helped by language, but it is also difficult to express in language. They have difficulty in reflecting on language itself, thinking, for example, of words like 'salt' and 'coffee' as inimicable in their particular context rather than defining them in terms of more general possibilities. 'You can't put salt in coffee!' Children of five also have difficulty in keeping the semantic context of a sentence constant while changing its form, and find passives difficult, since language is felt to reflect order in its internal structure ('he hitted me') and its overall form.[17] But even the semantic implications of words are at first simplified. Young children test and try out experimental statements that are not particularly supposed to mean anything. If children of seven are asked about the 'best' or 'worst' thing they have done they interpret the 'best' as the most successful or their favourite, rather than the most moral.[18] The 'worst' thing is interpreted as painful or unpleasant more than as bad. This does not mean that their lives are amoral but that they make a pragmatic interpretation of words of that kind. For young children words are to clarify, not to carry implied or ambiguous meanings. Words are there to do what they are ordered to do rather than to have an effect on other people. Children also relish the obscurity and ambiguity of language, as in puns.

Because of the inwardness of language children find it difficult to use verbal symbols as mediators in various tasks or experiments.[19] At the same time they find that linguistic sense and nonsense are difficult to tell apart, remembering a sentence that does not make sense as easily as one that does.[20] There are types of nonsense they find as easy to recall as meaningful passages.[21] Words create their own connections and their own associations in their minds. They are not just part of a semantic network of structured meaning.[22] Verbal stimuli can arouse purely verbal response.[23] This is because language is predicted before it is properly understood. Perceived and remembered material is fitted into pre-existing verbal clichés.[24] Words can create such powerful associations in themselves that they obscure physical information, as in the 'Stroop' effect, when words of colours like 'red' or 'yellow' written out in other colours cause all kinds of difficulties.[25] Word associations are the result of powerful verbal connections as much as of 'logical' categories.

Words create a world of their own but they also help create children's sense of their world. The juxtaposition between the world as it should be and the world as it is remains in constant balance; no amount of will-power or self-deception can create an arbitrary order. There are certain moments when the difference between a world of perfect patterning and one that is a sudden disappointment makes life difficult to bear. There can be few people who do not remember the first moment when an adult was particularly unfair, when the rules that had been so carefully built up were broken. The consequences do not have to be great for a child to feel betrayed. Such moments (one only needs to remind oneself of an early disappointment) stay in the mind even though the significance was not felt at first. Even before there is any hint at understanding, the sense of betrayal can be felt.

Of all the attempts to bring the world into a personal perspective, stories are one of the most important and revealing. They link the child's and the adult's attempts to understand. They are important even before the child can read, and they matter however they are used. Whether the story is as demanding as one by Henry James, or has the easier comforts of a romance, the need to impose some order, some kind of sense, unites them. Stories are a major way of bringing shape to a complex world, of entering it through understanding rather than through ignorance.

Children possess the desire to create simplicity out of all circumstances. The very earliest mistake a child makes, in his movement, his language or his understanding of concepts, is that of seeing things as being simpler than they actually are, of transferring one insight to a different circumstance. Children are not merely reacting simply, but imposing their own version of what they see, or hear, so that it begins to make sense. Children have a need for rules, for a clear sense of what is expected of them; they also need to create a sense of what they expect of the world. Their grammatical mistakes show the imposition of a clear pattern, and their utilization of the rules.

Children's need for patterns, therefore, is one that they impose, not one that is imposed on them. The outlines of stories, however complex, are always complete, for within their dimensions there is the sense of the ending, of the point at which, whatever the ambiguities, the reader or listener understands the whole context. Children's use of stories is an analogy of their reaction to their surroundings; it is an attempt to impose a series of simplicities upon the ambiguous and the complicated. The earliest perceptions are a matter of trying to limit all that is taken in until some order is imposed. Learning to be in the world of adults is a learning about limitations as much as about complexities. The complexities are those things perceived. The limitations are what we make of them and what we need to make of them.

The order that perception gives to the world is a personal one; it is nevertheless an order not merely idiosyncratically imposed, but dependent on what is seen. Thus the traditional dichotomy between 'nurture' and 'nature' is in many ways a false one when it is concerned with human development. That there is an 'inner' and an 'outer' is clear; that these are in tension is reasonable, but they are also in a kind of synthesis. For children parody rather than imitate their surroundings. Stories are a sign of such a sense of parody. The world is put into a transferred order by the way in which the reader is both part of, and an observer of, what is read. The story is itself a simplifying, a restructuring, an explanation, an easing and lightening.

Children's need for the security of a clear structure, of the sense of an ending, is not a matter of minor escapism.[26] Stories are not an alternative to the real world, with its muddles and disappointments. They are a reflection of the real world. Rather than being a distortion, they show that it is possible, even in the telling, to make personal sense out of a variety of different implications. Children listen, in a story, to concepts that they cannot possibly grasp by interpreting these new concepts in their own ways. Listening to stories gives children practice in interpreting experience, a practice that is as important as their learning to discriminate between different sensations, or the practice of learning how to handle objects in words. Children's natural relish for stories is a sign that some of their first instincts are concerned with an attempt to understand, to see a clear relationship between their own viewpoint and the world in which they find themselves.

The very first stories that children like are those to do with the everyday world. A story is an internalization of external events, and it becomes a way of understanding what has been taking place. It is difficult to make a clear distinction between children's own interpretations of what they are doing, in play, and the interpretations given in stories after the event. The story is different from the children's rehearsals of what they are doing because it is shared, a social as well as personal experience. Stories are a continuation of a child's experiments in speech and perception, but most of all in understanding. A story about domestic events reveals an interest in the events that goes beyond the routine. To a child such a rehearsal of events fulfils the complex process of seeing the world objectively, of knowing what to interpret, and of finding the means of interpretation.

Children's sense of structure is an interpretation of the world that is highly personal, but also to a great degree objective. The actual sharing of events, the understanding of consequences, the very action of reading or listening are not purely subjective acts. Too much has been made of the glib notion of identification, of the assumption that if children watch television they will be so emotionally caught up in what they see that they will ultimately copy it, or that if a child likes to read a story it is because he imagines himself the hero, or heroine. The use of material in play (as in pretending to be a space monster) and emotional projection into the identity of a character are distinct from each other. Children accept the ritual outlines of plot and the juxtaposition of good and bad for the sake of the coherence of the plot. They are also aware that the experience of story differs from real events.[27] The element of fantasy when people imagine themselves playing some mercurial role tends to come later in human development. The spirit with which young children approach stories is at once more simple and more complex: more simple because they retain the sense of a clear structure, and more complex because the relationship between the individual and the story is always a tension between self-awareness and the perceptions of a different interpretation.

Children's response to structure, revealed in stories, is significant. A child tells a story: 'and then ...'. His five-year-old fingers are working as hard as his mind as he fulfils his idea of what a story should be. 'And then ...' – in this phrase he knows he has captured the essence of story telling, of anticipation and excitement, of control and logical sequence. What he thinks about to fill the moments before and after the phrase is less important to the child telling the story than the idea of the story itself. Just as adults read countless detective stories, one after the other, without any scrutiny of their quality, so children have an unquenchable thirst for the ritual of the story. Stories can be badly told, and children will show their boredom or surprise, but the important point is that they should be told.

The ritual of a story is important for a child; for it is a ritual rather than a routine. To compare the adult taste for detective stories with children's tastes is clarifying part of the expectations that children have. The detective story ends by fulfilling the expectation: the end is always anticipated. For a child a story begins by fulfilling the expectation: the end is unknown. So the ritual of the story, with its sense of sequence and the control of anticipation, is itself a starting point for a child's understanding of the world. The control of the story, like the control of magic, lies in making order of whatever happens.

Of all forms of control, the most obvious is that of the story. Everyone is constantly using fiction, using the power of interpretation to rewrite the past. This is not something carried out only by historians, or the official chroniclers of repressive states, but the everyday and inescapable fact of all who talk about themselves. Interpretation and re-interpretation, changes of mood or the benefit of hindsight are all part of the control that makes the story different from the event, and necessarily so. Children are more aware of the necessity of such re-telling at a time in which there is little to re-tell, for they see that they can only make sense of the world by their own interpretation. They also know that they can only be made sense of if they can share the interpretation. Stories are the public side of a private dialogue. They make the inevitable re-interpretations clearer for being shared. Again, the difference between adult and child re-interpretations lies not just in the subject matter, but in the uses to which interpretation is put. The adult attempts to re-interpret the private experience against the common experience of the world. The child is trying to interpret the common world against his own experience.

The structure of a story is more than just a framework bricked out with ideas: it is the essential idea. It is impossible to separate the story from its structure; while there are many variations, they are all variations on the same essential structure, not a series from which to choose. One does not need to use the conventions to create the atmosphere of the story. 'Once upon a time' is a way of drawing attention to the idea of any story. The phrase 'once upon a time' is famous because it carries the essential idea behind any story, the juxtaposition between the context of the story and the world outside, between the moment of telling and the expanse of time before and after, between the time within the story and the infinite possibilities beyond. The phrase is a deliberate juxtaposition between two concepts of time, the one momentary and the other eternal. The convention of a story is that one acknowledges both; there is no pretence that *all* is contained but that there is some aspect of a story that relates to the world elsewhere. 'Once' is, therefore, not just an arbitrary moment taken from the whole of time, but also a complete and 'eternal' moment.

The story makes a convention of being complete, of being contained in a structure that has the inevitable beginning, middle and end. But the structure is more important than that. The structure is in evidence at every part of the story. Each cause has an effect, each action a consequence. 'And then' is a connecting thread, implied or written. For every story, however much it concentrates on one action, or however simple, is about how one thing leads to another. The very setting of the first paragraph can imply an instability, an alternative. The most primitive and the most sophisticated stories create a sense of pattern at every moment, a pattern that every reader or listener takes for granted but a pattern nevertheless. Once a start is made, something is going to happen that changes the opening; even if the end can be guessed, the reader needs to travel through certain stages to get there. The change from point to point is also a reminder of the sense of a story, of its implicit structure.

But the most abiding sense of structure about any story is the sense of the ending. The fact that there is an ending, that all can be, temporarily at least, bound up, pervades even the beginning.

The story is a whole, is a moment out of context. 'They lived happily ever after' is, like the conventional opening, a juxtaposition of two states, one temporal and one eternal. 'They lived' in their time, in their place, in their story. 'Ever after' places them out of time, living again and again, according to the needs of the story. But the ending, where so much of the *raison d'être* of novels can be, is also the implicit sense of completeness in the story.

Whatever the detailed structure, the sense of wholeness is an important ingredient in a story. Children are not articulate about their responses – are, indeed, never taught to think about them until they are taught to think about anything in the text *but* their responses – but they are aware of them none the less. The love of story goes deeper than a desire to be distracted; part of this love is of the structure itself. The variety of stories is infinite, they can be concerned with fantasy or everyday life, with adventures or domestic details, with animals or robots, but the linking theme is that sense of wholeness. To explain that children like fantasy is not to explain why young children like to have everyday details that they know to be 'real' repeated to them in the pattern of the story. To suggest that children like excitement does not explain why children like the same story repeated again and again, noticing any performance that is not word perfect. It is as if they are so interested in the overall pattern that they remember every detail that fits.

The mark of tragedy in some novels, and some plays, is the fact that the end, while resolved, is a merely ironic resolution that implies a different type of continuation. But for children the end has no such complications, for the ironic complication of the story lies in its existence itself, in its juxtaposition to reality. The 'optimism' of children lies in their delight in and expectation of the happy resolution.[28] But it is not wilful optimism nor ignorance that leads children to wish the structure of a story to be complete. The story is obviously in ironic counterpoint to the arbitrariness of everyday life; it doesn't shape life but shows an understanding of how life can be shaped. So it is the sense of completeness in a story that matters in itself; not optimistic in the sense of just the happy ending, but optimistic in the sense of retaining the belief that it is possible to achieve a solution. To be optimistic is to retain a sense of the possibility of justice, and the importance of a correct resolution. In children's subconscious analysis of their own experience they wish to see a coherence that shows how one event leads to another justifiably.

Nothing in a story is merely arbitrary to the reader, however inconsequential it might seem. The control of a pattern does not imply that every moment is inevitable, nor that the hero of a story does not undergo dangerous escapades or terrible experiences. Pattern lies in the fact that for every action there will be an inevitable denouement: not just a happy ending but a proper rounding off. At times the fulfilment of expectations might seem to be a dull and obvious pastime, although it pervades nearly all books, but it still pleases because of its sense of structure. The 'happy end' is the logical end, not just a way of taking away some of the putative terror. The ritual of right and wrong is believed in, *not* because of the sense of moral rectitude but because children understand the logic of stories. When groups of children were asked, individually, about different heroes and anti-heroes in stories about the Wild West and about space, they showed how deep this respect for the ending goes.[29] They defined the heroes as those who won: it was those who survived that were good. It might seem at first that this was an immoral or amoral stance, as if they were saying that the winner is always right. But in fact it shows a respect for the conventions of story. The 'bad' man is not a moral entity but a symbol that needs to be overcome. Any close analysis of a western, for example, leaving aside the clothes that characters wear, or the colour of their hair, or the number of their guns, shows how similarly the 'good' and 'bad' men behave. What is clear to all children is that the 'good' man is inevitably faster on the draw, cleverer or luckier than the 'bad'. He therefore survives. The structure of the story is more important than the moral judgement.

The interplay between the real and the fantastic is constant and subtle. Children do not simply accept and imbibe all that they hear; nor do they suspend all disbelief and enter into the complete world of the story. Stories are too important to them to be 'mere' fantasy. The relationship of the child with the story is, therefore, not with the particular point of view in the story, but with the story as a whole. Children do not simply identify with the one point of view expressed as the 'hero'. Their sense of structure means that they accept that the conventions of right and wrong and of proper solutions mean that there is a hero, but this is a structural rather than moral necessity. To a child the 'hero' is not, therefore, a formulation of all that is good or morally uplifting. The hero gives a point of view that holds the structure together: he is like glue. The idea of 'identification' is not therefore all that important.

To many commentators the role of fantasy seems to lie in the idea that the hero is emulated. Certainly there is a conventional wisdom that suggests, more quickly than reflection, that the danger of stories on television is that they might be copied, that fantasy will seem so real that it will turn into the lives of children. Numerous studies have concentrated on which of the characters in films children have watched, to prove whether they are fascinated with their own sex or the other. These have been extensions of the more conventional idea that the thrill of watching Batman, or the A Team, lies in a close identification with the actions of the eponymous heroes. This is then supposed to lead to imitation. The child who admired Superman would, supposedly, throw himself out of the window as if he also could fly; to watch the A Team is supposed to lead, inevitably, to the same violence they portray.

Fortunately the evidence that children do not merely copy what they see is overwhelming, even if many of us would like to think they did so, provided their model was ourselves. The fact of reading, or personalizing what is read, creates a more objective stance. The fact that the hero holds these events together does not mean that everything is seen from his point of view. The stories that young children prefer show that it is the meaning of the whole structure that interests them. They want to make sense of their world by having it interpreted. Saying 'is it true?' is not a subjective empathy with the hero or heroine but an attempt to assess the story as a whole. The question of 'truth' is one of whether the story gives a coherent account of how things happen. This is as 'true' of those stories that have animals as their leading figures as of any other. The fact that an experience put into animal dimensions has a semblance to the general human condition rather than to the domestic realities of their own lives makes this clear. The Opies have shown clearly that the use children make of fantasies is a type of 'ritual', not merely the sublimation of the stories' fantasy into their own lives.[30]

NOTES AND REFERENCES

1 McGinn, C. *The Subjective View: Secondary Qualities and Indexical Thoughts.* Oxford: Clarendon Press, 1983.

2 Not unlike Freud's notion of the 'id' and the 'ego'. Cattell, R.B. and Child, D. *Motivation and Dynamic Structure.* London: Holt, Rinehart and Winston, 1975, describes them as 'drives' and 'ergs'.

3 Klein, M. *The Psycho-analysis of Children.* London: Hogarth Press, 1975.

4 Salzberger-Wittenberg, I., Gianna, H. and Osborne, E. *The Emotional Experience of Learning and Teaching.* London: Routledge and Kegan Paul, 1983.

5 King, R. 'Multiple realities and their reproduction in infants' classrooms'. In Richards, C. (ed.) *New Directions in Primary Education.* Lewes: Falmer, p. 245, 1982.

6 Miller, G.A. *Spontaneous Apprentices: Children and Language.* New York: Seabury Press, 1977.

7 Chukovsky, K. *From Two to Five.* Berkeley: University of California Press, 1963.

8 See Siegal, M. *Fairness in Children: A Social–Cognitive Approach to the Study of Moral Development.* London: Academic Press, 1982.

9 Gibson, E.J. *Principles of Perceptual Learning and Development.* Englewood Cliffs, NJ: Prentice-Hall, 1969.

10 Piaget, J. *The Moral Judgement of the Child.* London: Routledge and Kegan Paul, 1932.

11 Cobb, E. *The Ecology of Imagination in Childhood.* London: Routledge and Kegan Paul, p. 18, 1977.

12 Research based on interviews with children of seven to eleven carried out in 1984–5 as part of a series of interviews concerned with children's political perceptions. (Publication is forthcoming.)

13 Goldman, R. and Goldman, J. *Children's Sexual Thinking.* London: Routledge and Kegan Paul, 1982.

14 Entwhistle, D.R. *Word Associations.* Baltimore: Johns Hopkins Press, 1966.

15 Osgood, C.E., Suei, G.J. and Tannenbaum, P.H. *The Measurement of Meaning.* Urbana: University of Illinois Press, 1957.

16 Wundt, W. *Frundzüge de Physiologischen Psychologie, Vol. 3.* Leipzig: W. Engelmann, 1903.

17 de Zwart, S. 'Developmental psycholinguistics'. In Elkind, D. and Flavell, J.H. (eds) *Studies in Cognitive Development.* Oxford: Oxford University Press, 1969.

18 Part of the research carried out on children's attitudes to questions of morality.

19 Flavell, J.H. 'Developmental studies of mediated memory'. In Reese, H.W. and Lipsitt, L.P. (eds) *Advances in Child Development and Behavior.* New York: Academic Press, pp. 182–209, 1970.

20 Unlike adults in experiment tests.

21 Miller, G.A. and Selfridge, J.A. 'Verbal context and the recall of meaningful material'. *American Journal of Psychology*, **63**, 176–185, 1950.

22 Deese, J. 'Influence of inter-item associative strength upon immediate free recall'. *Psychological Review*, **5**, 305–312, 1959.

23 Tversky, A. and Kahneman, D. 'Availability: a heuristic for judging frequency and probability'. *Cognitive Psychology*, **5**, 207–232, 1973; and Paivio, A. 'Psychological processes in the comprehension of metaphor'. In Ortony, A. (ed.) *Metaphor and Thought*. Cambridge: Cambridge University Press, 1979.

24 Compare Allport, G.W. and Postman, L.P. *The Psychology of Rumor*. New York: Holt Rinehart, 1947.

25 Stroop, J.R. 'Studies of interference in serial verbal reactions'. *Journal of Experimental Psychology*, **18**, 643–662, 1935.

26 It is a concept which remains central to literature; compare Kermode, F. *The Sense of an Ending*.

27 Cullingford, C. *Children and Television*. Aldershot: Gower, 1984.

28 Chukovsky, C., 1963, op. cit.

29 Cullingford, C., 1984, op. cit.

30 Opie, I. and Opie, P. *The Lore and Language of School Children*. London: Routledge and Kegan Paul, 1959.

CHAPTER 8
Making Sense of Experience

If evolution is to work smoothly, consciousness in some shape must have been present at the very origin of things.
William James, *The Principles of Psychology*, Vol. 1.

The adult's experience of the world differs from the child's experience in type, not quality. The adult imagination, with its powers of severe self-discipline, of ignoring all experiences that do not seem immediately to the purpose, of limiting itself to the matter in hand, is a way of allowing a fixed view of the world to control and organize what is perceived. The 'set' of mind dominates the actual experience. This means that habits are constant, and that experiences are less intense. Such a difference in immediacy marks out the difficulties in interpreting the more complex and variable responses of children. In their engagement with their surroundings their reactions are more obvious, more geared to all the nuances of the situation. The whole context of circumstances, including, for instance, the researcher as well as the experiment, informs the child's reactions. Sometimes the *context* of a task, such as problem-solving, can interfere with the task by distracting the child from the intended action.

Every instruction that is given to children rests on the assumption that they will ignore all the unspoken possibilities. When a teacher says 'stand by the door', she means 'get up quietly out of your seats without talking, and walk up to the door, forming a line behind each other without talking or poking each other' ... but only when she has made quite clear that the short instruction *means* a more detailed list of 'don'ts' is she likely to be understood. The move from one end of the room to another is for an adult a particular move to a goal; for a child it is much more of a possible adventure, through the exploration of things on the way or through an experimental series of hops and skips. None of the hidden possibilities is ignored. The conventional world, however, relies on the network of understanding of what is left out, as when a notice such as 'No one can get in to the theatre without a ticket' really means 'No one (except managers, actors, ticket collectors ...) ...'.

We take many things for granted that children do not. Perception is itself a process of analysis, both by synthesis and by reconstruction, and nearly always involves a choice of what to attend to and what to ignore.[1] Children learn to attend, or select for attention, according to both physical and semantic clues, but once accustomed to the latter they tend to rely on them far more than the former. Children gradually learn to ignore incidental details that were, at first, as important as the main points. But even in their perception of different clues, as in a film or a picture, there is a sense of order for them even if it is not the order we think is important. Children attempt to make some sense out of a constantly expanding amount of material. The complexity is at first perceived in their own surroundings, through associations with place, made more complex in terms of time and through the appearance, disappearance and re-appearance of people, and then made even more complex in terms of ideas and relationships.

Children's interpretation of immediate information is a rich one, full of the excitement of discovery and 'naive' only in the sense that they are not weighted with expectations of what they see. Their immediacy of interest includes taking words at their face value. When they hear a story which from its context clearly refers to the 'wing' of a house, rather than a bird, to a hare, rather than a hair, to a quay, rather than a key, children, while understanding the story through its context, nevertheless can retain the full force of the words in other senses, and can interpret them afterwards as in the wing of a bird, or hair or key. There is a constant juxtaposition between the need to place what they see and hear into the context of their experience, and their interest in the experience for its own sake. The palpable 'misinterpretations' derive from the fact that, although they are conscious of what they have so far learned, their 'set' of experience is constantly changing. The conscious effort of understanding means that they are more willing to *make* a new experience fit, however awkwardly, into their expectations, and are more able to absorb a new insight so that it changes their point of view.

People do not remember what they do not attend to. There are even occasions when we suddenly realize that we are being addressed and 'tune in' to what has just been said in an effort to recollect it. This shows a clear distinction between information that is processed and information that is ignored.[2] Children pay attention to a wider range of events. Children try to 'conform', in Kohlberg's term,[3] but find it difficult to know exactly what they are supposed to conform to. As they build up their experience and their interpretation of their experience so they understand the ambiguities between their own perceptions and conventional interpretations.[4] They are more interested in tactile words, such as 'cold' or 'hot', than they are in more abstract concepts, such as visual terms like 'bright'.[5] This is because they are engaged in exploring their own interpretation, not out of the limitations of their own egocentricity but through a logic that explores new ideas in terms of those already understood.

Because of the difficulties of discovering the natural logic of a child's understanding of his world – a lack of a common way of communicating such an understanding – it has often been supposed that children actually lack the capacity to use inductive reasoning, to pursue logic or to understand analogies, even though they could not survive in the world, or develop language, without it. Piaget's stress on a particular mode of scientific thought, and the influence of his theory that children failed to meet certain mental targets at certain ages, led to the duplication of a number of experiments designed to prove children's lack of certain types of reason. In the past few years, however, most of Piaget's experiments have been repeated with small changes designed to enable the child to understand what was being demanded, either through a clearer explanation of the requirement or by relating the experiment to something within a child's own experience.[6] Once children connect the abstract logic required of them in an experiment with the *real* problem that they meet with every day, they are far more successful. To make any sense of the world in which they live they actually *need* to understand all those laws of conservation that Piaget implied were beyond them. The fact that they do not consistently *display* such abilities, even in the face of the demands of an experimenter, should not lead one to suppose that they are not capable of understanding.

Children carry out difficult tasks when they can understand how the problem set them relates to their experience of the world. In one of the Piagetian tests, for example, Bruner found that the perceptual display (of quantity of water) can actually mislead their understanding.[7] In this test children are asked to state which is the larger quantity of water when it is poured from a wide glass into a tall thin one. If a screen is used so that children cannot see the liquid being poured from one glass to another, and the experiment is instead described, they do much better in the tests, since the words overcome the 'perceptual seduction'. At other times, however, because of children's lapses of concentration, or their interest in other things than the task in hand, they can *seem* stupid because they do not attend closely to the significant part of the instruction given them.[8] They can latch on to a particular part of the language, to a word that interests them; indeed they can be 'seduced' by the language as easily as the perception. This does not argue for an incapacity, but for attention to other things than what the researcher was looking for. Children also say 'I don't know' to avoid having to answer a question that does not interest them, such as 'And what did you do today?'

When children know what the task required of them consists of, they can do the famous 'conservation' tests as easily as they can display their use of deductive reasoning in their criticism of stories. What Piaget describes as a failure to reason, on the grounds that children are so egocentric they are incapable of seeing beyond their own needs, is actually a failure of communication with the child. Two sticks of the same length in alignment are *not* the same as two sticks that are out of alignment, but Piaget's test demands that they should say that they are the same. Water seen in a thin glass is not the same as water seen in a squat one. To a child, *any* change is relevant: why else should he be asked? As Donaldson points out, the same experimental task becomes easy to understand when turned into a game with a familiar object.[9] To a child *every* detail of evidence is potentially significant. To a scientist the height of reasoning is the ability to ignore everything but the narrowest interpretations of the task in hand. Children's tendency to associate, to seek unusual connections, to interpret in their own way, is a demonstration of a different aspect of logic. Children do not always understand the implications of what a researcher or a teacher is getting at, and are diverted from the task to the interpretation of the adult's request. Children are not attracted to *abstract* logic.

If p then q
Not q
therefore not p

might make absolute sense, but is not easy to follow for those unaccustomed to the style. Children find the same logic applied to real events perfectly comprehensible.[10] They can easily follow the fact that:

If there is a wedding there is a man involved
There is no man
Therefore no wedding

Children learn logic through the necessity of applying it to their environment. They do not divorce abstract problems from the circumstances in which they take place. The problem with some of the tests on which the assumption of children's ignorance rests is that they do not relate to children's actual capacities or actual needs. Children of three and a half carry out many of the tasks that were designed to prove that they cannot think rationally or see beyond themselves. Their rootedness in their own experience is a sign of strength rather than failure. When children are asked what can be seen on a three-dimensional model from the point marked by a letter, they understand what is being sought and give accurate, reasonable answers.[11] What children do not understand, since they are using their minds against real material all the time, are questions to do with the psychological abstractions.

We find that children of three can transfer the discovery of a rule to new circumstances, that they focus on distinctive features to facilitate their understanding. The 'mistakes' children make show the application of a logical choice, as they choose *certain* features to be significant. When there are alternative features that matter more – like the shape of the handle rather than the base in making the distinction between a cup and a mug – children will still have noticed other possible distinctions, such as size and texture.[12] Without the context of a question, without the knowledge of possible applications, problems can remain both abstract and meaningless, as if they were fanciful games being played to show up the foolishness of the listener: 'If a man travelling backwards through a tunnel at four miles per hour meets an oncoming express train on which an elephant . . .'.

The fact that children (like adults) find it difficult to adapt quickly to particular demands that remain incomprehensible to them does not mean that they do not learn in their own way. Their deductive reasoning is demonstrated by the way they criticize stories that are not logical, or when something seems missing. Their constant use of the question 'why?' is as much a part of their pursuit of a particular line of argument as it is of their desire for knowledge. They can tell when they are being fobbed off with a trite answer. But what they want to know relates closely to the world of their experience: their logic is applied. A problem presented to them in terms of envelopes or money is a reasonably easy task. The same problem presented in abstract terms of letters and numbers means little to them.[13] Children explore the dimensions of a problem, its associations with the world beyond and the meaning it has in relation to other events. For this reason children are as conscious of the teacher or researcher making a demand as of the demand itself, as they do not separate the context from the clues. Some might say that they are more easily distracted, looking for answers in all places but the most obvious, restlessly waiting for the examinations to be over, to go away, but their 'distraction' is as much a matter of being responsive to experience as it is of looking for a means of escaping the problem in hand. When children are 'tested' on their ability to use passive or active sentences, and are shown pictures that illustrate the different uses of syntax, they assume that the words being used refer to the pictures, since there would surely be no point in showing them the picture otherwise.[14] They are, after all, accustomed to seeing picture stories: the words always support the pictures and vice versa.

Children's mental energies are directed towards coming to terms with their experience, even if this adaptive process seems to be idiosyncratic. In testing, as in lessons in school, children spend much of their time trying to work out what the researcher or the teacher is attempting to elicit, and what will please. This takes their attention away from the actual problem presented to them.

This is the difference between children's coping behaviour and their behaviour in trying to avoid entry into a problem.[15] Many of the peripheral pieces of information (such as the circumstantial information that surrounds a typical mathematical 'problem') distract them from the task in hand. The more that is understood about the human mind the more complex it seems. Ironically enough, the development of microtechnology and the greater understanding of the intricacies of computing have led to a realization that the mind cannot simply be likened to a machine that processes information.

The belief that there is some perfect attainable intelligence which is slowly reached only through a series of immutable stages is no longer justified. The brain is capable of carrying out precise mathematics, but it is not only mathematical. It is through the discovery of the limitations of many of the standard tests of attainment that a greater desire to understand how children (or adults) function has developed.[16] Piaget's dominating influence arose because of the precision with which he measured his belief in the dominance of logic and mathematics.[17] His own biological training suggested that: 'It must be emphasised at once that the entire world of reality can be expressed in mathematical terms and, *a fortiori*, in logical terms. There is no known physical phenomenon which has defied expression in mathematical form'.[18]

The discovery of the limitations of mathematics to explain the mind has led to the questioning of many Piagetian experiments. The usefulness of many of Piaget's ideas and suggestions has been somewhat eroded by the rigidity and ubiquity with which they have been taken up and by the way in which a perfectly sound theory has been misapplied to realms it cannot adequately touch. On the development of scientific modes of thought Piaget remains most impressive, but he does not explain children's own logic or their inner worlds. Piaget's idea of structure embodies what for him are three fundamental ideas: wholeness (a form of *internal* coherence, without outside associations), transformation (as in language in relation to ideas) and self-regulation.[19] This idea of a strict autonomous structure to learning leads him to dissociate egocentric from socialized speech, as if children talking about a picture were undergoing an experience fundamentally different from responding to questions. The concentration of Piagetian thought is on a world where the empirical changes in the children's mentality are quite divorced from the social environment in which they live.[20] Once viewed in such a way it is easy to see why a theory of stages should follow, from the 'sensorimotor', through the 'preconceptual' and the 'concrete operations' phases to the goal of 'formal operations'. All depend on the demonstration of particular achievements or, more precisely, particular limitations. There are few tests that are designed to show egocentricity that have not subsequently been found wanting. A few subtle changes have shown children achieving mastery of just those tasks they were supposed not to be able to undertake.[21]

To understand the activity of children's minds we need to be aware of the subjective element. The tendency to try to find empirical measures of children's capacity to remember has created a model of children's performance that draws attention to deficiencies, as if they do not measure up to the ideal. In fact it is the very need of children to adapt in their own way to the circumstances, to internalize what they see and understand their relationship to the information presented to them, that makes them *seem* irrational. But this is partly because children are both thinking and learning to think. Their minds are so actively engaged that they continue to reflect on a range of new ideas even when teachers are asking them not to.

It is often difficult to understand the excitement or the mental power involved in coming to terms with the world, when there is no ready vocabulary to explain and communicate. We have to use words even to explain the states of mind that develop before, or below, linguistic abilities. Children's first approaches to language suggest some of the many possible misapprehensions open to someone to whom so many incidental clues (such as tone and gesture) are important and to whom some of the underlying concepts of words, their abstractions and generalizations, are not yet clear. Children appear to have difficulty with the distinction between the word 'ask' and the word 'tell'.[22] It is thought that this misinterpretation arises from misunderstanding of the complement clauses that the word 'ask' dominates, but it is more from the fact that to children the distinction between the two modes of address is in fact very slight.[23] Both words are after all used in the same way: the adult says 'ask John to come over here', and does not expect a polite refusal.

The distinction between what Skinner called 'Mands' and 'Tacts', between real demands and commands, however put, and the desire to inform rather than manipulate, is more significant than the words used since children can perceive the hidden intentions of language much earlier than the polite conventions in which the intentions are wrapped.[24] The action of language is its ultimate significance.[25] Children understand the tone of voice and the sense of the gesture as a means of contextualizing what the words actually say. Words to them are a reflection of action rather than a distancing from action; they are an intrinsic part of the environment rather than a reflection of it. When children of seven and under are asked what the word 'change' means they express it in terms of direct actions or as substitutions of one thing for another.[26] Only later, from the age of ten, is the concept of change treated as part of the more general order of things in terms of gradual transformation.

Children often grow accustomed to using an actual concept and to the general sense of particular words, without quite connecting the two. One example of this is the use of the simple words 'down' and 'up'.[27] The use of such words is far easier for children than the explanation of them in terms of opposites. They could be familiar with the words, and obviously have experienced the concept, but could not deal with the same things in terms of another, outside, abstraction, such as a test. But the language that is spoken by children reflects the nature of the events they describe. They do not comprehend the concept of a sentence which is so clearly demonstrated in the written word. For them the language that they use is an immediate counterpart to observed experience, with cause preceding effect, unlike the order of words used in written prose, which is often detached from the immediacy of events.

Children are rarely static in their observation of the world; they do not hold a fixed point of view into which perception is supposed to fit. Children see with excitement that many things are alive and that many events are formed not through growth but through the action of outside events. One might discuss such symptoms of 'animism' or 'artificialism' as primitive gestures if one did not perceive that children's need to find a frame of reference is constantly changing in the light of fresh experience.[28] The changes that children undergo, so carefully tabulated by Gesell,[29] reveal a constantly changing perspective, an ability to re-engage, to adapt again and again.

NOTES AND REFERENCES

1 As in the skill of reading; synthetic versus analytic types of analysis – breaking a word into its constituent parts, or building up a word from its phonemic and morphological components.

2 Norman, D.A. 'Memory while shadowing'. *Quarterly Journal of Experimental Psychology*, **21**, 85–93, 1969; and Moray, N. 'Attention in dichotic listening: affective cues and the influence of instructions'. *Quarterly Journal of Experimental Psychology*, **11**, 56–60, 1960.

3 Kohlberg, L. 'Development of moral character and moral ideology'. In Hoffman, M. and Hoffman, L. (eds) *Review of Child Development Research*, Vol. 1. New York: Russell Sage, 1964.

4 Asch, S.E. and Nerlove, H. 'The development of double-function terms in children: an exploratory investigation'. In Kaplan, B. and Warner, S. (eds) *Perspectives in Psychological Theory*. New York: International Universities Press, 1960.

5 Lesser, H. and Dronin, C. 'Training in the use of double-function terms'. *Journal of Psycholinguistic Research*, **4**, 285–302, 1975.

6 For example: Donaldson, M. *Children's Minds*. London: Fontana/Croom Helm, 1978; and Voneche, J.J. 'Conclusions'. In Modgil, S. and Modgil, C. (eds) *Towards a Theory of Psychological Development*. Windsor: NFER, pp. 765–787, 1980.

7 Bruner, J.S. *Beyond the Information Given: Studies in the Psychology of Knowing*. London: G. Allen and Unwin, 1974.

8 Donaldson, M., 1978, op. cit. Compare Egan, K. *Education and Psychology*. New York: Teachers College Press, 1983.

9 Donaldson, M., 1978, op. cit. Note the distinction Piaget's tests make between testing and reasoning.

10 Donaldson, M., 1978, op. cit., p. 80.

11 Donaldson, M., 1978, op. cit.

12 Gibson, E.J. *Principles of Perceptual Learning and Development*. Englewood Cliffs, NJ: Prentice-Hall, 1969.

13 Donaldson, M., 1978, op. cit. p. 80.

14 Turner, E.A. and Rommetveit, R. 'Focus on attention in recall of active and passive sentences'. *Journal of Verbal Learning and Verbal Behaviour*, **7**, 543–548, 1968.

15 Bruner, J.S., 1974, op. cit.

16 Cronbach, L.J. and Snow, R.E. *Aptitudes and Instructional Methods: A Handbook for Research and Interactions.* New York: Irvington, 1977.

17 Rotman, B. *Jean Piaget: Psychologist of the Real.* Brighton: Harvester Press, 1977.

18 Piaget, J. *Biology and Knowledge.* Chicago: University of Chicago Press, p. 339, 1971.

19 Piaget, J. and Inhelder, B. *Mental Imagery in the Child: A Study of the Development of Imaginal Representation.* London: Routledge and Kegan Paul, 1971.

20 Voneche, J.J., 1980, op. cit.

21 Borke, H. 'Piaget's view of social interaction and the theoretical construct of empathy'. In Siegal, L.S. and Brainerd, C.J. (eds) *Alternatives to Piaget.* London: Academic Press, 1978.

22 Chomsky, C. ' "Ask" and "Tell" revisited: a reply to Warden'. *Journal of Child Language,* **9** (3), 667–678, 1982.

23 But then such a lack of distinction between modes of word is observable in adults as well, in their confusion between 'lend' and 'borrow' and between 'teach' and 'learn', e.g. 'I'll learn you'.

24 Skinner, B.F. 'The science of learning and the art of teaching'. *Harvard Educational Review,* **24**, 86–97, 1954.

25 Searle, J.R. *Speech Acts.* Cambridge: Cambridge University Press, 1969.

26 Crowther, E.M. 'Understanding of the concept of change among children and young adolescents'. *Educational Review,* **34** (3), 279–284, 1982.

27 Clark, E.V. 'On the child's acquisition of antonyms in two semantic fields'. *Journal of Verbal Learning and Verbal Behaviour,* **11**, 750–758, 1972.

28 Compare the assumptions about children's 'animism', the mixing up of the world of fantasy with the real world, as if they assumed that all things are somehow living. This could be the transference by adults of the way in which stories are 'peopled' by creatures like Pooh Bear.

29 Gesell, A., Ilg, F. and Ames, L.B. *The Child from Five to Ten.* New York: Harper and Row, 1977.

CHAPTER 9
Friendships and Relationships

A man has as many social selves as there are individuals who recognize him
and carry an image of him in their minds.

William James, *The Principles of Psychology*, Vol. 1

There are many skills involved in making a relationship. When we
study the complicated ways in which adults give each other non-
verbal as well as verbal signals we are aware of the difficulties as
well as the subtleties that characterize new relationships.[1] Young
children continually explore the varieties of response to other
people: reading their faces, provoking different reactions, interpreting tone, analysing the sense of the words or the outline of the
voice, as well as trying to convey a similar range of expression even
before they can clarify or mask what they wish to say through
language. They often test a reaction by saying something designed
to shock or surprise, or trying a new idea while watching how a
parent will respond. The most laconic of verbal interchanges is
surrounded by a mass of possibilities, even when we choose to
ignore them.

Whether children are expansive or evaluative, whether they go
through periods of anxiety or of equilibrium, whether they play by
themselves with their toys or burst into activity, they are continually testing relationships.[2] Children's emotional development and
their gift for relationships is being developed all the time. Sometimes such development can atrophy. Interest in individual children by other people is one of their most important needs. We
know how much children suffer when deprived of such interest.
We also understand how children suffer when they are not given
the chance fully to pursue the possibilities of individual attachments. The variety of sustained relationships teaches children
how to change and how to respond to new people. It involves
forgiveness, sorrow and understanding, as well as the immediate
charms of acquaintance. It is through the demands made by other
people that children learn to 'unfreeze' a particular point of view

122

before changing to a new one.[3] Children need time to develop sustained relationships, and need a variety of them. Children need adults to act as thinkers as well as containers, to react to them as well as to absorb them, so that children do more than indulge in 'projective identification', seeing their own personalities reflected in others.

Learning obviously involves self-esteem. Many of the failures at school are failures of nerve, when children retreat from a problem rather than putting mental energy into it. This loss of self-belief is not just a reflection of other people's immediate attitudes, nor a matter of the teacher making it quite clear that she has low expectations. It is not just a matter of the opinions of the peer group, or parents. Self-esteem derives from confidence in making relationships, and from being expected to make relationships. It depends on symbolic interactions with other people, for friends do not just impose an opinion about success or failure, but reflect the child's concept of himself.[4] Children experiment with friendships and change their friends often. The sense of anxiety and insecurity is dependent not so much on self-approval or lack of it as on the freedom with which relationships can be made. The fear of new circumstances, a new class or a new school, comes from the fear of meeting new people, from the unfamiliarity of forming new roles with other people.

This insecurity is a characteristic not only of the very young but also of many adults: those who have never found themselves surrounded by the security of stable and coherent relationships remain shy throughout their lives. Very close relationships are not neutral; they include the exaggerations of hate as well as love, and reveal to the child the bad as well as the good. They include a sense of suitability as well as permanence and form the way in which a child understands the world. To allow this interplay of the inner world with someone outside is to allow a means of reconciliation between personal and impersonal points of view. The most important attitude that children can learn at an early age, the ability to accept doubts and uncertainties, derives from shared security. It is only through the knowledge that characteristics in others remain the same, despite changes in mood or circumstances, that children can accept some of the ambiguities that inevitably surround their own temporary certainties.

One of the most important shared experiences for young children is conversation (as well as story telling). The adult is useful not only as a conveyor of the words of a text, but as someone else reacting to the same experience, noting the pictures, commenting on the characters. Those children whose parents naturally share their enthusiasms with them, such as going to museums, sporting events or country houses, develop longer periods of interest and concentration. The relation of anecdotes, the sharing of interests and the telling of stories all have a significant part to play in children's development of attitudes. It is against other experience that personal guesses and ideas are tested.

The way in which parents react to events has a strong influence on their children. Boredom or impatience with a visit to a country house will soon cause the child to share the same indifference. Lack of enthusiasm is very influential. Parents can be indifferent to the child's interests as well as to their own, or they can be over-protective of the child's reactions so that children either feel inhibited from demonstrating what they think or take refuge in the experiences without sharing them. They can hide in comics or in day-dreams. Children require both the security of steady relationships and the objectivity that comes from articulating a shared experience. They spend time learning not only how to perceive other people, but also how to form some kind of opinion about them. Children do not merely recognize the familiar and dislike the unfamiliar. They are clearly more interested in some people than others, according to their style of approach – rejecting the overbearing or the self-indulgent ('oh, what a pretty little boy!') – and according to their characteristics. Children test their attitudes to other people, trying to find out how to make judgements, often exaggerating their own responses. It is as if they were using Osgood's 'semantic differentials': weighing up people against pairs of opposites and, having formed an opinion, taking sides.[5] Adults under that kind of scrutiny do not need to feel offended; children's judgements are not absolute but the testing of hypotheses.

The forming of attitudes to others is not only a matter of personal temperament or circumstances but also a result of particular decisions. Attitudes towards behaviour that is considered ordinary are attributed to the circumstances in which they are seen; attitudes towards behaviour that is uncommon are attributed to personal dispositions.[6] We therefore fit people into preconceptions of what is normal, looking for consistency of behaviour, as well as for the normality of behaviour, against which any distinctiveness stands out. The reasons for liking some people are not only because they reward us or because it is profitable to us to like them, but because some kind of equilibrium in the relationship has been established, or a neutral territory has been observed for long enough to leave the equilibrium undisturbed.[7]

Time and circumstances shared together can also be reasons for liking particular people. In all formations of attitudes to others there is an element of trying to fit new people into preconceived notions.[8] But these preconceptions are not just a matter of clear self-interest. Charm is a far more complicated commodity, depending not so much on the innate characteristics of a particular person as on both people understanding the same things in the same way. Some people are very good at adapting to others, at 'putting themselves out' to please. All children need to learn how to manage this in order to form relationships, to be interested in others for the sake of the pleasure of communication. They learn, almost as an art in itself, to keep a conversation going.

When we meet others for the first time we try to make them seem predictable in such a way that we can guide our own behaviour appropriately.[9] We not only observe other people's behaviour but attribute motives and intentions to them, and assess them.[10] We like others to the extent to which we share important attitudes and beliefs.[11] We like those who seem to admire, like or respect us.[12] And we also desire more than an individual relationship, wanting to be part of a recognizable group identity.[13] Adults are for the most part accustomed to the conventions of forming judgements and striking up conversations, even if they are not always very good at it, or do not wish to make use of it. Children, however, are both more active in their experiments in relationships, trying out different companions and groups, and more neutral, remaining sometimes dispassionate in the middle of a seemingly intense friendship. They are willing to test out a liking, to have a strong attachment, just as they can later form a one-sided 'crush'. But they can also remain indifferent to other people as they make up their minds about them. Like adults, children perceive others according to pre-set judgements based on associations – with the name, the accent or the clothes. But even more than adults, children perceive others according to the circumstances they are in, and according to what they are doing.[14]

Children make and test their judgements of other people not because they wish to impose a structure of expectations on what they see but because of their need to make their experiences and perceptions coherent. They need to be able to generalize, to choose the moment when it is possible to simplify the eternally complex and arcane into a coherent statement. No such statement, indeed no statement that attempts to sum up human experience, can be wholly true, or nothing but true, not even this one.[15] But children need to make such statements, while accepting the limitations of what they say. Children's simplifications of judgement are necessary; their judgement of right and wrong, between one category and another, is a necessary step towards the more refined, hidden and inactive moralities of the conventional world. Children make judgements, even cruel ones, against other people and other children, that they might afterwards regret, especially remembering how a particular person suffered. Sometimes this is defined as the cruelty of childhood, when a group can agree and act upon a dislike of an individual and feel justified in punishing him.[16] But it is also an attempt to impose an understanding on behaviour and on relationships, an understanding that comes about through rules, through contrasts between right and wrong. Children like to know where they stand with other people, admiring the teacher who is consistent, and both hating and despising the teacher who is not.[17] Their first taste of rules might come from their parents, but they soon need to learn the rules that attach to all relationships. In play such rules are clearly being tested. Children learn to create positions for themselves and others within the same conventions. They attempt to make judgements on others just as they look for the justification for others' judgements.

The question of these rules and the consequences of obedience and punishment goes so deep that Kohlberg tries to explain all young children's experience in those terms.[18] The sense of conformity is not just subservience to rules but also a discovery of what is acceptable. Children do not merely conform to avoid punishment. They will test how far they can go before being punished.[19] They try to appraise natural or unspoken conventions. They need to understand the rules, since they naturally believe that their world must make clear social sense. Their inner need for structure is displayed in their desire to see this structure visible in people's relationships. Their sense of acceptance of rules is to some extent demonstrated in their response to punishment. Far from making children more obedient, punishment can make them respond less and less quickly, with more inclination to rebel, both at home and in school. Punishment, when badly directed, can lead to a clash of wills, and to a child's deep sense of resentment.

When children exchange their points of view with others they are both exploring their own attitudes and allowing themselves to be convinced. It sometimes sounds as if the children in a group are echoing each other, even to the extent of exaggerating attitudes like snobbery, if that is the collective road down which they find themselves going. In the face of objections or contraries children can be very stubborn. They will continue to assert their point of view. But they are just as capable of changing their minds subsequently. This testing out, or exploration, of an opinion is part of their discovery that certain opinions define less than the whole of the world, but more than themselves alone. As part of the exploration of conflicting truths in the world, the peer group is very important. Like adults, children learn as much from anecdote and overheard remarks as from direct argument.[20]

A peer group is not only a sounding box for ideas, with simultaneous conversations on different subjects, but also a testing ground to see what it feels like to hold certain attitudes. Naturally, the sense of belonging gives the attitudes an emotional edge, for these are not carefully finished opinions, the result of complex thought, any more than most attitudes are. The emotional mood of people affects others deeply, even in a variety of different formal circumstances, but such effects are not necessarily long-lasting.[21] Such a range of different activities with their friends can distract from reflection but can also cause a different type of reflection in contrast. The influence of other children, and the need for relationships with them, begins early and causes a different kind of curiosity from that aroused by adults. Children need to learn how to play with the same toys in joint activities and how to distinguish between different levels of relationship. nurturing favourites and trying to avoid others.[22]

The way in which children learn from social events is a conscious abstracting of useful information, neither random nor merely reflecting what happens to them.[23] The way in which children react to groups depends on their size. Children of three or four will be quite happy striking up individual relationships in a group of ten or so, but once the same group is merged into a class of 30, the same group becomes dispersed into small cliques, according to particular friendships.[24] One of the most characteristic signs of the significance of the group from a teacher's point of view is the power it can have over the performance and attitudes of other children. Any group will tend to impose one standard as well as one attitude on all its members, a standard into which all will try to fit.

When children learn how to make judgements of others, and how to form emotional attachments with others, they are learning about their own point of view, as well as about conventional attitudes. Without individual views, the group norm might dominate a child's ideas entirely. Without others to share ideas with, a child is less likely to have ideas. Children have to learn how to foster relationships as well as how to understand the signs and signals that show awareness of other people. Even the most explicit form of communication, language, is enmeshed with half-hidden implications. Children learn that social language can be indirect, that 'could you open the door?' doesn't really expect the reply 'yes, I think I could'; that 'do you know the date?' doesn't want the answer 'yes, I do'. Just as there is a range of conventional signals through which people draw a conversation to a close on the telephone, so children need to learn this 'back channel feedback': 'Well . . . nice to talk to you . . . OK . . . right then . . . goodbye'.

Children also learn to make a distinction between the way that adults talk to them, and the way they are supposed to talk back. Only adults are supposed to say: 'What's your name? How old are you? Whose child are you?' They learn how to take turns when they talk, how to use different forms of the same phrase, and when different forms are appropriate. They learn how to cajole as well as ask. They need to learn, in fact, all those uses of language that others require: politeness as well as curiosity, the ability to fill a conversational gap as well as give an answer. Children learn the range of social conventions that are sometimes in marked contrast to the use of language by their teachers – 'Right! Now, Sheila, what have we learned about the Anglo-Saxons?' – and by their parents. Children need to learn a whole range of linguistic codes, not just public or formal, restricted or elaborated, but a means of communicating what is necessary both to the different circumstances and according to their own differing needs.

Of all the people with whom children come into contact, parents are obviously the most important, because it is with them that children first form a significant connection and because the parent functions as the child's first teacher, encouraging the child's language, curiosity and manipulative skills. Long before teachers come into contact with children, their parents will have made a crucial difference to their success or failure. It is partly because this fact is recognized that there will be a time when parents are once again in the forefront of education, not only recognized as such but encouraged to be so.[25] Despite the significance of this, parents are not yet a central part of the educational system. Despite the numerous roles they fulfil, from supporters to teachers of their own children, from teacher aides in the classroom to policy-makers, tensions remain between schools as isolated institutions and parents as rather shy outsiders. Parents tend to assume that 'real learning' starts with a 'real school', when in fact children's basic attitudes have been formed far earlier. But the parents' subconscious attitudes can be encouraged by teachers who do not want to be disturbed by parental influence or involvement on the grounds that it undermines professional autonomy and takes up time. The problem is that parents' influence on their children is not measured in the same terms that schools judge their success: reading skills or mathematics.

It is the underlying motivation that parents give that remains significant. They are not menials at the service of the teacher but people who, for better or worse, promote their children's attitudes to learning, just as they pass on their own assumptions about politics. Successful relationships between parents and teachers involved in children's learning have generally been in formal schemes such as reading, carefully measured and controlled.[26] But informal relationships between schools and homes have not generally been encouraged, and where they have, have not generally met with obvious success. Attitudes to education in the two groups remain very different. This is a pity. Children do not learn through the accumulation of information but through their attitudes to what they can do with the information they discover. In this sense parents are central to any education. They are the source of knowledge of a whole range of subjects expressly outside the school's curriculum: politics, society, attitudes to other people, other races, trades unions, peace and war, the meaning of life. . . . When asked to cite their sources for their opinions on any of these subjects children cite their parents.[27] There is no reason to doubt them.

Whether parents show a *laissez-faire* attitude or not they are helping to form the child's assumptions, reinforced by other children and other adults. Children of seven already have marked political opinions,[28] even if their view of political figures is still fairly optimistic, because of their love of natural order.[29] Nearly all children of eight express a preference for one of the political parties, despite their lack of ostensible interest in politics. What they learn does not depend on what they are told. They have opinions even if the schools have not told them what to think. Parents have a profound, subtle and unsurprising influence on how their children learn. The surprising fact is how little use has been made of this. In all the studies that are now taking place it is the parents who provide the most extensive environment for learning, for skills, for language and for the development of interpersonal abilities.[30] Children do not learn only when they are officially supposed to. They actively seek the kind of information they need, the kind that helps them understand the meaning of the world they are in, and the relationships that they are forming with it and within it.

NOTES AND REFERENCES

1 Argyle, M. *The Psychology of Interpersonal Behaviour*. Harmondsworth: Penguin, 1976.
2 See Gesell's 'norms'.
3 To use Lewin's model of attitude change.
4 As Berger, P.L. and Luckman, T. *The Social Construction of Reality*. Harmondsworth: Allen Lane, 1967, point out.
5 Osgood, C.E. 'An exploration into semantic space'. In Schramm, W.

(ed.) *The Science of Human Communication: New Directions and New Findings in Communication Research*. New York: Basic Books, pp. 28–40. 1963.

6 Jones, E.E. and Davis, K.E, 'From acts to dispositions: the attribution process in person perception'. In Berkowitz, L. (ed.) *Advances in Experimental Social Psychology*. New York: Academic Press, 1965.

7 Giles, H. and St Clair, R. *Language and Social Psychology*. Oxford: Basil Blackwell, 1979.

8 For example, Hamachek, D.E. *Encounters with Others: Interpersonal Relationships and You*. New York: Holt, Rinehart and Winston, 1982.

9 Called 'cognitive uncertainty theory'.

10 'Causal-attribution theory'.

11 'Similarity-attraction theory'.

12 'Gain–loss theory'.

13 'Intergroup identity theory'.

14 Bruner, J.S. and Postman, L. 'Emotional selectivity in perception and reaction'. *Journal of Personality*, **16**, 69–77, 1947.

15 Hence the favourite philosophic conundrum about 'truth': 'This is an untrue sentence'.

16 Some literary texts give an interesting insight into the judgements and actions of children, e.g. Hughes's *High Wind in Jamaica*.

17 Cullingford, C. 'Children's attitudes to teaching styles'. *Oxford Review of Education*, **13** (3), 331–339, 1987.

18 Kohlberg, L. 'Development of moral character and moral ideology'. In Hoffman, M. and Hoffman, L. (eds) *Review of Child Development Research*, Vol. 1. New York: Russell Sage, 1964.

19 Pollard, A. *The Social World of the Primary School*. New York: Holt, Rinehart and Winston, 1985.

20 Katz, E. and Lazarsfeld, P.F. *Personal Influence: The Part Played by People in the Flow of Mass Communications*. Glencoe, IL: Free Press, 1955.

21 Compare Schachter's 1964 experiments: Schachter, S. 'The interaction of cognitive and physiological determinants of educational state'. In Berckowitz, L. (ed.) *Advances in Experimental Social Psychology*, Vol. 1. New York: Academic Press, pp. 49–80, 1964.

22 Mueller, E. and Lucas, T. 'A developmental analysis of peer interaction among toddlers'. In Lewis, M. and Rosenblum, L. (eds) *Friendship and Peer Relations*. New York: Wiley Interscience, 1975.

23 Turiel, E. *The Development of Social Knowledge, Morality and Convention*. Cambridge: Cambridge University Press, p. 33, 1983.

24 Smith, P. and Connolly, K. 'Experimental studies of the pre-school environment'. *International Journal of Early Childhood*. **10**, 86–95, 1978.

25 Cullingford, C. *Parents, Teachers and Schools*. London: Robert Royce, 1985.

26 Hewison, J. 'The evidence of case studies of parents' involvement in schools'. In Cullingford, C., 1987, op. cit., pp. 41–60.

27 Research in Oxfordshire and Berkshire 1985–6. (Publication is forthcoming.)

28 Connell, R.W. *The Child's Construction of Politics*. Melbourne: Melbourne University Press, 1971; and Greenstein, F.I. *Children and Politics*. New Haven, CT: Yale University Press, 1965.

29 Hess, R.D. and Torney, J.V. *The Development of Political Attitudes in Children*. Chicago: Aldine, 1967.

30 Tizard, B. and Hughes, M. *Young Children Learning*. London: Fontana, 1984.

CHAPTER 10
Styles of Thinking

No doubt it is often *convenient* to formulate the mental facts in an atomistic sort of way, and to treat the higher states of consciousness as if they were all built out of unchanging simple ideas. ... But ... we must never forget that we are talking symbolically, and that there is nothing in nature to answer to our words.

William James, *The Principles of Psychology*, Vol. 1.

Thought is not easy to define. It cannot be understood as a simple process at which people are bad, mediocre, good or excellent. There are many different types of thinking. Even at high levels of concentration there are some people who learn information in an ordered, accumulative way, who will learn a passage from the beginning to the end and remember the significant facts in the given order; there are others who take in the information as a whole and superimpose their own structure when they remember it.[1] Some types of thinking are diffusive and others concentrated. The precision of logic is a different kind of thinking from richly imprecise associations. These distinctions refer not just to the common antipodes of thought and feeling or reason and emotion, but also to different ways of approaching, and categorizing, the same material. Cognitive processes vary. Guilford made the distinction between convergent and divergent thinking, between the seeking out of new connections and new ideas, seeking similarities in diverse categories, and the ability to explore material within a set framework.[2] The thinking that embraces fantasy, dreams, images and hallucinations remains a style of thinking for all its contrasts to logical realism. Creative thinking can often be more profound than 'critical' thinking.

Children use many styles of thinking to understand their world. The more 'creative' modes of thought are as helpful to them as 'scientific' reasoning. Their ability to concentrate on empirical connections within the boundaries of precise information presupposes a given set of conditions, such as the ability to read extensively and an adequate grasp of given facts. Children need to predict and guess long before they feel they have all the relevant information. They test the distinction between truth and false-hood because they cannot assume that they know all the answers or that they know all that they need to know. Children's logical mistakes derive from their own view of the connections between ideas. They have no choice but to be 'divergent.' Later they learn the particular style of concentration on the matter in hand that underlies academic enterprise. Later they learn to ignore the messy ambiguities that surround living problems, but muddle the clarity of thought for thought's sake. Yet those who have learned how to refine their minds with the logic of a closed system, whether it be mathematics or some other system of symbols, will be the first to point out the need for the creative act, for intuition, for the chance associations that cannot be drawn on at will. The mind continues to function on more than one level. Indeed, it is this more complex concept of mind that makes it unique, despite the fashion to expect it to be more simple.

When the mind engages on a task it responds to the stimulus, but also controls it; the process of associations works in two directions. No thought is altogether mechanical. There is a dif-ference between the learning of information, reading, marking and inwardly digesting new material, and the learning of new ideas through experience. But sometimes too much is made of the difference between 'reception' and 'discovery' learning and between 'rote' and 'meaningful' learning, since they act together. Nothing can really be learned without some personal discovery or connection, even if the connection is one that does not last or seems meaningless. It is possible to learn a series of dates and then forget them; the mechanical nature of the exercise might make the learning seem no more than 'rote'. But to re-member even nonsense is to call to mind other powers of mne-monics, recreating a picture, or some other connection with the far reaches of the mind. Rote learning often refers to material that holds no interest to the child and that the child views with indifference. Yet all material has some personal connection, or else demands such a level of interest that it becomes like a new symbolic language.

William James makes the important distinction between acquaintance *with* material and knowledge *about* material.[3] Chil-dren receive information all the time. They think about this information. But all depends on how determined they are to be engaged fully in understanding it. To all children words have both connotative and denotative meanings. The word 'father' denotes 'parent' and 'male', but also associations with 'kind' or 'stern'. There is little that children learn at first that does not contain both these semantic differences. As children get older they learn to separate the two modes of thought, using one for some circumstances but not others. They learn to adapt at school to a particular demand and use their minds with less cognitive application at home.[4]

Awareness of information or acquaintance with information does not imply that use is made of the information. The meaning of information can be either analytical or operational, either referring to the characteristics of the information, such as its component parts or phonetic form, or referring to the way in which the meaning works.[5] These two levels of meaning, the general and the particular, are always operating at the same time in the characteristics of a word and its reference. While the ability to generalize from one circumstance to another is essential, there will always be, in any information, particular characteristics that cannot be transferable. Ausubel even questions whether *general* principles of science have any application to understanding the ideas of any *particular* science.[6] And yet the knowledge of how to operate and how to apply the mind is essential in the approach to any new material. Every time a new sentence is read there is a degree of anticipation, of guessing based on previous experience. Just as the mind chooses which way to perceive the Neckar cube, so it chooses how to interpret new information.[7]

By 'thinking' we normally mean a demonstrable performance of something abstract. Children of five are capable of understanding the concept of thought and also of proving that they can understand it.[8] But thinking, defined as the application of the mind to a particular task, does not describe the constant activities of the mind, both awake and asleep. Even when reading a book the mind can wander; we think of other things. When the task in hand, taking the dog for a walk or having a bath, leaves the mind free, not all that takes place can be thought of as 'formal' thinking. We know something about the learning that takes place as we read a book. We know less about the learning that occurs as we concentrate on actions. But it is the connection between these levels of thought that is at the heart of learning.

The choice between whether we think, in the formal sense of the word, or whether we do not remains to some extent with us all our lives. Young children are forced into using their minds to the greatest of their capacities by their responses to the world, until as they grow older much of this intelligent activity is diverted into finding ways of avoiding thought. The reason for the divide between thinking and contemplation, between active reasoning and passive reception, lies in the great divide into which our culture is riven, between reasoning and feeling, between ratiocinative skills and entertainment.

Thinking has a poor reputation. It is often assumed to be a gift, unavoidable to those who have it and unattainable by those who do not. Thinking is often envisaged as a detachable ability, a technique, a fluency, that can be admired for its own sake. The whole education system as perceived in society is dependent on pupils' capacity to perform in examinations in such a way that their ability to demonstrate their skill is made manifest. The subject taken in an exam, or its relevance to our expectations of life, is considered less important than the level of achievement compared to other people's performance. For some people the first class honours degree is the supreme moment, the fulfilment of life, as well as a passport to other things. The man denoted as 'brilliant' for his displays of wit and admiration of the 'razor-sharp' mind are both part of the recognition that there is a skill to be admired for the smoothness of its working rather than the success of its application. There is no doubting the recognition that some people have very much more analytical power than others. There is doubt about the uses to which it is put.

While the ability to think clearly, sharply and quickly is easily recognized there must be some disappointment about the difference between the gifts of the mind and the limitations of its application. It is always a puzzle to discover a critic of literature who makes sensitive, discriminating, moral judgements of other people's work in writing, and applies none of them to his own life or work. It is a disappointment to note how brilliance – in government, industry or education – often remains brilliance without any subsequent success or achievement. There are several problems with cultural notions of thinking. One is the assumption that only a few have the capacity. While it is demonstrably true that some are indubitably more intelligent than others, in many people the capacity to think is never fully realized. Thinking involves not only the application of the mind but also the demonstration of its powers. It is only by constant practice, by continually choosing to use the capacity, that thinking continues to develop. It depends upon the desire and the need to think. Children learn to divert their thinking into strategies of avoidance and to separate the particular skill of thinking from the rest of their lives.

The divide between thinking and feeling is a cultural divide between work and play, as if it were pointless to expect pleasure from the application of the mind, and as if it were pointless to assume that entertainment should involve thinking. But the other great problem with ideas of thinking is a popular tendency to link it strictly to memory. Knowledge of historical dates or lengthy quotations can be impressive in itself as well as an integral part of the ability to think, but it is not the only aspect. The real mastery of the mind does not come solely from mnemonics or the recall of facts under pressure. Thinking might be an essential skill but the purpose of learning is to use the skill, to show greater self-know-ledge, more wisdom and the capacity to deal with others.

Learning is unavoidable in the very young. It can be a delight to those who are growing up, and it should have a clear purpose. But even the application of the mind to demonstrating an almost abstract set of logical steps is surrounded by a whole set of attributes: confidence, satisfaction and desire. Thinking cannot produce whatever is demanded of it. Our growing knowledge of the computer demonstrates the difference between notions of information processing and the actual idiosyncratic workings of the brain. Neither the more broadly defined concept of learning nor the narrower ability to think are just a performance for the 'brilliant'.

Nevertheless, 'thinking' is a distinct skill, not wholly dependent on subject matter or on memory. It is possible to learn how to learn, just as it is possible to choose to apply the mind. Much learning is actually concerned with the skills of studying, the techniques of increasing the efficiency with which we approach problems. There are textbooks that show how it is possible to take thinking skills further.[9] There are also texts that show how the capacities to think and learn can be applied to the emotional development of the individual.[10] We think of 'thinking' as an ability, but we know that learning is both an inevitable process – for bad as well as for good – and one that depends upon what we wish to make of it. Carl Rogers reiterated some principles of learning, starting from the recognition that all human beings have a natural potential for learning.[11] He underlined the personal nature of learning by making his principles depend on the relationship between the individual and the subject matter: on the emotional, personal approach of the individual to the information.

Learning depends on the desire of the individual to learn, when the subject seems relevant and does not threaten self-belief. Learning not only involves seeing the usefulness and the purpose of what is learned but is enhanced when the learner is active and when learning is at least partly self-initiated. Learning the capacity to be open to change is an outcome of the individual's creative independence, his self-esteem. The real point of learning, and of the development of learning, is the constant redefinition of the self in relation to the world.[12] This reason for learning remains constant from the moment of birth.

Sometimes it seems as if nothing could be more distinct than the uses of learning and the games that are played with learning. A young girl, being asked what she wanted to be when she grew up, answered 'a speller', since that is what she was demonstrably best at and most praised for in school. An eight-year-old boy in a classroom, on being asked what he was writing about, looked at the questioner with scorn and said 'this is English'. A statistician can be so caught up in the intricacies of the subject for its own sake that any possible application becomes meaningless. It is hard to avoid allowing the demonstration of an ability to be more powerful than its use. But even the narrowest definition of 'thinking' should not lead us to suppose it is one character, one stereotype, to be applied to different areas of information. When any application of the mind is analysed we see how varied are the approaches to, and the demands on, different types of material. The distinction between 'convergers' and 'divergers' is partly that between mental tuning to a conventional intelligence test and the ability to adapt to the varying demands of other people.[13] 'Convergers' are characterized as those who can limit themselves to the demands of the task within its own context. 'Divergers' are those who can make mental leaps and associate diverse ideas. The notions that people are 'introvert' or 'extrovert' are not just those of fixed character traits but can denote different ways of approaching new material.[14]

Different kinds of material demand different styles of learning. It is tempting to suppose that one can make a clear distinction between the skills demanded by the arts and sciences, but this is partly a result of the association of scientific thinking with detachment, and according to many distinguished scientists does not do justice to the creativity and guesswork involved in science. Once the purely 'academic' is celebrated, whether in history or particle physics, it is difficult to avoid being caught up in the excitement of scholarship for is own sake, and the famous theological debates of the middle ages about how many angels could dance upon the head of a pin are not unlike the subject matter of intense academic controversy today.

Those who approach an academic subject for the first time find it very difficult to understand what it contains, what it is for. They cannot see why some people should see so much in it, and make so much complexity out of what seems to the uninitiated a simple matter of common sense. It is only when details become significant that the subject becomes complicated. There might be a number of abstruse languages used in communication, from chemical symbols to musical notation, but the characteristics of the types of thinking involved are often the same. Although there is a tendency to respect a subject for its obscurity – the more abstruse the better – insight into that subject is a matter of understanding its particular language, and its style as well as its relevance. Young children's developing concentration on the particular, and their ability to ignore irrelevant digressions, become gradually transformed into the capacity to concentrate, to stick firmly to the matter in hand.

One of the difficulties of understanding any subject is that it appears to have internal consistencies and distinctions, like a language, but also to have inherent contradictions and tautologies. Subject matter is rarely more precise than language. Young children have difficulties with mathematics because 'add' and 'plus' and '+' are all different ways of saying the same thing, but seem to be different. Children also have their *own* definitions and understandings of concepts that are supposed to be simple. Children have 'alternative frameworks' in their understandings of concepts such as 'force' and 'gravity'.[15] What de Bono calls 'lateral thinking' is itself part of children's approach to any perception and to any subject.[16] They find it hard to ignore the distracting or to avoid the remote association.[17] While the 'perfect' academic subject, such as classics, is one which seems to have no possibilities of change, or of being undermined by the complexities of everyday reality, and while we admire the skill of thinking demonstrated in the confines of a game as complete in itself as chess, there are obscurities, ambivalences and difficulties that pervade almost any intelligent act, from the awareness of the connections made by the classicist between the study of the past and the present to the self-consciousness or psychological exhaustion of a chess-player.

The ambiguities of language are obvious, but the difficulties with semantics lie not only in the words but also in the syntax. Just as there are transformational rules that convert structure into meaning, so almost any set of propositions is open to interpretation at a number of different levels. Any analysis of learning therefore needs to take account of differences of circumstance, aptitude and task and also of variations in the different kinds of interaction appropriate only to that moment.[18] Cronbach and Snow, in their analysis of instructional treatment and aptitudes, show how inadequate are the simple notions of measurement applied to the great variations of performance over time and the differences between each task.[19] But this is another way of drawing attention to the different styles of learning, to the tensions between rote and meaningful learning and between concept formation and problem-solving. The variations of learning lie in personal factors and in the circumstances, in the intellectual ability, motivation and interest of the pupil, the materials and the teacher.

Understanding of the capacity of the mind to absorb and make sense of new information is complicated by the fact that people are as capable of being bored or oversaturated as they are of being exhausted by an overload of information. Experiments on the brain's capacity show that there is a limit to the amount that it can take in at any one time. But these experiments do not concern themselves with information of the kind likely to be encountered in real life, such as minutes, reports or presentations. The means by which people organize material are not always conscious deployments of methods of organization. They can include obscure connections, journeys through associations and personal interests or the chance business of skimming and skip-reading. Although repetition is normally thought to help learning, it can also be a hindrance. Seeing a painting enough times to make it familiar can increase people's liking of it, but only if the painting is fairly complex. Simple paintings, like simple music, that are easier to grasp at first, tend to be increasingly disliked on repeated acquaintance.[20] Even young children only like the repetition of certain kinds of material and prefer the repetition of words to the repetition of the crudest pictures.

There are difficulties present in the most familiar material. A reader can follow the wrong track in a passage of prose, however carefully it is written. Readers habitually pick up enough hints to support the first statement seen and mistake an introductory remark for a whole statement. This more hazardous side of learning is as much a part of the substructure of thinking as those moments of utterly lucid concentration. When Weiner wrote about the four causes of success or failure in learning he referred to the expected factors of ability, effort and the difficulty of the task, but added 'luck' as equally significant.[21] It is because of the distinction between the ability to apply the mind and the fact that we do not bother to do so at every instance that advertisers have rather simple behaviourist designs through 'triggers' or associations. They demonstrate their belief in the subliminal, and in people's capacity to react automatically and without careful thought.

The problem with the clearest manifestations of the ability to think clearly and logically is that it is easier to do so with an academic problem than in the complexity and ambiguity of actual circumstances with all their variables of personality and time. The popular instinct which suggests that the man who 'thinks too much' is not really fit for the actions of the world is a reflection of the distinction between self-contained tasks and real consequences. Displays of cerebral power can be observed most easily in conditions that are safely different from the obscurities of information (made obscure by presenting either too much or too little) and from psychological disturbance. In other circumstances even what seems a most impressive grasp of facts, and a type of ready insight that makes other people wish they had thought of thinking and saying it first, are as much a result of the underlying factors of reasoning – confidence and psychological distance – as they are of memory and articulacy. Just as an emotional attachment to a cause can inhibit rather than help arguments for its espousal so an emotional investment in real decisions makes them more difficult than theoretical ones. But the theoretical appears attractive because of the ease of demonstrating intellectual command. The tradition of admiring the academic, as opposed to the practical, runs very deep. Academic disciplines that deal with practical factors are not as admired, not only because of the self-protecting self-interest of tradition, but also because of the attitudes towards thinking that make such a skill understood by its performance – the ability to make sense of a finite, controllable amount of information.[22] It is far simpler, for example, to understand the 'syntagmatic' – links between consecutive utterances or links between speakers – than the 'paradigmatic' – the adaptability of children who use different styles of language for particular circumstances.

'A grasp of the facts' often appears to be the essence of 'a good mind'. But even memory is divided into the kind that can be tested and the kind that is dominated by particular attitudes. The ability to recognize and store the salient facts of a document and to be able to 'place' them is demonstrated in the conditions of the examination hall and in committees. The relationship between the types of recall needed for a short time span (the understanding of a document) and for a larger time span (an examination) is a closer one than might at first be apparent. In each case there is a propensity to arrange what is heard or read into some kind of manageable sequence. But even then it depends on the personal way in which the information is ordered. There is a selectivity of response in every act of remembering, when the familiar can be easily passed by and only the unfamiliar recorded.[23] Once even a sentence is read it is passed into a line of meaning which is very difficult to disentangle or reinterpret.[24] The 'grasp of facts' is a personal grasp. Anderson and Bower argue that most facts are represented in memory as a complex network of propositions.[25]

It is far easier to test the mind when it is functioning at the height of its powers on a set task than when it functions normally. Learning is, unfortunately or not, more difficult to measure since it includes all the other subliminal forces that subconsciously influence the individual mind. We take for granted the fact of individual differences and different levels of ability, but we also know that these differences are not just a matter of chance, as if some genetic fairy godmother places her magic wand on the brain of particular infants. The relationship between success in examinations and family background is so close that we need to understand better what it is that gives some people the ability to comprehend new material, analyse complex issues, remember an impressive array of facts and know how to gain access to information. It is sometimes suggested that what is being measured, or the discriminations being made between people, depends too much on the superficialities of language and home background.[26] Bernstein's distinctions between different uses of language, even if the matter of 'restricted' or 'elaborated' codes has often been applied in a simplistic way, do reveal a genuine problem.[27] When the terms 'formal' and 'public' language were still being used there was a sense of the realization of social control over speech.[28] As in the case made by Vygotsky, the point of a 'public' language is that it is the easiest way of communicating shared attitudes and renders the closer definitions of ideas and perception unnecessary.[29] Even the invention of a world like a 'Sloane' (as in Ranger) or 'Hippie' creates a sense of an immediate public cliché that is readily understood without further definition. But then language has the power to obscure as well as to clarify, to lie as well as to enlighten, to control as well as to release. Language itself can be used as a means to avoid thinking just as it is the one universal means of demonstrating it. The differences between people's use of language are not just a matter of background or accent – what could be more 'restricted' than the linguistic code of 'Sloanes' – but are a matter of the different uses to which language can be put. The problem is that people's reactions sometimes suggest that thinking needs to be demonstrated in a particular style, that 'intellectuals' need to speak with a recognizable accent.

The one 'style' in which thought can be clearly demonstrated is in language, and yet the irony is that many of the thinking techniques designed to explore different styles and abilities do their best to avoid language as much as possible. This demonstrates a suspicion of anything that is not clearly complete in itself, but also demonstrates some of the ambiguities of thought. Whether one chooses to argue that language precedes thought, or vice versa, the fact that one is dependent on the other is not in dispute.[30] Furthermore, the importance of language to thought lies not just in the utterances, the means of communication, but also in the internalization of hypotheses, of categorization.[31] The rehearsal of ideas and the reflection upon events are matters of internalized language, of guesses and predictions. Whether we try out this internal reflection deliberately or not, we are continually rehearsing our ideas, either strengthening prejudices or changing them. But internal thinking 'games' are not just demonstrations of ability, but a necessary condition for growth. Poor reasoning is caused more by lack of application or by 'psychological aberration' than by ignorance or defects of intelligence.[32] It is possible to use the ability to think not only for its own sake but also as a practical means of enhancing self-understanding.

NOTES AND REFERENCES

1 See also Chapter 14.

2 Guilford, J.P. *The Nature of Human Intelligence*. New York: McGraw-Hill, 1967.

3. James, W. *The Principles of Psychology*. New York: H. Holt, 1890.

4 Lenneberg, E.H. and Lenneberg, E. *Foundations of Language Development: A Multidisciplinary Approach*. New York: Academic Press, 1975.

5 Ogden, C.K. and Richards, I.A. *The Meaning of Meaning*. New York: Routledge & Kegan Paul, 1938.

6 Ausubel, D.P. *Educational Psychology: A Cognitive View*. New York: Holt, Rinehart and Winston, 1968.

7 Foss, D.J. and Hakes, D.T. *Psycholinguistics*. New York: Prentice-Hall, 1978.

8 Compare Bowey, J.A., Tunmer, W.E. and Pratt, C. 'Development of children's understanding of the metalinguistic term word'. *Journal of Educational Psychology*, **76** (3), 500–512, 1984.

9 For example, de Bono, E. *The Use of Lateral Thinking*. London: Cape, 1967; and *Teaching Thinking*. London: Temple Smith, 1976.

10 For example, Berne, E. *Games People Play: The Psychology of Human Relationships*. London: André Deutsch, 1966.

11 Rogers, C. *Freedom to Learn*, 2nd Edition. Columbus, OH: Merrill, 1979.

12 Compare Cobb, E. *The Ecology of Imagination in Childhood*. London: Routledge and Kegan Paul, 1977, with the introduction by M. Mead.

13 Hudson, L. *Frames of Mind: Ability, Perception and Self-Perception in the Arts and Sciences*. London: Methuen, 1968.

14 Eysenck, H.J. *Readings in Extroversion and Introversion*. London: Staples Press, 1971.

15 Watts, M. 'Alternative frameworks'. *Times Educational Supplement*, 19 March, 38, 1982.

16 de Bono, E., 1967, op. cit.

17 Mednick, S.A. 'The associative basis of the creative process'. *Psychological Review*, **69** (3), 220–232, 1962, actually draws attention to this ability as the essence of creativity.

18 Note how more and more complex attribution theory became: see Kelley, H.H. 'Attribution in social interaction'. In Jones, E.E., Kanouse, D.E., Kelley, H.H., Nisbet, R.E., Valms, S. and Weiner, B. (eds) *Attribution: Perceiving the Causes of Behaviour*. Morristown, NY: General Learning Press, 1972.

19 Cronbach, L.J. and Snow, R.E. *Aptitudes and Instructional Methods: A Handbook for Research on Interactions*. New York: Irvington, 1977.

20 Krugman, H.E. 'Affective response to music as a function of familiarity'. *Journal of Abnormal and Social Psychology*, **3**, 388–392, 1943.

21 Weiner, G. 'A theory of motivation for some classroom experience'. *Journal of Educational Psychology*, **71**, 3–25, 1979.

22 Goodson, I. *School Subjects and Curriculum Change*. London: Croom Helm, 1982.

23 Compare Bartlett, F.C. *Remembering: A Study in Experimental and Social Psychology*. Cambridge: Cambridge University Press, 1932.

24 Kimball, J.P. 'Seven principles of surface structure parsing in a natural language'. *Cognition*, **2**, 15–47, 1973.

25 Anderson, J.R. and Bower, G.H. *Human Associative Memory*. Washington, DC: Winston and Sons, 1973.

26 See the controversy and arguments surrounding this summarized by, for example, Stubbs, M. *Language and Literacy*. London: Routledge and Kegan Paul, Vol. 1, 1963, Vol. 3, 1975.

27 Bernstein, B. *Class, Codes and Control*. London: Routledge and Kegan Paul, Vol. 1, 1963, Vol. 3, 1975.

28 See Bernstein, B. 'Aspects of language and learning in the genesis of the social process'. *Journal of Child Psychology and Psychiatry*, **1**, 313–324, 1961, for the first formulation of the thesis.

29 Vygotsky, L.S. *Thought and Language*. Cambridge, MA: MIT Press, 1962.

30 Many philosophers could be invoked, e.g. Searle, J.R. *Speech Acts*. Cambridge: Cambridge University Press, 1969.

31 Fodor, J.A. *The Language of Thought*. Brighton: Harvester Press, 1976.

32 Wilson, J. *Discipline and Moral Education: a Survey of Public Opinion and Understanding*. Windsor: NFER Nelson, 1981.

CHAPTER 11
The Role of Schools

The pursuance of future ends and the choice of means for their attainment are thus the mark and criterion of the presence of mentality.

William James, *The Principles of Psychology*, Vol. 1.

Schools are peculiar institutions, as most people in them would concede. They are also easily misunderstood. They are a comparatively recent phenomenon, and in their present form the result of the rise of industrial organizations and the subsequent belief in the value of institutions. Like other institutions of the nineteenth century, schools were seen as compensations for, as well as refuges from, the ills of industrial society. They are still viewed with mixed feelings. On some occasions schools are seen to be the great hope of social change. On other occasions schools are assumed to do nothing but maintain the social status quo. Sometimes schools are blamed for not making great differences to the attainment of pupils. At other times they are blamed for trying to. They still fill an uncomfortable, even fragile, place in the structure of society.

Sometimes schools suffer in the perception of society because all learning is associated with them. It has been suggested that for every one who wishes to teach there are approximately 30 who do not wish to learn. Schools also suffer from the individual human tendency to deny that anyone has helped them in their education, and to say with Churchill: 'I am always ready to learn, although I do not always like being taught'. With the National Curriculum, the status of schools is even more formalized.

The fact that schools are an important part of the first quarter of people's lives, and the fact that they exist primarily to help foster the aspirations of civilized society, do not automatically mean that they are treated with great respect. Despite the obvious importance of their role, schools (and those in them) do not appear to be treated with respect. This is partly because people do not like to

147

think of themselves as beholden to others and partly because schools are seen as symbols of a particular kind of learning, cut off from parents, from the community and from many other types of human experience. Many people look back on their own schooling with a sense of contrast with other experiences. A few will feel nostalgia, many more a sense of loathing, but the kind of experience that schools symbolize does not *seem* to link with any other. Schools seem a world apart. The demands made on both teachers and children are often greater and usually different from those in any other circumstances; the emotional strain, the clearly defined demands, the lack of connection with the community at large and the acceptance of buildings and equipment often inadequate and run-down all mark out schools as unusual institutions.

Because schools hold such a powerful position in society, they are open to abuse. They can be blamed for all manner of things by those who have left them. The years of close interest in, and knowledge of, schools are either those of childhood or those of parenthood, when the relationship with schools is rarely easy. Too much has been hoped for from schools, as well as too little. The idea that schools could, in their isolation, transform society is as fashionable a belief as the opposite one, that schools make no difference at all. Both fashionable simplifications miss the subtle and vital role that schooling, in the broadest sense, plays.

As it became clear that early influences on children were important, that home background made crucial differences and that it was not possible to use crude social engineering to change the inequalities of society, there grew up an inappropriate disillusionment with the education system. The understanding of the processes of learning should have led to a greater rather than a lesser belief in the importance of education and in its possibilities. The more we understand about how people learn, in terms of relationships, attitudes and inner needs, the more interesting is the part that schools play, not less. Schools are neither institutions devoted to the measurement and display of innate abilities nor the only means of conveying knowledge and testing what has been remembered. Schools are not there only to deliver the national curriculum and measure the attainment of their pupils. Schools fulfil the more important role, in relationship with the home, of forming attitudes and creating expectations. They might not always be encouraged to do so, they might even be subsconsciously resented for doing so, but they cannot help having an important influence on the children in their care. This influence arises from the way in which children's learning abilities are fostered.

One of the early examples of the rediscovery of the differences that particular schools can make is the research that led to *Fifteen Thousand Hours*.[1] Using an approach that was not based on a particular pre-judged hypothesis, the research made it clear that secondary schools in London differed greatly in their pupils' success and behaviour. The differences were not due to distinctions of home background or to the conditions of the buildings. Children's successes or failures were found to relate far more closely to the character of the institutions themselves, to the staff and their attitudes and expectations. The relationships between the pupil and the teachers were found to be of great importance; children were being helped or hindered by different schools, depending on their 'ethos'. The ways in which schools made a difference, even at the secondary stage, were found to be caused by a number of factors, not just the obvious ones usually measured, like scholastic attainment or absenteeism, but attitudes to learning, pupil participation and the relationships of the staff to each other.[2]

To show that individual schools made a significant difference at primary as well as at secondary level, Mortimore and his colleagues took a similar approach in research that led to *School Matters*.[3] They concluded that there were twelve significant factors that made schools effective, factors that had a great deal to do with the attitudes of the people who make up the school community, attitudes to each other and to learning.[4] The sense of unity of purpose, through leadership and the involvement of all staff contributing to a positive ethos, was one recurring theme. Another was open communication between teachers, pupils and parents, so they all knew what was expected of them and how well they were doing. The other major theme was a sense of structure, so that each lesson would be clear in its intellectual objectives. The differences in pupils' attainment were a result of differences in those more subtle levels at which all learning actually takes place. Most studies of schools come to the conclusion that what happens on the surface, in terms of easily quantifiable measures, such as standard attainment tasks, exams or 'time on task', is not nearly as significant as the more complex social interactions and children's reactions to them. The question remains whether the clear tasks set by the National Curriculum, with examples of good practice and the need both for clearer assessment of individual pupils and greater collaboration between teachers, will make a significant difference.

Even those who attack the concept of schools recognize the significance of their influence over children's attitudes. Gramsci might have seen schools as symbols of hegemonic control of one social class over another, but he also recognized the power of moral and intellectual persuasion.[5] Those who excuse the drastic limitations of resources given to schools also argue that the effect of schools is not dependent solely on such matters as the existence or non-existence of buildings and money, although they do help. Comparisons between different local education authorities show wide variations between the amounts of spending and the kinds of success that are measured in examination results.[6] Simple measures of class-contact time or numbers of bodies are not factors that go to the heart of the individual school and its influence. But given the way that institutions work, resource constraints can make subtle and essential differences to the inner life of the school, to the relationships between colleagues and their attitudes to their work. Resources themselves do not make a school, but lack of them can lead to internecine strife, a doubling of time spent on meetings and paperwork, or attempts to prevent the development of new and creative ideas. It is at this level that effects will then be felt by the children, if not at once. Resources do not, in themselves, make a school, but lack of resources prevents a school becoming what it could be.

The recognition of the social autonomy of the school has not always led to an understanding of its particular influence, but there is general recognition that individual schools are characterized not in terms of an imposed curriculum but by the processes employed in children's learning.[7] Any national curriculum with clear objectives is bound to succeed on one level, but will always depend on or be undermined by the realities and idiosyncracies of individual learning. Atmospheres might be difficult to measure but they are none the less pervasive.

Schools are not clusters of individuals working on separate tasks but interdependent systems in which children and teachers together create a way of working in which problems are solved, and in which the individuals depend on the organization they share.[8] The life of an institution is made up as much by an emotional climate, a sense of purpose and identity, as it is by the environment or by the processes of decision-making or learning. Organizations, in the real sense, are the result of personal constructs, serving individual purposes.[9] The 'structure' is a description of the behaviour of people within an organization.[10]

The institution of a school is important because it is both a collective influence upon and a reflection of the needs of individuals. Little learning is carried out in isolation from other people. Although it is possible to pore over a text in a lonely garret, what is learned in that way normally only makes sense when it is shared with other people, when it bears a relationship to the needs for communication. This is why the overheard remark, or the implicit opinion, generally has more influence than delivered facts.[11] Schools would not be so important were it not for all the normally unmeasured aspects of learning.

It is sometimes difficult to imagine the importance of the inner world of schools when the way in which they present themselves as institutions seems so formal and distant, and so different from other physical environments. The gaunt Victorian building with high windows, looking like a miniature lunatic asylum with separate gates for two different types of inmate, still tends to be associated with ancient notices saying 'No parents past this point'. The squat, single-storey temporary-looking buildings, with windows almost inviting the immediate creation of even more fresh air and tiles reminiscent of public conveniences, are reminders of the role of the State in other people's education. The new open-plan designs, with their maintenance-demanding but ostensibly money-saving lack of corridors, suggest not only views on how to organize the way children learn but views on how little it should cost to help them do so. Buildings are symbolic of external attitudes to school.

Part of the real atmosphere of a school, as well as part of the influence, is the way in which the buildings are actually used. The effect of a different environment on children is demonstrated by the difficulty many of them have in adjusting to a new school, or in transferring from primary to secondary school.[12] The difficulty of adjustment and the fact that many children begin to do worse work after the transfer is a result of a change in organization, a change in the type of demand and a change in relationship with their teachers.[13] Those children who improve on going to a new school have made an assessment of their previous performance and are determined to do better, seeing a change in environment as an opportunity to do so and implying that they had despaired of any change in their previous circumstances. But every new circumstance, of class or school, can also bring about a sense of helplessness and vulnerability.[14]

Much more is known about the ways in which teachers use the school buildings than about the way in which children react to them, although we know that children do react strongly and emotionally to different atmospheres.[15] Some children react against certain types of building,[16] or reveal different aspects of creative endeavour according to whether the environment looks formal or informal.[17] But these responses to different environments, as the terms 'formal' or 'informal' suggest, are ones that include not only the amount of decoration, the crowdedness of the room and the spacing of the desks, but also the approach of the teacher.[18] Schools that do not contain a series of enclosed rooms give teachers an opportunity for open planning and flexibility,[19] even if most teachers still work independently.[20] Headteachers like open-plan schools more than teachers do, since it is usual for a teacher to prefer to control her own contained spaced, to create an atmosphere that is distinct and easily manipulated.[21] The children, meanwhile, pick up the attitudes subconsciously, if not often openly, revealed by the teachers.

The difficulty of separating the tasks of schools from the circumstances in which these take place argues for the importance of other influences in a school beyond the communication of information. Learning includes the absorption of atmosphere. The way in which a teacher organizes the class is central to the conveying of information. When space is carefully thought out as a means of promoting learning there follows an improvement in the way children learn, not only because of the abilities of the teacher but also because of the actual management of the classroom, individual attention and the clarity of expectations.[22] Sometimes the way in which the environment is designed is countered by the actual use made of it, as when junior schools form mixed ability classes but when a quarter of the teachers in them assign the children to groups depending on their attainment.[23] Each teacher tries to find the best, or the easiest, method of organizing the classroom. It is not a simple matter to see the effects on the ways in which children learn since one cannot judge what a child is learning by the amount of time that is being spent on a particular task. The recording of time spent on a given syllabus obscures the fact that children can appear to be busy, or even hide in a pretence of busyness, without any real learning taking place.[24] But one of the signs of effective classroom management is the amount of time a teacher spends in significant individual dialogue with pupils.[25]

Some of the insights derived from the recording of pupil interactions with each other and with adults, and of the activities that they are engaged in, reveal the nature of children's learning in school. The attention paid to the ways in which teachers ask questions shows how few questions that are put to children demand individual thought.[26] They require the ability to guess what the teacher wants to hear and the knowledge of the right answer. The questions are nearly all 'closed', where there is only one right answer ('What is a watershed, Simon?') and even if they are ostensibly 'open' – trying to encourage a more individual response ('What do you think of the book?') – they are virtually always interpreted by children as being closed.[27] The curriculum seems to children to consist of a 'closed' body of knowledge to be acquired.

Even before the advent of the National Curriculum, the 'core' curriculum was already a clear entity, with two-thirds of the time in primary schools being spent on mathematics and English.[28] For every minute devoted to the spoken word there are ten minutes spent on writing. The teacher's attention is directed at the whole class for 80 per cent of the time but only about two per cent with any individual.[29] The lack of individual attention arises partly because of the practical difficulties of having about 30 children confined in a small space. Despite the attempt to bring a more liberal organization into the classroom, the degree of formality remains high, not only in a traditional curriculum of set subject matter, but also in the expectations of children. Sometimes the very existence of 'open plan' as an environment can mean that more rather than less formal teaching takes place: teachers in open-plan schools can spend almost twice as much time presenting information as those in self-contained classes.[30] Teachers in open-plan schools were found to talk for nearly half the available time rather than a little more than a third of the time in self-contained classrooms.[31]

The question of formality and informality in a classroom is a vexed one and answers to it raise more questions. All teaching is formal to a certain extent. Any class of children with their multifarious requirements demands careful organization, for children appreciate a clear structure. They want to know what they are expected to do for their own sense of security. The school as an institution is not only formal in the way it conveys public information: it has the means of influencing those within it in many 'informal' ways. But the way in which schools are generally organized shows how the system constrains certain activities. Many studies have found that nearly a quarter of a teacher's time is spent on administration.[32] They also show that teachers find it far easier to cope with closed, contained environments, whatever their philosophy about the autonomy of the individual child. To some extent the structures implicit in the National Curriculum, with set targets and assessment tasks, give the teacher a defined role that makes her even more 'formal'.

The role of a teacher in assessing each child's needs, knowing what task to set, making sure the task is understood and appropriate, and then evaluating it before creating a new task is very demanding. It is no real surprise that many sit behind their desks trying to respond to children as they queue up. The class seems to work hard, but as Bennett and Desforges show, much of the work being carried out is misunderstood and ill-matched to the needs of the pupils.[33] Given the nature of schools, this is not really surprising; nor is it merely the fault of the teachers. Such a mismatch between what the pupil ought to be doing and what he actually does is a result of rather mistaken views about learning. Many of the tasks that teachers are expected to set are meaningless in the eyes of the children: they never connect in any practical way with all that the children wish to know. Children might see learning as the imposition of a set curriculum, so that by the end of years of schooling a pupil will emerge with the skills necessary to carry out various tasks and acquire a job, but this is not the way learning actually takes place. We can go on criticizing teachers or schools for all we are worth, but what we expect of them conflicts with what we know about the individuality of learning. The problem is that the higher the expectations of the individual teacher, the more there is a potential failure. To do an ordinary job is easy, for it means being unaware of what *could* be happening. To do a good job is to be aware of the difference between attainment and potential.

A fair proportion of children's mental energy in school is spent trying to guess what is being demanded of them, in anticipating and avoiding these demands and in attempting to understand the ethos and implicit expectations of the school. One might think that if the same amount of energy were spent on fulfilling the tasks required by teachers the results would be far more satisfactory, but just as young children learn to guess and predict ways of interpreting work to please the teacher, so older children naturally look for underlying motives, for the generalizable insights that clarify a whole field of study and that avoid too many demands. Some children very quickly learn the significance of assessment tasks and gear *all* their work to tests. No one wants to spend a long time arriving at a solution when the solution can be found easily, unless there is pleasure in the task itself.

For most children, the tasks given them in school are not viewed with any joyful anticipation. The teacher is expected to police the tasks to see that they get done. Children do not always know why this is so, although they accept the teachers' assurance of the necessity, and there is not always such pleasure that they would wish to take work home with them. Many of the tasks presented to children remain opaque in their purpose, with no more explanation of immediate relevance than the promise that as a result of doing fifty 'divisions' some undefined benefits will accrue or a target will be met. Children's desire to conform, to fit into a firm framework, does not mean that they acquiesce unthinkingly to all that goes on, but that they look at it the more carefully to enable them to understand what is required of them.

Despite this close scrutiny of the school, much of what takes place remains obscure to children. The habit of schools of relying on implied codes of behaviour, of using a language of a kind not used elsewhere and of holding a series of clearly held beliefs about children – which ones are virtuous and which are not – constitutes a problem in the minds of anyone entering an institution. Such codes are made formal by the publication of the results of tests. The sense of comparison and competition then makes the formal ethos of schools even clearer in the minds of children.

In a school children have to learn new codes of behaviour. The kind of language used by many of the teachers is symbolic in itself. It does not always demand a response. It is not geared to communicate to any individual. It commands rather than tries to persuade. It is language spoken for the sake of filling space, almost like the language of a chat show. The catch is that children are supposed to respond to it occasionally at particular times, although the language is not usually directed at them. The series of statements, closed questions and commands might suddenly be directed at an individual, at you. The trick of survival is to know how to anticipate when this might happen.[34] The public nature of school language is a question not of its form, its syntax or vocabulary, but of the milieu in which it takes place and the uses to which it is put. The understanding of different codes of language is made the more difficult because of the constant shift between the use of language as a means of learning and its use as a communication system in a school.[35] Children have to learn which questions are to be ignored and which should be answered, which are implied commands and which are explicit ones, often depending on where the transaction takes place as well as the tone of voice. Language is, after all, both social and individual.[36]

Children's bewilderment with school is not often allowed for because schools tend to assume that their purpose is either obvious or implicit. Children themselves have an explicit sense of the purpose of the school as a conveyor of skills and knowledge for the sake of a job, a view they share with their parents.[37] But they do not experience this purpose within the school quite so simply. School remains unfamiliar territory, never really secure. They try to find some aspect of school that makes sense and around which they can operate.[38] Children are not really inwardly satisfied with the conventional wisdom that sees school as a place of competition through exam success, even if that is often the only purpose presented to them. Schools are as much social centres as centres of learning.

Children are often aware of the ambiguities of school even when they do not possess the means of conveying this awareness. Children also try to find their own means of coping with school. They know that some of them will be favoured by teachers if they do not make too many demands. They know that girls do not have to work so hard because teachers assume that they are working diligently because they are quiet.[39] They see that those who do not conform tend to be regarded as backward and that there are important distinctions made between those children with high and low status, however 'child-centred' the regime.[40] They ride some of the ambiguities by creating and changing groups, so that they can help and protect each other. They know that they must avoid being trapped in certain groups, that non-conforming 'gangs' are so much in trouble with the teachers that they are in danger of losing all social consensus in the school. They also learn to avoid being associated with the hard-working quiet 'goodies'. They learn, in fact, how far they can manipulate teachers, when to take what the teacher says seriously and when she can be teased. They learn to play the system and know exactly how far to go and what they can get away with.[41]

When children gain social knowledge, they do so by abstracting it from events that take place around them and to them.[42] They learn from school all kinds of social signals, the utility of the implied instruction and the importance of close observation of others' behaviour. One aspect of schools about which children learn fast is the fact that rewards and punishments depend largely on competition. Although teachers feel and express the sense that they are concerned to help each child individually, and that they are not there to foster the idea of one child's superiority over another, the children are, by the age of eight, in no doubt about individual comparisons, about what they think of each other and what the teachers think of them.[43] This is not the result of the elaborate grading system of assessment tasks, but an awareness by children that schools actually embody the first step towards future rewards, towards success or failure. Some children, on seeing and experiencing this, make that realization an excuse to drop out of competition.[44] They compare themselves with each other, and

157

understand implicit labels. Those 'standstills' often observed in children, the periods of relative inaction and lack of progress, can be either a sudden lack of motivation or a period of taking stock, of refusing to continue the same kind of endeavour as other children. However 'hidden' the system of streaming, with letters of classes according to the teachers' initials, children always know which children are labelled in which way, not only passing on the information but generating their own system of labels. They also assume that some of them are born clever or stupid and that there is nothing they can do about it. The general cultural stress on competition, on winning and on rewards is associated in children's minds with the microcosm of the school. Just as children convey a laconic sense that some people are bad (few children think of themselves as wholly good), so they accept the use of labels such as 'stupid'. 'You shouldn't be talking to me: I'm one of the stupid ones.'

Once children accept labels like 'failure' this becomes part of their social network. Often the culture of a school includes the idea that it is quite a good thing not to work, or that the only point of any work is to pass exams. This is why 'swots' are often despised; and those that do well are seen as 'goodies'.[45] But this sense of individual labelling and failure is not surprising given the cult of individualism that pervades many aspects of school life: the lack of help to others,[46] the importance of personal success with the teacher and the absence of any explanation of the social functions of education.[47] Children's learning styles are often geared to the interpretation of individual teachers' expectations. Quiet or solitary children are less aware of teachers than either the 'attention seekers' or the 'intermittent workers.'[48] Those who are most demanding or most difficult are the ones most aware of teachers (and vice versa) and aware of the potential for exploitation. Once children have been embedded in a peer group or in a style of relationship with teachers it is very hard for them to change.

Attitudes to work become a permanent and important feature in children by the age of eleven.[49] The rewards that children then derive are from their peer group, and from other sources of satisfaction both within and outside the school. It is as if they were leading a double life, fulfilling all the ostensible requirements, but applying their minds to other things. They get used to the fact that they do not need to concentrate, that to try hard can lead to the possibility of real failure since those who do not try are not really 'failing'. Those children who inwardly retire from competition seem to take melancholy pleasure from their failure, but in recognizing it as failure blame the school rather than themselves. Their inability to adapt is a matter not just of misunderstanding the tasks set them, but also of being unable to please and reward the teachers in the ways in which they observe other children doing.

Some schools are clearly more effective than others. But they all suffer from the same problem, through no fault of their own. Learning is not really geared to the conventional methods of teaching, nor is teaching geared to children's styles of learning. Whatever the teachers might wish to do to help the social abilities and the individual autonomy of the children, schools are still organized in a way that runs counter to their implicit aims. No school can wholly escape this phenomenon. They vary in size and react to similar events differently but in each of them is the difficulty of giving the individual child both an environment in which he can continue his learning and the social purpose which would make sense of education.[50] Schools differ in the nature of teachers' and pupils' involvement in the process of learning. There can be four variables according to the low or high contributions of teacher or pupil and the relationship between them. A high contribution by a teacher combined with a low contribution from the pupil can be considered the traditional model of teaching; a low contribution by the teacher with a high contribution by the pupil is the conventional idea of the progressive. But real success depends on the combination of high involvement by both pupil and teacher, and this is difficult to achieve. Classrooms are complex systems that superficially look simple, full of different sources of information, some more useful than others, crowded with different and conflicting individual needs, even if all children are supposed to be going through the same process.[51] We believe we know all about what children ought to learn in terms of the National Curriculum, and we have great experience with different methods of presentation. Yet we sometimes forget to ask whether the task of the teacher in a large class is one that really fits the nature of learning. Children go on learning, but much of what they learn is accidental. In the circumstances it is remarkable how well schools perform.

NOTES AND REFERENCES

1 Rutter, M., Maughan, B., Mortimore, P. and Ouston, J. *Fifteen Thousand Hours – Secondary Schools and Their Effects on Children*. London: Open Books, 1979.

2 Rutter, M. 'School effects on pupil progress: research findings and policy implications'. *Child Development*, **54** (1), 1–29, 1983.

3 Mortimore, P., Sammons, P., Stoll, L., Lewis, D. and Ecob, R. *School Matters: The Junior Years*. London: Open Books, 1988.

4 The twelve factors are: purposeful leadership of the staff by the head-teacher; the involvement of the deputy head; the involvement of teachers; consistency among teachers; structured sessions; intellectually challenging teaching; the work-centred environment; limited focus within sessions; maximum communication between teachers and pupils; record keeping; parental involvement; and positive climate.

5 Gramsci, A. *Selections from Political Writings*. London: Lawrence and Wishart, 1977.

6 Lord, R. *Public Money*. London: Buckingham Place, 1983.

7 Bolam, R. *School-focussed In-service Training*. London: Heinemann Educational, 1982. See also the sociological work of Sharp and Green (note 40) and King, R.A. *All Things Bright and Beautiful? A Sociological Study of Infants' Classrooms*. Chichester: Wiley, 1978.

8 Schmuck, R.A. 'Organisation development for the 1980's'. In Gray, H.L. *The Management of Educational Institutions: Theory, Research and Consultancy*. Lewes: Falmer Press, pp. 130–162, 1982.

9 Nias, J. *Primary Teachers Talking: A Study of Teaching as Work*. London: Routledge, 1989; and Nias, J., Southworth, G. and Yeomans, R. *Staff Relationships in the Primary School*. London: Cassell, 1989.

10 Gray, H.L. *The Management of Educational Institutions: Theory, Research and Consultancy*. Lewes: Falmer Press, 1982.

11 Compare the work on propaganda carried out by, for example, Katz, E. and Lazarsfeld, P.F. *Personal Influence: The Part Played by People in the Flow of Mass Communications*. Glencoe, IL: Free Press, 1955; and Hovland, C.I. *The Order of Presentation in Persuasion*. New Haven, CT: Yale University Press, 1957.

12 Galton, M. and Willcocks, J. *Moving from the Primary Classroom*. London: Routledge and Kegan Paul, 1983.

13 Measor, L. and Woods, P. *Changing Schools: Pupil Perspectives on Transfer to a Comprehensive*. Milton Keynes: Open University Press, 1984.

14 Salzberger-Wittenberg, I., Gianna, H. and Osborne, E. *The Emotional*

Experience of Learning and Teaching. London: Routledge and Kegan Paul, 1983.

15 There is surprisingly little academic research on this subject as well, although fiction has dealt with it with insight and erudition for years.

16 Neill, S.R. and Denham, E.J. 'The effects of pre-school building design'. *Educational Research* **24** (2) 107–111, 1982.

17 Thomas, N.G. and Berk, L.E. 'Effects of school environments on the development of young children's creativity'. *Child Development,* **52** 1153–1162, 1981.

18 Or the wall-displays. Compare Cullingford, C. 'Wall displays: children's reactions'. *Education 3–13,* **6** (2), 12–14, 1978.

19 Rintoul, K.A.P. and Thorne, K.P.C. *Open Plan Organisation in the Primary School.* London: Ward Lock Educational, 1975.

20 Bennett, S.N. *Teaching Styles and Pupil Progress.* London: Open Books, 1976.

21 Bennett, N., Andreae, J., Hegarty, P. and Wade, B. *Open Plan Schools: Teaching, Curriculum, Design.* Slough: NFER, 1980.

22 Nash, B.C. *The Learning Environment: A Practical Approach to the Education of the Three, Four and Five Year Old.* Toronto: Collier Macmillan, 1979; and Nash, B.C. 'The effects of classroom spatial organisation on four and five year old children's learning'. *British Journal of Educational Psychology.* **51**, 144–155, 1981.

23 Lunn, J. 'Junior schools and their organizational policies'. *Educational Research,* **24** (4) 250–261, 1982.

24 Galton, M., Simon, B. and Croll, P. *Inside the Primary Classroom.* London: Routledge and Kegan Paul, 1980; and Galton, M. and Simon, B. *Progress and Performance in the Primary Classroom.* London: Routledge and Kegan Paul, and see the work of Bennett and Desforges (note 33) where they question the impact that what is observable has on the actual performance of the child.

25 Meadows, S. and Cashdan, A. *Helping Children Learn: Contributions to a Cognitive Curriculum.* London: David Fulton, 1988.

26 Flanders, N.A. 'Teacher influence on pupil attitudes and achievement final report'. *Co-operative Research Program Project, No. 397.* Minneapolis: University of Minnesota, 1960; and Barnes, D., Britton, J. and Rosen, H. (eds) *Language, the Learner and the School.* Harmondsworth: Penguin, 1969.

27 In a small-scale research project in Cumbria it was clear that children of eight did not think it was *possible* for there to be such a thing as an open question from a teacher.

28 Galton, M. *et al.,* 1980, op. cit.

29 Ibid.

30 Ellison, M., Gilbert, L.L. and Ratsoy, E.W. 'Teacher behaviour in open area classrooms'. *Canadian Administrator,* **8** (5), 17–21, 1969.

31 Bennett, N. *et al.,* op. cit.

32 Compare Desforges, C. and Bennett, N. 'Understanding classroom learning: an ecological approach'. In Richards, C. *The Study of Primary Education*, Vol. 1. Lewes: Falmer Press, 1984.

33 Bennett, N. and Desforges, C. *The Quality of Pupil Learning Experiences*. London: Lawrence Erlbaum, 1984; and Meadows, S. and Cashdan, A., 1988, op. cit.

34 See the careful manipulations by children of this system: Pollard, A. *The Social World of the Primary School*. London: Holt, Rinehart and Winston, 1985.

35 Barnes, C. *From Communication to Curriculum*. Harmondsworth: Penguin, 1976.

36 Vygotsky, L.S. *Mind in Society*. Cambridge, MA: Harvard University Press, 1978.

37 Cullingford, C. ' "I suppose learning your tables could help you get a job" – Children's views on the purpose of schools'. *Education 3–13*, **14** (2), 41–46, 1986; and Cullingford, C. 'The idea of the school: the expectations of parents, teachers and children'. In Cullingford, C. *Parents, Teachers and Schools*. London: Robert Royce, pp. 131–152, 1985.

38 Compare Francis, H. *Learning to Read: Literate Behaviour and Orthographic Knowledge*, London: G. Allen and Unwin, 1982.

39 Compare Davies, L. 'Gender, resistance and power'. In Walker, S. and Baston, L. *Gender, Class and Education*. Lewes: Falmer Press, 1983.

40 Sharp, R. and Green, A. *Education and Social Control: A Study in Progressive Primary Education*. London: Routledge and Kegan Paul, 1975.

41 Pollard, A., 1985, op. cit.; and Sluckin, A. *Growing up in the Playground*. London: Routledge and Kegan Paul, 1981.

42 Turiel, E. *The Development of Social Knowledge: Morality and Convention*. Cambridge: Cambridge University Press, 1983.

43 Cullingford, C., 1985, op. cit.

44 Compare the work of C. Dweck.

45 Turner, J. *Made for Life: Coping, Competence and Cognition*. London: Methuen, 1980.

46 Compare the tradition of independence in English schools – 'doing one's own thing' – compared to mutual co-operation in Russian schools: Bronfenbrenner, U. *Two Worlds of Childhood*. London: Allen and Unwin, 1971.

47 Hargreaves, D.H. 'A sociological critique of individualism in education'. *British Journal of Educational Studies*, **28** (3), 187–198, 1980.

48 Galton, M. and Simon, B., 1980, op. cit.

49 Galton, M. and Willcocks, J., 1983, op. cit.

50 Bussis, A.M. and Chittenden, E.A. *Analysis of an Approach to Open Education*. Princeton, NJ: Educational Testing Service, 1970,

51 Doyle, W. 'The use of non-verbal behaviours: towards an ecological model of classrooms'. *Merrill-Palmer Quarterly*. **23**, 179–192, 1977; Doyle,

W. 'Classroom tasks and student abilities'. In Peterson, P.L. and Walberg, H.J. (eds) *Research on Teaching*: *Concepts, Findings and Implications*, Berkeley, University of California Press, 1979; and Doyle, W. *Student Mediating Responses in Teacher Effectiveness*, Denton, TX: North Texas State University, 1980.

CHAPTER 12
The Sense of Self

We see no reason to suppose that self-love is primarily, or secondarily, or ever, love for one's mere principle of conscious identity. It is always love for something which, as compared with that principle, is superficial, transient, liable to be taken up or dropped at will.

William James, *The Principles of Psychology*, Vol. 1

Children's performance in schools depends on their self-confidence and on the motivation with which they approach their work.[1] If their curiosity is aroused, they will pursue a subject at length and devote great energy to it; if the subject seems irrelevant they will display equal energy in trying to avoid working. Children learn not only as a result of their interest in what is presented to them, but also as a result of their attitudes towards working and towards themselves. Self-esteem and self-awareness are subtle developments of the personality, and not a matter of simple confidence or lack of it.[2] Children's sense of their personal characteristics or personal faults can be profound and well thought out, even if sometimes mistaken. They show an ability to interpret and apply events to themselves that is part of their striving towards an understanding of their place in the world. Their learning of 'objective' fact is itself dependent upon their own sense of self and their confidence in their relationship to others.

Each human being has a sense of personal identity in relation to society. Some manage to retain a simple coherence that allows them to be perfectly in tune with their place in their surroundings. Others quickly discover a distressing dichotomy. But their sense of self is the basis on which all other relationships depend, even if it is not consciously examined. Even states of drunkenness or drug-induced forgetfulness, which seem the most determined efforts to escape from oneself, are acute reminders of self-consciousness and bitter self-appraisal.

Philosophers' natural fascination with the most central of human questions, that of personal identity, does not always examine the everyday actions that take people through their lives, but we do not need to take the extreme view of the world as depending entirely on our perceptions to admit the singularity of each person's experience.[3] Our own individuality we take for granted, and accept easily. We might ignore the individuality of others but we are still forced to accept it. Once having realized the power of our own moods and often arbitrary relationship to the world, we have already accepted the premise of the first and most profound of philosophical questions. Given the importance of understanding one's self, and the meaning of our lives, it is the more surprising that this subject is rarely examined as part of the education system.

Children learn, at school and at home, a series of attitudes towards themselves and others, towards their work and its relationship to society. They cannot help but measure learning against their personal needs. They do not appear to be self-conscious, and certainly do not set out to reflect upon themselves, but their learning implies a changing relationship with, and a changing understanding of, the world around them. The end of learning is not the curriculum but what is made of it. Those children who can achieve success within the examination system are learning distinct attitudes to themselves and society. To be psychologically an individual depends on self-consciousness, on the general social inheritance and on transcending the circumstances in which individuals are placed.[4] Each individual will interpret individually what is given, whether encouraged to do so or not. Each individual will establish the unique relationship he or she possesses to others and to society as a whole, whether mature and positive or not.

Children's needs to understand the social environment are acquired very much earlier than when they manifest their understanding in public terms, such as voting in elections. They strain to place themselves in some personal construct of their surroundings at an early age, and soon put their perceptual needs into a social framework. Very young children are sometimes pictured, in their inarticulacy, as being utterly egocentric, consumed only with personal, simple needs. At other times they are presented as beings without any self-consciousness, purely interested in the palpable manifestations of a world outside them. Both views can be held to be true, but both leave out that essential human quality, that of self-awareness. Egocentricity is, after all, carefully developed and nurtured as people grow older, whether it is turned to self-knowledge or to narrow self-interest. The first sign we see of human capacity is the singularity of each relationship. The second sign is the need to make this singularity more open and more communicable, especially in story. Children are learning in school to interpret, and be interpreted by, the society in which they are placed.

The structure of the individual personality is made up of a mixture of the personal and the universal. The social world is a personal matter and understood in a personal way. Children reveal, through their analysis of the rules of society, not an eccentric or naive view of the meanings of these rules, but a personal sense that rules have meanings. The issues at stake are not those of political parties, but those of personal meanings.[5] When Erikson analyses the changes that people manifest in their views of society he makes it seem inevitable that there are stages of understanding through which people have to go to achieve true wisdom, but he also shows how important are some of the earliest attitudes towards others.[6]

The question of trust or mistrust relates not only to the acquisition of food or warmth but also to a sense of a greater social order. Each personal understanding has its roots in social order, whether this personal awareness is that of trust, guilt, shame, inferiority or isolation. The awareness of other people, including parents and other children, is part of the developing awareness of social structures. Even the most 'primitive' reactions to moral order, in Kohlberg's sense, such as those of obedience to avoid punishment, show a concern with relationships that continues even when they are abetted by more 'moral' considerations.[7] The child's first awareness of a world in which there is a sense of order is like the later awareness of the universal value of the individual: both transcend that sense of a rigid order that is easily imposed, and both go beyond the stress of the purely instrumental in human action. The desire for order is as instinctive as the desire for individual autonomy.

The difficulty in making a true distinction between the personal and the public is often cited as marking a peculiar limitation on children. Like adults, children take what happens personally; they do not make a simple distinction between the structure of facts and their relationship to the individual personality. For a young child the universal is important. For this reason children have more than simplistic political or moral attitudes. Six- and seven-year-olds are more impressed by the moral obloquy of the accidental breakage of a whole dinner service than by the deliberate destruction of one cup. By the age of eight children are more aware of the motive behind the act.[8] To younger children, as with the drink/drive law, the consequences of an action are more significant than the reasons for it. To the older child the deliberate breaking of an object seems more culpable than the accidental breaking of many. Younger children express these attitudes because they assume that the world has an order of its own, universally moral. For younger children nothing appears purely accidental, nothing undeliberate, so that being stung by a wasp, for example, seems to be 'their fault.'

Children manifest a curious mixture of attitudes, both subtle and pragmatic. When asked questions about personality or individual differences they give answers that show both realism and imagination. They are matter-of-fact about the mechanics of dying or of burial, and are not afraid of it. At the same time they still spend much energy trying to work out the meaning of dying.[9] They are aware of the fact that there is no one else exactly like them, and yet do not feel themselves to be special. They have a pragmatic awareness of birth, and the fact that they are the results of their parents wanting a child; and yet still need to ponder the fact of birth against the often covert stories told to them.[10] While misled about the facts of life, children nevertheless dwell with personal concern on issues like the threat of nuclear war.

One of the ways in which people learn to cope with and communicate their understanding of the world is by making a clear distinction between the objective and the subjective. It has often been pointed out how Western culture has made a god of objective reality, with the touchstone of philosophy being not reason but empirical fact. Such a determination to test the pulse of sensation against the verifications of science has often been the subject of satire. But many of the most important insights into human nature cannot be made through the application of empirical tests alone. Philosophers have long doubted whether the most rigorous applications of logic or the analysis of language can afford to leave out the notion of the subjective, that sense of self which does not lend itself to the formulations of objective observation.[11]

The most analytical scientists are aware of the limitations of attempting to apply the logic of data processing to the complexities of the mind, especially with the increasing understanding of alpha waves and the different hemispheres of the brain. The discovery that the left hemisphere of the brain, connected to the right side of the body, is concerned with logic, analysis and verbal and mathematical reasoning, and that the right hemisphere is involved with synthesis, spatial awareness and imaging, not only gives the view of humans' two opposed modes of consciousness an empirical basis, but reveals how much of the sense of our individual nature has not been subjected to analysis. The problem with understanding the subjective is, of course, that by its nature it cannot easily be communicated. The sense of self is at once private and public, logical and illogical, associative and sequential, a mixture of the objective and the subjective, of outer relationships and hierarchies of value, and inner analyses of previous experiences and present needs.

The two different modes of consciousness are not to be analysed in a linear, logical way. But for children as well as for adults, more than we would readily admit, the different modes of consciousness are all interwoven: the explicit with the tacit, the intellectual with the sensuous, the sequential with the simultaneous, the verbal with the spatial, the intellectual with the intuitive, the creative with the receptive.[12] Children learn how to translate their feelings into the form that culture demands of them; but this means that they learn not only to understand themselves and their places in the world but also how to limit their experience according to the normal demands of communication. They learn what to ignore. They learn that schools are implicitly designed to bypass certain tracts of experience.

Children involve themselves with different modes of learning, using their minds subjectively, but they also learn that there are many areas of learning about which they are not expected to communicate. One of the reasons why children give such laconic answers to fundamental questions of belief is that they know that they are not really expected to talk about them in adult society.

Although they are taught to please their teachers and are polite to the questioner, they know that there must be a peculiarly scientific reason for asking questions of the kind that are not empirically verifiable.[13] It is as if people were given a cultural licence to think about the meaning of their lives, and talk about it only when they are given philosophical or political techniques to do so. Some of these techniques are not always appropriate to the concerns to which they are applied. Children are not prevented from being fully and personally engaged in reflection, but their thoughts seem quaint to those whose cultural experience leads them to recognize the techniques themselves more readily than the answers to difficult questions.

For all the attractions of the ratiocinative, people learn to cope with their lives on a more subjective level. Crick and Mitchison interestingly suggest that dreams are a form of 'unlearning', that dreams are the way in which the brain makes connections of all the experiences that are useful, and refines out of the immediate consciousness all the information that does not relate to previous experiences.[14] But one does not need to use dreams to see that such a creation of semi-random connections which are refined by experience takes place all the time, in a way that does not lend itself to the formality of logical judgement. The difference between those who tend to be 'convergent' and those who tend to be 'divergent',[15] between those who are more emotionally inhibited, good at conventional tests, at mechanical and technical logic, and those who are better at open-ended tests, with unconventional individual attitudes, is a difference that depends on the habit of holding on to the other types of thinking that part of their culture suggests they suppress.[16] The distinction between the inner and the outer, between an awareness of a personal reflection of the world and the world as an objective order, is shown in children's developing concept of the word 'change'. At seven they see it as referring to themselves, to actions performed, to a substitution of one state for another. After the age of ten they see the word in a less active sense, as part of general transformations that do not affect them.[17]

The individual sense of self is both an essential fact and a developing sophisticated concept. To understand children we need to see how the innate sense of personal being is balanced by the sense of forces beyond their immediate control, both social and genetic. Some of the innate drives that children possess, with their instincts of self preservation or of gratification, are both intensely personal and general. Their personal feelings include displays of pleasure that seem so natural a response to gratification that Freud was led to suggest a series of oral, anal and phallic stages of subjective drives.[18] But their personal feelings are also dependent on social circumstances, not just in the sense of physical needs, but in terms of mood. Children are noticeably quick to reflect a prevailing atmosphere, to be aware of mood and tone. This awareness of personal feelings as a result of other people's expectations never completely leaves us. In one series of experiments, for example, some students were shown to respond to the mood of an individual leader until they were either euphoric or depressed, even when they knew that they were being led on.[19] But then we know how quick people are to pick up a prevailing mood and to imitate others when they think it is the right thing to do, following the lead of the figure in authority, or fitting into what is assumed to be the general expectation of a crowd.[20]

Erikson suggests that the underlying conflicts are all battles of personal feelings in relation to other people.[21] From basic trust, to a sense of integrity, the individual learns gradually to be aware of him or herself, always with the same desire not to separate the self from other people, since it is impossible to define the self except in relation to others. Children's awareness of their own feelings includes the definitions of the feelings of others: of other objects, as well as people. Their view of sex and marriage might be romantic and 'backward' but it is a result of a mixture of personal feelings and observation, rather than a result of discussion or analysis.[22] Many of the matters that concern adults most closely, from religion to sex, are observed and discussed by children in an implicit, informal way.

The earliest years of learning are necessarily about the concept of the world, about attempts to structure experience into sense. Later, this process becomes more conscious of itself, despite the counter pressure not to examine such issues. Sometimes this personal sense of learning is manifested in a steady unchanging determination to succeed; sometimes it is no more than a mood. Students intent on learning are as susceptible to changes of mood as anyone else. Students feeling elated learn far more success-fully than those who are depressed, obviously concentrating better, making clear evaluations and remembering more.[23] The difference between the cognitive task and the emotional attitude towards it can often become a conflict.[24] This reiterates the importance of attitudes towards learning and the need to avoid the tendency for children to feel failures, finding themselves alienated from all that goes on around them.

Children's self-concept includes an evaluative element and is closely related to academic achievement.[25] Their self-concept survives when they have forgotten dates, theorems or definitions. The self-concept is not to be confused with self-esteem despite the close relationship between them. Self-esteem depends much more on the way in which the individual feels himself to be assessed by other people whom he respects. Self-concept is far more concerned with a person's analysis of his own performance, and the difference between hope and result. Children who are rated as clever in classes can nevertheless begin to give up their cleverness.[26] Children tend to think of ability as a fixed commodity as if there was nothing they could do about it. Many children who, with the first flush of self-conscious optimism, keep their attention alert and their curiosity at its fullest, begin to lose that use of their own capacities as they learn to compare themselves to other people. When children see the classroom as the place where standard assessment tests advertise the difference in fixed abilities, they are as likely to give up trying if they think they are clever as they are if they are considered stupid, because they prefer not to compete, not to have to strive to overcome the competition.

Younger children experience learning as a matter of exploration, of understanding new ideas, of becoming more personally involved. They think that 'ability' depends on hard work alone and are concerned to try their hardest. As they become older most children lose this assumption and lose confidence in the face of a different view of learning that is presented to them, a view that stresses abilities and overcoming opposition in competition. In such conditions many children do not even want to be challenged; they put less and less effort into what seems a potential threat to their self-esteem. The youngest children have an optimistic view of their own ability. This diminishes as they work their way through school.[27] The youngest children still retain the attitude that learning is exploration rather than competition. Older children learn how to label and rate themselves according to the implied criteria of capacity laid down by teachers, their peers and themselves. There are, of course, some who thrive on competition.

Children's motivation towards learning depends not only on other people's views of their ability but also on the connection between their formal learning and their own experiences. The normal context of learning, of applying the mind, is not the classroom in the school, but conversations with others and material presented on television, in books, magazines or advertisements. Children's attitudes towards learning are formed partly as a result of these experiences, and are then applied to the different challenges of school. Many children find it difficult to use their minds differently when the teacher suddenly challenges them to pay particular attention. They have generally been learning at a very different level at home, and in a different way, but learning nevertheless. They learn information, but they also learn attitudes towards information, and most significant of all, attitudes towards learning.

By the age of eight, children have quite an accurate knowledge of political vocabulary, but they also learn that they are not to trust politicians and that politics is not a particularly interesting subject anyway.[28] Their interest in politics depends largely on how much their parents talk to them about politics and this generally is not very much. They pick up information of the kind that is constantly thrust at them, but without the organizing interest that makes it significant. Most eight-year-olds know the name of the Prime Minister; even more know the name of the President of the United States. But the important matter that they learn is not so much the information but the values that go with it. Children want to have benevolent attitudes towards authority and the structures of society, but they are generally discouraged from having an interest in social organizations or the way they are run. They therefore learn to pay indifferent attention to the material of television, and are then expected to pay attention of a quite different kind to the work that is presented to them in school. The problem with such academic schizophrenia is that it does not draw together the different capacities of children, and lets them divide the tasks that demand attention from those that they are usually engaged in. It gives children the excuse not to apply their minds.

Children can choose whether to apply their minds or not. They do not 'think' all the time, in the sense of being engaged in concentrating on a particular task. A child often seems to refuse to apply what has just been learned, and can seem for hours to be in a daze of inattention. The learning of curiosity is one of the most telling and long-lasting acquisitions of children's early years. The fact that so many children do not go on believing in their abilities, or do not want to continue to explore things in any depth, is because their abilities have not been encouraged. This habit of attention is crucial from the age of one. From the age of seven to eight, a child starts to demonstrate much more than learning through self-absorption and the exploration of his own feelings and opinions.

The sense of criticism and the understanding of the limitations of some adult values (the unfairness of individuals on one level, the lack of justice in the law on another) begin to manifest themselves at first in an incoherent way. This incoherence is a result of the bewilderment felt when a sense of order, or natural justice, is confronted by the realities of the social world, by greed and selfishness. Criticism emerges first not through analysis as much as through a sense of shock. It takes time for children to adjust to the motives underlying the mechanics of society. Children at such a time also begin to lose confidence in their own ability, and become acutely aware of other people as well as of being judged themselves. By the age of eight, children seem to make the choice between application or lack of interest, as if they want to retain their optimism or not. At this age the sense of complex values and the difficulty in interpreting the word 'truth' are made manifest. It is at this age that children point out their awareness of the fact that advertisements have designs on them. Around the age of eight, children learn to apply their critical sense through the logic of organizing the classifying clues into hierarchies of the type used in Twenty Questions.[29] They replace the awareness of a political world of heroes with a more critical and disinterested understanding of the political phrases used by different parties. A shift of emphasis takes place, with the acquisition of more precise conceptual categories of the kind that adults find easier to understand.

While children learn to use the conventional terms that are required for the lucid communication of common beliefs, this does not mean that they have lost touch with their continuing curiosity about the world, or their drive to find meaning in it. For this reason the way in which they shift from natural, unfocused curiosity to a more self-conscious critical awareness is very important, for the link between the drive to know and the way in which this drive is to be formulated to satisfy the demands of others is not always obvious and never automatic. In their early years children respond to experience, and find that curiosity is demanded of them naturally; but after the first years, learning needs to become an acquired habit, a sustained curiosity that can often be in contrast to the tasks demanded of them when a particular way of working seems more important than what is learned. For young children all they learn has some kind of meaning; the distinctions between the applied and the theoretical are not made. Only moments of stress show their tendency to withdraw from the demand. But from the age of eight, children see some kinds of demands being made on them not as impossible but as meaningless. Their own natural curiosity about facts can become a hobby divorced from set tasks. They begin to develop different styles of criticizing: cautious, calculating and impulsive.[30] They also learn not to bother to criticize.

Children's individual characteristics, their interest in other people, their temperament and nature, are all easy enough to see almost from the first weeks. But their styles of learning become manifest later. Some children show a marked propensity for using a vocabulary that consists largely of naming words, of labelling, of choosing the right word for an object.[31] Other children are more inclined to use words that make demands for action: 'give me more!' rather than 'a house!' As children become older they tend to be better with either of two semantic fields. Some children are good at 'paradigms', collections of a similar type that have a number of associations with each other. 'Man, boy, girl, woman' are a human paradigm, with cross-classifications and associations like 'sex' and 'maturity'. Other children are more inclined to understand 'taxonomies', which are classifiable by distinct properties, just as copper, lead, zinc, gold and silver are all 'metals' that can be classified by individual chemical properties.

When children acquire both an attitude towards learning and a particular style of learning, they acquire a habit that underlies all they do. This 'habituation' is not a passive automatic response of the organism but a state of expectancy delicately tuned to the recurrence of circumstances.[32] It is a matter of expecting things to happen, of hoping for particular levels of demand, of assuming that what is being analysed will fit into their own style of thinking. Much of what children learn from books or television is not as much a matter of information as of the assumptions underlying it. The discarding of new and challenging information takes place because of the tendency for hypotheses to 'fixate after receiving a minimum of confirmation'.[33] The same habit of expectancy in perception is revealed in the acquisition of new knowledge: opinions are there to be confirmed rather than changed.[34] Material that seems to suggest a new challenge is more easily discarded. Children learn not only how to take in new information but also how to reject it. They remember what they choose to remember according to their learning style. Just as children learn to read because they understand the purpose of reading, so they learn to approach new material of any kind through the way in which they think it will fit, or challenge, what they already know. No learning is automatic. It is painfully acquired, rejected or desired.

NOTES AND REFERENCES

1 The literature on this matter is quite weighty, so much so that it is a matter of surprise to find how rarely it seems to be taken into account.

2 Turner, J. *Made for Life: Coping, Competence and Cognition*. London: Methuen, 1980; and Burns, R.B. *Self-Concept Development and Education*. London: Holt, Rinehart and Winston, 1982.

3 The Berkeley tradition of associative philosophy and linguistic analysis on the one hand; numerous ethical texts on the other.

4 Harré, R. *Social Being: A Theory for Social Psychology*. Oxford: Blackwell, p. 23 and p. 212, 1983.

5 The fact that many children do not have a strong sense of political parties does not prevent them having a sense of the world of politics and some strongly held beliefs.

6 Erikson, E.H. *Childhood and Society*. New York: Norton, 1950.

7 Kohlberg, L. 'Moral stages and moralization: the cognitive-developmental

approach'. In Lickona, T. (ed.) *Moral Development and Behaviour, Theory, Research and Social Issues*. New York: Holt, Rinehart and Winston, pp. 31–53, 1976.

8 Piaget, J. *The Moral Judgement of the Child*. London: Routledge and Kegan Paul, 1932.

9 Research based on interviews with 120 eight- to eleven-year-old children on their attitudes towards morality and blame. (Publication is forthcoming.)

10 Goldman, R. and Goldman, J. *Show Me Yours: What Children Think about Sex*. Harmondsworth: Penguin, 1988.

11 For example, Harré, R., 1983, op. cit.

12 Polanyi, M. *The Tacit Dimension*. London: Routledge and Kegan Paul, 1967.

13 One of the reasons why children are rarely asked questions is that the temptation to deal with evidence that can be submitted to factor analysis in a computer and scored in terms of correlations is so strong that there is a suspicion of 'soft' information that does not lend itself to such analysis.

14 Crick, F. and Mitchison, G. 'The function of dream sleep'. *Nature*, **304**, 111–114, 1983.

15 The terms used by Hudson, L. *Frames of Mind; Ability, Perception and Self-perception, in the Arts and Sciences*. London: Methuen, 1968.

16 It is worth noting that the 'artistic' is often praised as *separate* from the 'normal' demands of the exam system.

17 Crowther, E.M. 'Understanding of the concept of change among children and young adolescents'. *Educational Review* **34** (3), 279–284, 1982.

18 Freud, S. *Civilization and Its Discontents*. London: Hogarth Press, 1973.

19 Schachter, S. 'The interaction of cognitive and physiological determinants of emotional state'. In Berkowitz, L. (ed.) *Advances in Experimental Social Psychology*, Vol. 1. New York: Academic Press, pp. 49–80, 1964.

20 Latané, B. and Darley, J. 'Determinants of bystander intervention'. In Macauley, M.E. and Berkowitz, L. (eds) *Altruism and Helping Behaviour*. New York: Academic Press, 1970; Milgram, S. *Obedience to Authority: An Experimental View*. London: Tavistock, 1974.

21 Erikson, E.H. 1950, op. cit.

22 Goldman, R. and Goldman, J. *Children's Sexual Thinking*. London: Routledge and Kegan Paul, 1982.

23 Hettena, C.M. and Ballif, B.L. 'Effects of mood on learning'. *Journal of Educational Psychology*, **73** (4), 505–508, 1981.

24 Eysenck, H.J. *Readings in Extroversion and Introversion*. London: Staples Press, 1971.

25 Shavelson, R.J. and Bolus, R. 'Self-concept: the interplay of theory and methods'. *Journal of Educational Psychology*, **74** (1), 3–17, 1982.

26 Stipek, D.J. 'Children's perceptions of their own and their classmates' ability'. *Journal of Educational Psychology*, **73** (3), 404–410, 1981.

27 Wixson, K.K. 'Questions about a text: what you ask about is what children learn'. *The Reading Teacher*, **37** (3), 287–293, 1983.

28 Survey carried out in Oxfordshire, especially in selected primary middle and preparatory schools in Oxford, Spring, 1985.

29 Mosker, F.A. and Hornsby, J.R. 'On asking questions'. In Bruner, J.S., Olver, R.R. and Greenfield, P.M. (eds) *Studies in Cognitive Growth*. New York: Wiley, 1966.

30 Winkley, D.R. 'Children's response to stories'. DPhil thesis, Oxford University, 1975.

31 Clark, E.V. 'Some aspects of the conceptual basis for first language acquisition'. In Schiefelbusch, R.L. and Lloyd, L.L. (eds) *Language Perspectives: Acquisition, Retardation and Intervention*. Baltimore: University Park Press, pp. 105–126, 1974.

32 Pribram, K.H. 'Neurological notes on the art of educating'. In Hilgard, E. (ed.) *Theories of Learning and Instruction*. Chicago: Chicago University Press, p. 80, 1964.

33 Bruner, J.S. *Beyond the Information Given: Studies in the Psychology of Knowing*. London: G. Allen and Unwin, p. 81, 1974.

34 Compare the literature on propaganda, especially as carried out by Hovland and others on propaganda in the Second World War.

CHAPTER 13
Teachers and Learning

Experience is trained by *both* association and dissociation . . .
William James, *The Principles of Psychology*, Vol. 1.

Teachers influence their pupils. Sometimes this is obvious, and sometimes it is unacknowledged. But teachers are also the creations of their pupils. They are surrounded by respect and suspicion. The more that individuals resent being taught the more they will blame teachers for trying to impose learning on them; the more they respect learning the more they will assume that they have achieved what they know despite, not because of, the attention of teachers. Teachers have a great deal of power and yet work in such conditions that it seems absurd to think that an individual teacher could make a difference to others. This combination of respect for power and a sense of suspicion makes teachers uncertain of their roles.

The sense of an equivocal role is fostered in teachers partly because of the peculiarities of classroom life, when the duty to cajole, interest and develop about 30 children who might not see the point of their being there demands a level of emotional strain that is unusual. It also partly derives from the fact that schools are relatively small organizations in which personal relationships are very important.[1] In the different approaches schools take to class and team teaching there are many more common organizational similarities than differences.[2] Attention to the management of schools tends to focus on the role of the headteacher and on the organizational structures, as if all types of organization were similar, but the *raison d'être* of schools makes them essentially unlike any other type of organization. While it is sometimes tempting to think of schools in terms of products and outcomes, clearly measured, this type of analysis does not take us very far.[3]

The particular nature of teaching is pointed up by examining the changing roles of headteachers. They have all had experience of managing classrooms, of developing the curriculum and of inspiring other people. They have then been promoted into a position in which they are to appoint and discipline staff, control finances and respond to every demand made upon them by the Education Reform Act. Where once they were considered to be responsible for the curriculum of a school, they have become accountable to one given to them. This creates tensions. One crucial distinction between alternative approaches to leadership (and to any teaching) is that between the autocratic and the democratic. Some headteachers naturally assume that they are in command and should be obeyed; others stress the need for greater participation by all members of staff.[4]

Some headteachers have exaggerated characteristics, such as those who lock themselves away in their studies and hate to see anyone and those who want to know exactly what is going on at any moment and who dominate the school with their presence. Between the two extremes are any number of possible variables. Yukl gives three degrees of leader influence over group decisions, from initiating a structure, to involving others, to centralizing the decision-making process.[5] Nias discusses the 'passive' head who gives more freedom than the teachers want, the 'Bourbon' head who is socially distant and very authoritarian, and the 'positive' head with high professional standards.[6] Hersey *et al.* characterize four styles of leadership, ranging from delegating decisions and participating with staff, to 'selling' ideas to staff and to telling them.[7] Heller characterizes headteachers as military leaders ('running a tight ship', respected, distant) or as missionaries (relying on charisma and fragmentary enthusiasm), as entrepreneurs (conscious of image building and publicity, and out of touch with the classroom) or as artists (with untidy organization but involved with personal development).[8] Such analyses of the ways in which a personal approach to organization creates particular effects are closer to the actual muddles of real events than any of the 'structural' outlines that posit simple causes and effects. Understanding the influence of personal approaches brings one closer to seeing the way in which the individual pupils react. They might not analyse the cultural effort of a school but they become aware of it, and analyse enough of it to survive.

Children, in observing different approaches to leadership, also understand the difference between ostensible policies of democracy and involvement, and the actual realities.

Headteachers are not the only people to whom pupils react, even if there is more of a collective mythology built around their characters. Each teacher also creates a style of her own, and children learn to recognize the style, and know how to handle it, while imbibing some of the teacher's underlying attitudes to work.[9] Children's knowledge of human nature, as well as deriving from the developing relationships with their friends, is also formed through the observation of teachers' abilities, or inabilities, to understand and encourage pupils' interest in what they are learning. The effects of different kinds of teachers, in terms of children's progress in mathematics, language and other topics, were analysed by the 'Oracle' project at Leicester University.[10] Teachers were characterized as belonging to one of six different types, which bear a fairly close resemblance to the ways in which headteachers are categorized. The 'group instructors' wanted children to work on their own, with few demands made on the teacher; they wished to delegate learning. The 'class inquirers' were clear and lucid in explaining work to the whole class, so that children worked for the most part with little personal contact with the teacher. Then there were the 'infrequent changers', who set carefully thought out tasks to the children and participated with them with a high degree of individual attention. The 'individual monitors' told children one by one what they should be doing and spent much of their time marking work and telling children what to do next. The 'habitual changers' switched from class teaching to individual work unpredictably as a result of the behaviour of the class, spending much of the time on topic work. And the 'rotating changers' organized their classrooms so that groups of children could work on different subjects at the same time, moving to a new topic at a given signal. Some of these styles are more successful than others, not only in terms of achievement but also in children's attitudes towards their work.[11]

The differences between the styles of organization result in marked differences in the ways children learn, in their level of boredom or their self-esteem. If one takes an example of a teacher working in the 'individual monitor' style, it is possible to discover, as do Bennett and Desforges, that the teacher can be unaware of what the pupil is doing, and what mistakes he is making.[12] As a result of this the pupil can become indifferent to the possibility of learning anything. Although teachers characteristically see themselves as responding to the individual needs of children, they actually spend a lot of time confined behind a desk. The children then spend much of their time in classrooms doing anything but structured work. Teachers want to be able to diagnose their pupils' work, but find they have little time for doing so, or for practising it. Children soon learn to accept that marking is a routine, the display of a tick or gold star, which merely acknowledges that they have fulfilled a task that has been set. There is rarely time for individual diagnosis or discussion.

One of the major problems for teachers is the conflict between what they would like to do and the realities of the classroom. Every teacher wishes to respond to individual needs, because it is much closer to the ideal of learning and because it is far more natural than the imposition of will on a recalcitrant group of people. And yet the task of teaching in the circumstances of school often demands a style of behaviour that contrasts with other human relationships. There is no retreat from the difficulties of the classroom. The emotional demands on teachers to respond individually but not personally means that their task is often far more taxing than it seems. Children see teachers under stress. It is no surprise that some teachers would like to withdraw from the difficulties of teaching by concentrating only on 'delivering' the curriculum and suggesting that the pastoral side is better handled by others. Teachers look for relief from the difficulty of their role, including the possibility of remaining distant and unconsulted. But learning is pastoral. There is no escaping the actual demands, the perceptions and the strain on the individual. The approach to children that suggests that their needs do not matter as far as the teacher is concerned, and that she is only there for those who have enough interest in her subject, is merely another attitude to the pastoral, a particular role to play.

Teachers face great insecurity and great suspicion. They know that the pupils' and parents' reactions to them are ambiguous and sceptical. Some teachers have a tendency to see themselves as foster parents, trying from a disinterested point of view to overcome the problems of home. This is a natural temptation for anyone in that position, as well as impossible to carry through. Teachers do not usually feel that directive activity is the best use of their time and yet it is the only way in which they can cope with the demands of the classroom.[13] As a result of the constant contrasts to what they feel they ought to do, teachers tend to revert to what is safest and well tried, or become indifferent to lack of success. Once a particular method of teaching becomes routine it is very hard to change. Even teachers who use the newest published projects to help them teach rarely use the different aims and objectives set up in those projects.[14] Student teachers revert to the practices they find easiest to cope with, practices they find 'safest' in terms of classroom management, even if they begin their teaching with the best of intentions and a fresh outlook on the difficulties.[15] More tellingly, teachers revert to the style of teaching that they have observed when they were in school themselves. All the different possibilities of teaching style, the discussions, the ideals, the understanding of methodology and the reasons for it are actually translated into the practice of the distant past remembered from years earlier. The personal experience of watching different teachers is more influential than later attempts to develop a new style. For it is a personal style and mannerism that teachers learn rather than the application of particular methods, just as it is the personal style of the headteacher that is influential, not the management structure itself.

Teachers are constantly learning new roles. This is partly because of changing circumstances and partly because of the nature of teaching. The role of the class teacher is not what it used to be. Increasingly there are other people in the classroom, from parents to ancillary workers.[16] Increasingly the teachers are seen as consultants and specialists in the primary school as well as in the secondary. Teachers are becoming more formally assessed as well as being caught up in elaborate assessment procedures. But the changes that have followed the introduction of a National Curriculum highlight the constant ambiguities of the teacher's role. However strong the tradition of pastoral care, teachers are also expected to represent a national body of knowledge, to pass on to parents statements of comparable assessment. There is always a tension between concern for the individual child, imparting the necessary skills and attitudes that will allow the pupil to direct his own learning, and the passing on of a formal body of knowledge. Although the greater personal rewards, and successes, derive from putting the child's interest first, it seems like an impossible task to many, especially in the light of increased involvement by inspectors, governors, parents and headteachers.[17]

The influence of the teaching styles of teachers on their pupils is one example of learning through close observation of someone else's performance. Children's ability to parody, to create their own version of other people, is manifested in the way they analyse and copy the characteristics of their teachers. They might not always demonstrate their awareness of the personal habits of teachers, by betting on a number of times a teacher says 'right' or the amount of time that can be wasted by side-tracking them, but they can produce a shrewd parody almost at will. This insight into the personality of the teacher matters to the pupils; on this insight depends their own style of response. They learn what they can get away with and what to avoid. The personal style of a teacher is of more importance to the pupils than the subject matter she is conveying. Furthermore, teachers develop reputations for the particular services they supply: they are soon expected to play a role. The teacher might think she has given a brilliant lesson, or a dreadful one because she is not feeling well, but although the pupils will pick up the mood, the lesson will be just another example of the same teacher's characteristic routine.

To children the distinction between 'formal' and 'informal' approaches in the teacher's style is almost meaningless. Superficially the word 'formal' suggests children sitting silently in rows, and the word 'progressive' nothing but disorganized chaos. But children know it is possible to create chaos when 'formally' in rows, and that working on individual tasks can be fiercely well organized. However hard teachers try to convey a sense of informality, children continue to guess what the teacher wants and direct as much energy to anticipation as to the work itself. The teacher's 'open' question might require children to come up with their own solution, to think of something that is not either right or wrong, but to children virtually all questions given by teachers, and most other adults, are 'closed', however they are phrased. The ostensibly 'open' question is only more difficult because children at first cannot see what answer the teacher wants. Children know, from the reaction of the teacher, that some answers are more pleasing than others, and that answering a question in class is a kind of public performance. Class discussion is then a peculiar task, requiring pupils to predict what the teacher wants to know. 'Indirect' teachers, in Flanders's term, might ask more questions than 'direct' teachers but, to the children, they make the same demands.[18] Teachers who ask most questions are found to be the least likely to receive questions back from the children, and also the least likely to get any elaboration on the answers or to receive any kind of spontaneous comments.[19] Asking lots of questions is not the answer to the desire for 'open' communication. Children assume that the teacher has organized all the knowledge under discussion into a structure.[20] This means that they assume that she is looking for the right answer. They tax their minds trying to predict not what the answer is as much as what the teacher wants to hear. This means that teachers need to make elaborate efforts to create sustained and demanding conversations with individual children.[21]

Children's expectations of formality in teachers gives an important clue to their learning habits, early ingrained. A teacher's concern for the individual learner is a demanding intellectual one rather than anything sentimental. Much has been made of the concept of starting to teach from 'where the child is'. If interpreted to mean engaging the child's personal and involved interest this is a good thing. But it can also imply a lack of demand and a narrowness of focus that diminishes a child's awareness of the whole world beyond his immediate environment, a world of intellectual depth as well as cultural richness. For children like to have demands made on them that are clear, formal and explained. This can be demonstrated by the research that has taken place on the early stages of reading. Each child finds his own means of learning to read, but is also helped most when he is taught formally, whatever the particular method used. The more direct and clear the instructions the more successfully children overcome reading difficulties.[22]

The first few minutes, or even lessons, of contact between a teacher and a group of children can be very much easier, as well as more difficult, than subsequent engagements. The group has not yet worked out how to react to the new presence: the pupils have not learned to anticipate the teacher's expectations. It is almost like a normal meeting, which is why new student teachers sometimes begin by trying out new ideas and different approaches before reverting to more standard expectations, including those of the pupils. As they become understood so they tend to retreat to more conventional routines of management. It is for this reason that up to a quarter of every lesson is spent on 'administration', on the routine organization of controlling the amount of paper, the distribution of pens or the tracing of lost compasses.[23] To a great extent children expect a teacher's time to be taken up with the matters of management; for them it becomes a way of passing the time, of avoiding work.[24] Pupils' engagement in a lesson has been found to be generally higher when teachers move directly into tasks than when they began with some preparatory outline of what is to follow.[25] Teachers are often taught to introduce the subject, to give an outline of what they will be dealing with so that their pupils know what to expect. But to the pupils this is as much a part of administrative padding as the guest lecturer who begins warming up with a few jokes about his journey. Children learn to understand the codes used by teachers, and learn what they can safely ignore.

There are many signals used by teachers that they expect their pupils to understand. Non-verbal communication is used primarily to keep control and manage the classroom.[26] Children are therefore constantly aware of what the teacher wants of them. They are also aware that the teacher is assessing them. Seligman *et al.* showed that teachers usually evaluate their pupils' ability according to their voices and their physical appearance, as well as (or in spite of) their written work.[27] Edwards found that in Dublin teachers' inferences about poor vocabulary, fluency and pronunciation gave unfavourable evaluations about the pupils' personalities and their performance.[28] This common, perhaps unavoidable, phenomenon is often based on assumptions about home background. The most 'common sense' explanations of success or failure tend to be not just ability and motivation but also home background and parental attitudes.[29] Given the whole tenor of society it is hardly surprising that teachers should reflect common attitudes, but they also display the human tendency to label, to come to conclusions quickly and then to defend their position once they have made up their minds. At the beginning of the year many teachers are able to give very acute analyses of individual children by the end of the first day – which child will be a quiet worker, which one is clever and which will cause trouble. By the end of the year, however, one finds that the teachers can give exactly the same opinions about exactly the same children on whom they pronounced so quickly. They might, of course, have been right at once.

Labelling people might be a general characteristic but in the conditions of the classroom it can become a forming influence. In their book on self-fulfilling prophecy, Rosenthal and Jacobsen opened up an important area of learning and teaching.[30] They suggested that teacher's expectancy itself made a difference to pupils' performance: that teachers having formed impressions of them changed their behaviour according to this impression and that children became aware of these attitudes and expectations and responded to them. The suggestion that one could mislead teachers into a different (higher) expectation by giving false information about the pupils' home background is hardly an answer, since the problem is deeply embedded in a range of more complex attitudes, towards work, towards behaviour and towards other people. Asch showed that pupils' reactions to other people could be easily influenced by a previous description of them in which either of the words 'warm' or 'cold' joined a list that included 'intelligent, skilful, industrious, determined, practical and cautious'.[31] Kelley found that students who were told that their teacher was 'cold' participated far less in a seminar than with a teacher previously pronounced 'warm'.[32]

Children's reactions to teachers are personal, but they are also subject to rumour and the overheard remark. But it is teachers who must subtly alter their behaviour towards individual children and communicate their expectations to the child.[33] One of the most striking marks of the professionalism of teachers is their ability to adapt to individual children. In a class of 30 the teacher will know, when there is some kind of disturbance, which child to ignore, which to console and which to tell off, with a remarkable degree of instinctive awareness. This professional expertise changes and develops as teachers learn from their experience of teaching. When they have taught for a long time the focus of attention turns increasingly away from the teachers' own performance to an awareness of what the pupils are doing.[34] They also change from trying to transmit large quantities of fact to concentrating on a few principles that underlie learning.[35] The other side of such development is the danger that teachers know how different techniques work so well that their work becomes a routine.

Teachers' views of children depend partly on the views they have of their own role, and on the conditions they feel they wish to create in their classrooms. As in all social actions that include subjective meanings teachers tend to present a view of children as innocent; to be protected, to be happy and to be obedient.[36] They see themselves as adapting to the children, encouraging their innocent play on the assurance that children will find their own fulfilment as a natural course of their development.[37] At the same time teachers actually see creativity not as a spontaneous overflow of powerful feelings but as reading ability and hard work.

The various attitudes teachers display can be suggested by their attitudes to two variables: to the child and to the curriculum. Some teachers take the view that the children they teach in primary schools are innately gifted, that they only need opportunities to display their natural abilities. Other teachers take a more jaundiced view, feeling that children are not very clever, and that they need a lot of judicious instruction as well as encouragement to do well. The distinction between these views of the child is far more important than that between 'traditional' and 'progressive' approaches to teaching. The other important variable in teachers' approaches is whether they view the curriculum as a means to an end, as a tool which children must learn to use, or as concerned with the development of the whole child. This distinction between pragmatic and holistic approaches is more significant than the kinds of classroom organization employed. In observation and questioning of a group of teachers,[38] it appeared that teachers of primary school children (eight to eleven) were fairly equally divided between the four possible combinations shown in Figure 4.

The performance of teachers who assumed that the children were clever and yet took a pragmatic view of their subject was in marked contrast to those who shared the pragmatism of taking

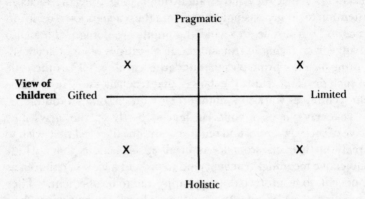

Figure 4

their subject as a tool but who did so because they felt their children were too limited for them to do anything else. Other teachers who believed in the pupils' essential limitations nevertheless wanted to help the development of the whole child. This group also contrasted with those teachers who assumed innate abilities in children and saw them developing through an holistic approach to the curriculum.

Children's views of teachers are sometimes in marked contrast to teachers' views of themselves. Staff think that the most important element in the school is staff co-operation. The pupils think that their development comes first, and that no one else really cares about them.[39] The difference in outlook might seem obvious but it is implicit rather than spelled out. Children do not feel that their own motivational style is understood by the teachers but they do feel that there is a lack of concern for their personal responsibilities and relationships to others.

When children are asked about their perceptions of school they do not say much about the institutional restrictions on their relationship with their peers, but more about the friendliness or distance of the teachers.[40] Their greatest suspicion is of teachers who are 'unfair' or 'uncaring'. Children are aware of a teacher's lack of interest in them by the way in which they are addressed.[41] But while children tend to worry about teachers being 'unfair' they nevertheless expect them to fit into a particular model: they expect them to be authoritarian, to make decisions, to impose order and structure.[42] There are certain phrases they associate with teachers, such as 'right', which according to the tone of the voice means anything from 'stop what you are doing' to 'now I'm going to introduce something new'. They feel that 'do it again' is the most characteristic saying of teachers.[43] And they see teachers as evading the issue just as they evade things themselves, avoiding the teacher's eye in case they are asked a question. The reaction to particular teachers and the response to the idea of a teacher are held together not only by the reputation teachers carry, but also by the 'ripple effect', the teacher's influence related to pupils other than the one she is addressing.[44]

The ways in which teachers maintain control and give instructions tend to be oblique. This is because they show a characteristic leaning towards making requests when they are really giving instructions, and because they ask many questions that do not require an answer, such as 'Are you getting on with your work?' They give instructions by, as it were, thinking aloud – 'I do hope that no one is going to spoil our story' – and ask questions that it would be foolish to answer – 'Are we going to make a lot of noise?'[45] Children learn the ways teachers use language and how they control through the use of eyes and gesture, because it is important for them to understand the teacher, to predict the mood, to guess her intentions. And because the teacher is a scarce resource it is seen by some children to be necessary to acquire some form of power over her, while it is equally necessary for others to remain obscure and ignored.[46] Certain types of pupil – attention seekers and intermittent workers – create more intense relationships with teachers, either with the purpose of seeking out more involvement or by judging how to avoid doing too much real work.[47]

Children need to understand their teachers, not only because they have to learn to cope with the peculiarities of the school as an organization but also because so much of what is learned derives from personal influence. Children are occasionally conscious of admiring particular adults. They will tend to model themselves on the characteristics of their favourites. But at a less obvious level children are constantly learning attitudes as well as gestures from a whole range of teachers. They are aware of the ways in which different people are performing similar tasks. Teaching is often likened to acting; but the theatrical nature of teaching depends on the fact that there is a permanent, sophisticated audience closely observing the personal characteristics of teachers. One of the main facets of what is observed is the extent to which teachers both give themselves to others and retain their own personality.[48]

Children's liking and admiration of teachers depends on the degree to which the teacher is friendly and the degree to which she is trusted. She is expected to be scrupulously fair, to the point of formality, interested in the individual and clear in explaining her subject. She is supposed to be approachable but not too ardent in seeking a relationship. This duality of integrity and unselfishness is at the heart of charisma. While the notion of charisma is normally applied to someone set apart from the 'ordinary man' in an almost superhuman way,[49] or to a 'protean' character with authoritative ordering,[50] charisma is actually far more of a balance between distance and closeness, the willingness of a person to be both distant enough to be admired and friendly enough to be liked. In this sense many teachers have charismatic qualities for the children with whom they are in contact

NOTES AND REFERENCES

1 Note how different schools are from other organizations, which have more autonomy and a far clearer indication of how to measure success and failure. One of the most impressive analyses of the peculiarity of academic institutions is actually concerned with American college presidents: Cohen, M.D. and March, J.G. *Leadership and Ambiguity*. New York: McGraw-Hill, 1974.

2 Paisey, A. *Small Organisations: The Management of Primary and Middle Schools*. Windsor: NFER Nelson, 1981.

3 The American model of measurement by time spent on tasks was fleetingly popular but soon became regarded as meaninglessly superficial.

4 See the models given by Cohen, M.D. and March, J.G., 1974, op. cit., p.38, which range through the roles of entrepreneur, administrator, mediator, democratic representative, manager of consensus, catalyst, judge and decision-maker.

5 Yukl, G. 'Toward a behavioural theory of leadership'. In Houghton, V. *The Management of Organisations and Individuals*. London: Ward Lock, 1975.

6 Nias, J. 'Leadership styles and job-satisfaction in primary school'. In

Bush, T., Glatter, R., Goodey, J. and Riches C. (eds) *Approaches to School Management*. London: Harper and Row, 1980.

7 Hersey, P., Blanchard, K.H. and Natemeyer, W.E. *Situational Leadership, Perception and the Impact of Power*. La Jolla, CA: Learning Resources Corporation, 1979.

8 Heller, H. 'Management development for headteachers.' In Gray, H.L. (ed.) *The Management of Educational Institutions: Theory, Research and Consultancy*. Lewes: Falmer Press, pp. 219–244, 1982.

9 Teachers very quickly reveal whether they are trying to fill up time, or wait for the end of the lesson, or whether they have an enthusiasm for their subject. Some things are impossible to disguise.

10 Galton, M. and Simon, B. (eds) *Progress and Performance in the Primary Classroom*. London: Routledge and Kegan Paul, 1980; and the other books deriving from the 'Oracle' project.

11 It is clear that children are very acute in their knowledge of a teacher's role, both personally and in terms of the style of teaching: Cullingford, C. 'Children's attitudes to teaching styles'. *Oxford Review of Education*, **13** (3), 331–339, 1987.

12 Desforges, C., Bennett, N., Cockburn, A. and Wilkinson, B. 'Understanding the quality of pupil learning experience'. In Entwistle, N. (ed.) *New Directions in Educational Psychology 1. Learning and Teaching*. Lewes: Falmer Press, pp. 161–172, 1984.

13 Wood, D., McMahon, L. and Cranstona, Y. *Working with Under Fives*. London: Grant McIntyre, 1981.

14 Galton, M. and Moon, B. (eds) *Changing Schools ... Changing Curriculum*. London: Harper and Row, 1983.

15 Dreyfus, A. and Eggleston, J. 'Classroom transactions of student teachers in science'. *European Journal of Science Education*, I (3) 315–325, 1980.

16 Cullingford, C. *The Primary Teacher*. London: Cassell, 1989.

17 Broadfoot, P. and Osborn, M. 'Teachers' conceptions of their professional responsibility: some international comparisons'. *Comparative Education*, **23** (3), 287–302, 1987.

18 Flanders, N.A. *Teacher Influence on Pupil Attitudes and Achievement*. Co-operative Research Project No. 397. Minneapolis: University of Minnesota, 1960.

19 Wood, H. and Wood, D. 'Questioning the pre-school child'. *Educational Review*, **35** (2), 149–162, 1983.

20 Wixson, K.K. 'Questions about a text: what you ask about is what children learn'. *The Reading Teacher*, **37** (3), 287–293, 1983.

21 Meadows, S. and Cashdan, A. *Helping Children Learn: Contributions to a Cognitive Curriculum*. London: David Fulton, 1988.

22 Somerville, D.E. and Leach, D.J. 'Direct or indirect instruction? An evaluation of three types of intervention programme for assisting students with specific reading difficulties'. *Educational Research*, **30** (1), 46–53, 1988.

23 Bennett, N., Andreae, J., Hegarty, P. and Wade, B. *Open Plan Schools: Teaching, Curriculum, Design.* Windsor: NFER, 1980; and Desforges, C. *et al.*, 1984, op. cit.

24 Hence the anticipation children have of secondary schools, where they assume that a lot of time will be taken up moving from one classroom to another, settling down and finding books.

25 Brophy, J., Rohrkemper, M., Rashid, H. and Goldberger, M. 'Relationships between teachers' presentations of classroom tasks and students' engagement in those tasks'. *Journal of Educational Psychology*, **75** (4), 544–552, 1983.

26 Doyle, W. 'The use of nonverbal behaviours: toward an ecological model of classrooms'. *Merrill-Palmer Quarterly*, **23**, 179–192, 1977.

27 Seligman, C.R., Tucker, G.R. and Lambert, W.E. 'The effects of speech style and other attributes on teachers' attitudes towards children'. *Language in Society*, **1** (1), 26, 1972.

28 Edwards, J.R. 'Judgement and confidence reactions to disadvantaged speech'. In Giles, H. and St Clair, R. *Language and Social Psychology*. Oxford: Blackwell, pp. 22–44, 1979.

29 Kozeki, B. and Entwistle, N. 'Describing and utilizing motivational styles in education'. *British Journal of Educational Studies*, **31** (3), 184–197, 1983.

30 Rosenthal, R. and Jacobsen, L. *Pygmalion in the Classroom.* New York: Holt, Rinehart and Winston, 1968.

31 Asch, S. 'Forming impressions of personality'. *Journal of Abnormal and Social Psychology*, **41**, 258–290, 1946.

32 Kelley, H.H. 'The warm–cold variable in first impressions of persons'. *Journal of Personality*, **18**, 431–439, 1950.

33 Hargreaves, D.H. *Interpersonal Relations and Education.* London: Routledge and Kegan Paul, 1972.

34 Pye, J. *Invisible Children: Who Are the Real Losers at School?* Oxford: Oxford University Press, 1989.

35 Larsson, S. 'Learning from experience: teachers' conceptions of changes in their professional practice'. *Journal of Curriculum Studies*, **19** (1), 35–43, 1987.

36 King, R. 'Multiple realities and their reproduction in infants' classrooms'. In Richards, C. (ed.) *New Directions in Primary Education*. Lewes: Falmer, pp. 237–246, 1982.

37 King, R.A. *All Things Bright and Beautiful? A Sociological Study of Infants' Classrooms.* Chichester: Wiley, 1978.

38 Research carried out in Cumbria with 40 teachers in 1978.

39 See the work of Galton, M., Bennett, N. and Desforges, C.

40 Kozeki, B. and Entwistle, N., 1983, op. cit.; see also Donaldson, M. *Children's Minds.* London: Croom Helm, 1978, on teacher 'egocentricity'.

41 Getzels, J.W. and Smilansky, J. 'Individual differences in pupil percep-

tions of school problems'. *British Journal of Educational Psychology*, **53** (3), pp. 307–316, 1983.

42 Giles, H. and Smith, P.M. 'Accommodation theory: optimal levels of convergence'. In Giles, H. and St Clair, R. *Language and Social Psychology*. Oxford: Blackwell, pp. 45–65, 1979.

43 Nash, R. 'Pupils' expectation of their teachers'. In Stubbs, M. and Delamont, S. (eds) *Explorations in Classroom Observation*. Chichester: Wiley, 1976.

44 See the work of Galton and Hargreaves, e.g. *A Challenge for the Comprehensive School: Culture, Curriculum and Community*. London: Routledge and Kegan Paul, 1982.

45 Kounin, J.S. *Discipline and Group Management in Classrooms*. London: Holt, Rinehart and Winston, 1970.

46 See Pye, J., 1989, op. cit.

47 Galton, M. and Simon, B, 1980, op. cit.; and Croll, P. *Inside the Primary Classroom*, London: Routledge and Kegan Paul, 1980.

48 See Borowitz, E.B. 'Tzimtzum: a mystic model for contemporary leadership'. *Religious Education*, **69** (6), 687–700, 1974.

49 Shils, E. 'Charisma, order, status'. *American Sociological Review*, **30**, 199–213, 1965.

50 Weber, M. *The Theory of Social and Economic Organization*. New York: Oxford University Press, 1947

CHAPTER 14
The Developing Learner

A curious peculiarity of our memory is that things are impressed better by active than by passive repetition.

William James, *The Principles of Psychology*, Vol. 1.

Learning is a reflection of character as much as a reflection of ability. It does not consist of a steady accumulation of knowledge, but of change, adaptability and the ability to question and rethink. The refusal to learn, to change one's mind, and the refusal to question given assumptions is often a more marked characteristic of the human temperament than any desire for wisdom. The capacity to retain a set of beliefs in the face of the clearest evidence is a significant characteristic even of the clever man.[1] As much energy is spent adapting new information into a strongly held frame of reference as is spent absorbing new information. Real learning is never passive. Some things might be learned unintentionally, but they also depend on the willingness of the recipient to absorb something new. The learner needs either to want to learn or to be willing to learn.

The problem with learning is that once a framework of beliefs is established and a style of thinking fixed it becomes far harder to learn something really new. This is why we so often have to come to the conclusion that 'people don't change'. The means of adaptation and the ability to rethink a position fade. In contrast to the many experiments with meaning that young children demonstrate, even to the extent of misinterpreting rules or applying them incorrectly, adults tend to feel that their own set of beliefs is as firmly established as concrete foundations. Children characteristically acquire from their schooling an attitude towards learning and a style of learning of their own. They learn (or not) how to make use of new information and how to apply it to themselves. After a few years they also learn how to rely on a particular method of learning. They become used to recognizing instantly what interests them. By the time a student is following a specialized course at university he will be characterized by a distinct learning style, a style that often underlies his choice of subject as well as his success in it.

The relationship between learning styles and the curriculum is complex. Perhaps too much is made of the curriculum and modes of knowledge, and not enough of the fact that each part of the curriculum tends to depend on different approaches to learning. A particular subject or discipline not only attracts a particular temperament but also imposes a style of learning that the student likes or rejects. Different kinds of knowledge – aesthetic, moral, linguistic or mathematical – are manifestations of different styles and requirements of learning. Attempts to find some kind of common core below all subjects, such as some general principle of learning, have not been very successful, not because it is difficult for teachers to adapt to new principles, but because all students exhibit different ways of learning, differences and specialisms that naturally affect teachers even more.[2] Even the youngest children show quite distinct attributes in their approach to new material; their personal styles differ. These differences are a matter more of temperament than of ability. Rules of child development are most helpful when they can account for the variety of styles of learning. The various parts of the curriculum can be seen, in a sense, as distinct exemplars of style.[3]

One of the most difficult matters in devising a curriculum, whether on a national or a local scale, is that it is easier to think in terms of 'content' and subjects than in terms of the more holistic learning of principles and their application. What at first seems simple and attractively measurable, like the core subjects in a national curriculum, becomes more complicated when looked at more carefully. The way in which the National Curriculum was introduced is an example of this, as each subject group began to find common ground and sought for demonstrations of pupil learning that are very hard to assess. Then followed the almost inevitable attempts of subject groups to claim all knowledge as their own, so that the whole curriculum could be absorbed in, say, technology. It is not so much the presence of cross-curricular *issues* that reveals that learning is not fragmentary or compartmentalized, but the fact that at the heart of any curriculum are the *skills* that need to be learned.

For teachers the greatest difficulty is to understand and make use of the different learning styles of the children in their classrooms. In one way teachers show themselves to be remarkably sensitive to the individual children's needs. But it is far harder for the teacher to present an appropriately demanding task according to the needs of the individual. Teachers are often criticized for not matching the tasks to children's ability, but the differences in children's learning characteristics are such that it is very difficult, in normal circumstances, to do so. The notion of children's learning, as a matter of importance in its own right, is not usually acknowledged. This is for reasons of tradition, because of the weight given to examinations and the amount of attention paid to the curriculum and its 'delivery'. To understand the proper 'match' between the child's needs and the appropriate 'task', the teacher needs to know about the characteristic ways in which children learn.

Teachers are naturally far more aware of the relationship between themselves and the children than they are of the children's relationship with their own work. Adaptability to other people is part of a learning style. Some children require particular attention; others quietly get on with the job. Some work better by themselves; some better with partners. They respond to the teacher in different ways. Galton and Simon noted different pupil types: those who seek attention, those who are quiet and collaborative, and those who are either intermittent or solitary workers.[4] These are observations of the ways in which children work in relation to the teacher and the rest of the class, rather than the ways they approach different kinds of material. Pupils seek a clear indication of the rules, of the expectations under which they should work, and try to create a particular relationship with the teacher that is a characteristic of their own.[5] In a small way students try to cajole their way into the good graces of new knowledge – they like it to come easily, they like to know only what they need to know and to feel that they have acquired it without effort.

This sensitivity for relationships, expressed by teachers and students in different ways, is also shown in children's treatment of each other. Children, like adults, prefer to acquire knowledge and ideas by themselves rather than obviously through the medium of teachers. But they do respond sympathetically to other children, who are often far quicker to understand their style of learning and therefore their difficulties. When children are allowed to teach each other in small groups, they turn out to be very successful.[6] In some experiments in American schools it was found that children made far greater progress through helping each other than through other initiatives, such as smaller class size or the involvement of others in the classroom. Comparisons of different methods of encouraging children to help each other show that they are all a most effective way of teaching.[7] In small groups, or individually, children show an awareness of other's learning problems that allows them to support and help each other develop more successful means of learning. No one would suggest that these children have the knowledge of adult teachers; and one would not wish to compare their grasp of the subject to that of any consultant. But learning depends as much on the way it is transmitted and received as on the availability of knowledge.

Styles of learning are to some extent associated with the requirements of the task: whether there is a need to emerge with a particular solution or a new idea, to grasp an unrelated series of propositions or to comprehend a logical sequence. For this reason children are much better at some tasks than others, for each of them gradually evolves his own pattern of learning. There are a number of general differences that characterize styles of learning. Some tests suggest that students can be identified by whether they are 'independent' or 'collaborative' learners, whether they are 'avoidant' or 'dependent', and whether they are 'competitive' or 'participant'.[8] These variables are concerned with the ability to work with others, to accept help, with whether there is a degree of independence that makes it easier to master some tasks than others. The Dunn learning style inventory seeks to discover whether students are driven to learn through sociological needs, physical requirements, their own emotionality or the immediate environment, again tracing essential differences in terms of immediate, short-term gratifications, or more complex and personal long-term goals.[9] Johnson sought out distinctions between students who are spontaneous workers and students who are more systematic, between those who internalize and those who externalize.[10]

One of the recurring differences in the ways children learn is the question of whether they are motivated by immediate needs, or whether they have longer term strategies in mind. This is not so much a conscious decision – 'I will think of the ideal!' – more a different way of manifesting personal motivations, often subconsciously. For many students the ability to focus on present and future needs simultaneously, to hold concurrent interests, to appraise the environment and use intuition at the same time, are some of the different ways of going about similar tasks.[11] In his questionnaire Kolb divides students on a matrix, between the concrete and the abstract conception of the task and between the active and reflective observation, to discover whether they hold the characteristics of the theorist or doer, the brainstormer or the person who translates theory into action (Figure 5).

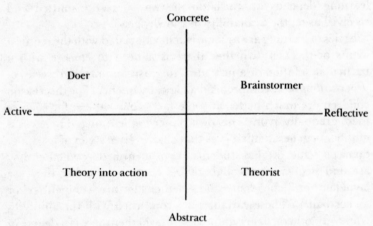

Figure 5

The division of personality into activity and reflection is as old as the analysis of people in terms of humours and as constant as the image of the 'academic' or the 'egg-head' inhabiting a kind of unreal world, as opposed to the 'practical, realist' man of action. These different typologies imply different ways of approaching new material and different ways of making use of it. Learning is itself a kind of action. The approach to ideas, from the 'over-cautious' or 'non-committed' to the 'hustler' or the 'plunger', is a matter of balance between the suspension of judgements and the guessing of what the point is so that one can make a strategy, or framework, for the subsequent analysis of the text.[12] Fransson described four different types of response to the analysis of a document: two ways of being 'conclusion-orientated' and two ways of being more concerned with the description of the text rather than coming to conclusions about it.[13] Whether students wished to describe the text or come to conclusions about it, they could do so in a detailed or a generalized way. When Entwistle put together questionnaires to discover students' approaches to learning he relied on four different factors: a 'deep' approach, concerned with the meaning of the text; a 'surface' approach, concerned with reproducing the text; organized study methods; and 'stable extraversion', the ability to form rapid conclusions, often through personal associations.[14]

All these typologies of learning tend to rely on an essential duality between exploration of the text for a meaning that binds the whole together and an attempt to reproduce and memorize the text according to its own rules and structure of presentation. Svenson used the terms 'holistic' and 'atomistic' to clarify the distinction.[15] Pask and Scott described the difference as that between 'holistic' and 'serialist' learning.[16] The holistic strategy is to look at the whole area being learned, to try to probe beneath the surface, so that an interpretation can be made in such a way as to summarize the essential points. The serialist relies on trying to understand the text in the order in which it is presented. Such crucial distinctions are also reflected in the work of Hudson,[17] with his distinction between convergent and divergent thinking, and de Bono,[18] with his interest in lateral thinking. In the many different types of learning there remains a great measure of agreement that underlying all of them is the distinction between 'deep' and 'surface' learning. Kagan *et al*. saw the difference as that between reflective and impulsive learners.[19] Witkin *et al*. made the distinction between field-independent and field-dependent styles.[20]

These different styles of learning are not only used consistently by different people, they also make a crucial difference to the success or failure of learning. Either type of learner learns best when he is given material that matches his own style of learning.

Matching material to children's or adults' needs demands an awareness of learning strategies. Some people seem stupid when confronted with material of an unfamiliar kind. According to their habitual methods of approach many people will feel justified in not being able to engage even in trying to learn unfamiliar material, such as maths for a historian or literature for a scientist. It is not that they are incapable of applying their minds differently but that they are not accustomed to the habit of doing so. It is very easy to let the mind become tuned to a particular way of thinking, even to the point of being reflective without concentration, or letting the mind 'go blank'. Learning the appropriate approach to various kinds of material is not only important in itself but also colours the student's perceptions of teaching and assessment.[21]

Underlying different styles of comprehension are different levels of approach. There are, indeed, pathological forms of the same types of learning, when, for example, serial or 'operation learners' turn their interest in distinct parts into an obsessive concern for detail in such a way that they are unable to see the relationship of one part to another; or when holistic or 'comprehension learners', who are only interested in formulating a viable insight, jump to instant and superficial conclusions.[22] Every method of learning has its own dangers. Students can be so caught up in the needs of a syllabus that they are unaware that there is anything beyond a series of set tasks. They can be so particular about those things they want to know that they approach all learning as a matter of self-indulgence. The academic perspective that leads a student to be so obsessed with the relationship of one part to another that he forgets that there is any possible application for the learning is well known. But learning a little can also be a dangerous thing in another way, since it is a means of bending all facts to suit a particular purpose. Listening to arguments between politicians is a way of discovering how the same information can be used to support contrary positions. This is not a deliberate series of lies, or even a verbal game, but a condition in which all new information is made to fit into a pre-arranged structure. It is the triumph of prejudice over facts. But at a less extreme and less public level everyone knows the desire to create personal associations, and to have prejudices confirmed.

Up to a point such restructuring of new information is necessary, for no new fact exists in abeyance, in an unconnected void. To make sense it needs to become part of an already existing hierarchy of assumptions. Children reading stories show associative ability: they interpret and speculate around the story in a way that takes them beyond the evidence, they amplify, often showing great insight doing so, and they are inventive in their understanding of character and plot.[23] Often the seemingly minor, irrelevant detail becomes closely observed. The associations made by readers can be not only a necessary step towards the realization of meaning but also the manifestation of an interpretative ability that shows great insight. They can also be signs of impulsive amplification and distortion of the material.

Learning how to learn is a part of personality and character. Students are characterized by their own styles and by the ways in which they develop them. They all go through fairly similar experiences in their attitudes to new material or a new subject. At first the new material or approach seems so obvious that there seems little point in it, since the idea of thinking about the new subject is so alien that there appears little to think about. After a time the student knows so much about a subject, without organization, that he is again inarticulate, even if for reasons of knowledge rather than ignorance. Only deep knowledge of a subject leads to the ability to explain it simply. To achieve this requires a painful series of questions and questionings, wondering what there is in a subject, realizing that it is more complex than it seemed at first, having patiently to divest the mind from the temptation to jump to conclusions, and then to hold and make sense of a mass of details in such a way that one is able to convey the essence of it simply.

This process of discovery is common to all stages of learning and depends on the amount of respect or interest the student has in learning. Perry suggested that the student would begin with the assumption that there was only one right answer, that he would then understand diversity but despise it before accepting that 'anyone has the right to their opinion'.[24] He would then go on to see all knowledge as depending on the context, before seeing the need for personal commitment despite the contextual nature of knowledge. This understanding of the relationship between commitment and knowledge arrives only through the process of learning.[25] It is often assumed, for all the love of generalization and assertion, that learning is a matter of rote, or memory, of being good at *Mastermind*. For those who continue to learn, nothing could be more misleading.[26]

The final outcome of learning, the communication of ideas, the changed attitude or behaviour or the elucidation of the text, lies in action. At first the action consists of improving on practice; later it is a matter of being able to change a pattern of behaviour, or an organization. The kinds of skills that emerge with learning include the capacities to have concurrent interests, to focus on the present and the future simultaneously, to be able to use intuition, to be aware of circumstances and to combine commitment and adaptability. The first concerns for learning are with the self, with what can be derived from learning. Gradually the interest in the task itself takes over. Ultimately the concern for self and the task are joined by a curiosity about the impact of ideas on other people.

The processes of learning are also those of becoming a mature person. The necessary irony that underlies the tension between understanding the misery of the world and still believing in it, between seeing the depravity of behaviour and still forgiving it, also forms the accumulation of new ideas and facts. As in the Platonic stages, we learn to collect new information for its own sake before we make facts fit a passionately held belief. And only then do we see how to understand how knowledge and a point of view balance each other, how we need to retain a sense of our own purpose and mode of action in relation to other people, while understanding the completeness of their point of view.

NOTES AND REFERENCES

1 Hovland, C.I. and Kelley, H. *Communication and Persuasion: Psychological Studies of Opinion Change*. New Haven, CT: Yale University Press, 1953.

2 For example, Bruner, J.S. *Towards a Theory of Instruction*. Cambridge, MA: Harvard University Press, 1967. 'Man: a course of study' does have clear and sensible aims.

3 Alexander, R.J. 'Teacher education and the primary curriculum'. In Richards, C. *New Directions in Primary Education*. Lewes: Falmer Press, pp. 135–155, 1982; and HMI Primary Survey, 1978.

4 Galton, M. and Simon, B. *Progress and Performance in the Primary Classroom*. London: Routledge and Kegan Paul, 1980.

5 Pollard, A. *The Social World of the Primary School*. London: Holt, Rinehart and Winston, 1985.

6 This is not the old 'Lankasterian' model of pupil-teachers, but something more intimate.

7 For example, Bronfenbrenner, U. *Two Worlds of Childhood*. London: Allen and Unwin, 1971.

8 Riechmann, S.W. and Grasham, A.F. 'A rational approach to developing and assessing the construct validity of a student learning style scales and instrument'. *Journal of Psychology*, **83**, 213–223, 1974.

9 Dunn, R., Dunn, K. and Price, G.E. *Learning Styles Inventory Manual*. Wichita, KS: Price Systems, 1975.

10 Johnson, A.F.; described in Ferrell, G.B. 'A factor analytic comparison on four learning styles instruments'. *Journal of Educational Psychology*, **75** (1), 33–39, 1983.

11 Kolb, D.A. *Learning Style Inventory: Technical Manual*. Boston, MA: McBer, 1976.

12 Heath, R. *The Reasonable Adventure*. Pittsburgh: Pittsburgh University Press, 1964.

13 Fransson, A. 'On qualitative differences in learning: effects of motivation and test anxiety on process and outcome'. *British Journal of Educational Psychology*, **47**, 244–257, 1977.

14 Entwistle, N.J. and Ramsden, P. *Understanding Student Learning*. London: Croom Helm, 1982.

15 Svensson, K. 'On qualitative differences in learning: study skills and learning'. *British Journal of Educational Psychology*, **47**, 233–243, 1977.

16 Pask, G. and Scott, B.C.E. 'Learning strategies and individual competence'. *International Journal of Man-Machine Studies*, **4**, 217–253, 1972; and Pask, G. 'Conversational techniques in the study and practice of education'. *British Journal of Education Psychology*, **46**, 12–25, 1976.

17 Hudson, L. *Frames of Mind*. London: Methuen, 1968.

18 de Bono, E. *Teaching Thinking*. London: Temple Smith, 1976.

19 Kagan, J., Rossman, B.I., Albert, J. and Phillips, W. 'Information processing in the child: significance of analytic and reflective attitudes'. *Psychological Monographs: General and Applied*, **78**, 1964.

20 Witkin, H.A., Moore, C.A., Goodenough, D.R. and Cox, P.W. 'Field-dependent and field-independent cognitive styles and their educational implications'. *Review of Educational Research*, **47**, 1–64, 1977.

21 Entwistle, N.J. and Ramsden, P., 1982, op. cit.

22 Ramsden, P. and Entwistle, N.J. 'Effects of academic departments on students' approaches to studying'. *British Journal of Educational Psychology*, **51**, 368–383, 1981.

23 Winkley, D.R. 'Children's response to stories'. DPhil thesis, Oxford University, 1975.

24 Perry, W.G. *Forms of Intellectual and Ethical Development in the College Years: A Scheme*. New York: Holt, Rinehart and Winston, 1970.
25 Again, this involves the Platonic stages of learning: compare Egan, K. *Educational Development*. New York: Oxford University Press, 1970.
26 Salgo, R. 'Learning about learning'. *Higher Education*, **8**, 443–451, 1979.

CHAPTER 15
The Uses of Learning

Nothing can be perceived twice over without being conceived in entirely
different states of mind.
William James, *The Principles of Psychology*, Vol. 1

The uses of learning range from the individual's search for happiness and meaning to society's need for technological skills.
Learning is the skill that enables an increasing accumulation of
knowledge and of wisdom. In many societies, knowledge gives
power. Knowledge makes it possible to gain positions of authority
and to be paid for the information one possesses. The battle for
supremacy over other nations, both in war and in trade, is based
on the application of technological advances. The realization of
the power of learning occasionally provokes governments into
displaying an interest in education systems they generally feel play
a secondary role in their priorities. But when there is a political
and publicly expressed interest in education it tends to concentrate on measuring outcomes, invariably blaming the education
system for not providing society with the skilled manpower that it
demands. About the process of education, the essentially personal
and less accessible core, there is less interest. Education in the
broad sense is a subject that clearly does not engage the excited
attention of many people, or of many politicians. It does not merit
headlines in newspapers, except on those few occasions when it is
an issue on which votes are won.[1] And yet learning is at the heart of
any civilization. It is what gives purpose and meaning to life.
Education is the very centre of all initiatives to change society,
to improve the conditions in which people live, to enhance the
value and pleasure of life, and it is almost deliberately ignored.
Why?

One reason for the dichotomy between the significance of education and the lack of interest is the fact that the dual purposes of
education – for the individual and for society – have never been

resolved. Every politician needs to think of the outcomes of learning: for example, whether people will be brought up to respect the law, or whether they will be able to manipulate information technology in an efficient way. From this point of view education is the clearly defined transmission of those things that people should know. It is a form of control, of manipulation for the sake of desired outcomes. It should enable others to think in the same terms as the politician, whatever the political persuasion. But from the point of view of the individual, including the same politician, learning has a very different purpose.

We are all convinced that we learn by ourselves and yet assume that other people have to be taught. We all have a natural tendency to assume that other people are easily corrupted by bad examples while we are unaffected. The assumption that television influences and manipulates is one easily made about other people, whether it is for good or bad, and yet we know how little affected each of us personally remains. Children parody this adult self-deception when they state that they would censor the very programmes that are their own favourites.[2] It is natural to assume that we are all self-made, beholden to no one else. There are few people who do not instinctively feel this. We know how much depends on our own efforts and how much depends on how we have used the experiences and opportunities afforded us. We also like to be in control and hate the thought that we might be learning things by chance rather than through a deliberate act of will.

One of the most deeply held beliefs about learning is the assumption that learning is undertaken 'for its own sake'. We readily become consumed in the control of forms of knowledge that have no personal bearing, even if they can be used to escape rather than enhance self-knowledge. On the other hand, learning appears to have distinctly utilitarian purposes when we see some of the outcomes: a better degree than someone else, a qualification that leads to a job, the failure to be employed, or being punished for being bottom of the class. But the idea of learning as a marketable commodity and the idea of learning for its own sake both leave out the use that learning can be to the individual and to the quality of thought. Learning is never for its own sake in the sense of some higher reach of abstraction that enables each person to escape the realities of life. Learning continues to have a distinct purpose for the individual and for the individual's relationship to others.[3]

Self-knowledge is not just the end of learning or a refinement of learning. It is also a tool and a means of learning in itself. Every result of learning, whether it be the application of the mind to machinery or to economics, includes some kind of self-knowledge. We know that confidence in oneself underlies every part of learning and our attitudes towards ourselves continue to affect the way in which we take in new information, or assess new acquaintances. It might sometimes seem that within particular conditions of work there is little chance for anything personal to enter into the normal currencies of business, but this is part of a self-imposed mythology of work, although some cynics might suggest that a lack of self-knowledge is essential for the single-minded drive necessary for political success. Self-knowledge is not just a medium for success, and nor does it depend just upon self-consciousness. The kind of self-knowledge that learning gives is neither solely about the individual nor solely about society but is about the relationship between the two.

One of the difficulties that children face in school is the ambiguity between the moral purposes of education, presented briefly in assemblies, and the lack of any moral or social context in the vast bulk of the curriculum. Subjects are presented as if their purposes, linguistic or mathematical, scientific or creative, were obvious. But children are not alone in this lack of clarity. In the many discussions about the curriculum little time is given to the question of what learning is for. Instead we are generally offered either the requirements of the state – vocational preparation and employability, the three Rs and computers – or the assumption that the traditional disciplines have been good for people and will continue to be so.[4]

There are many questions about the purpose of the curriculum that need to be addressed at a more fundamental level than in terms of aims, goals and objectives.[5] Bruner's attempt to define a purposeful curriculum in 'Man: a course of study' suggested not only that children were more capable of thinking than they are normally allowed to show, but that they should know some general truths about mankind.[6] When Lionel Trilling questioned the assumption about most curricula that they should be 'relevant' to the modern world, that all learning should be at the service of making people adapt to the circumstances of the time, he was suggesting that this assumption is usually unexamined or superficial.[7] Bantock continues to argue that the purpose of education is to continue the concept of civilization at its best, at least for a few.[8] But the curriculum that is generally offered at school and university rarely suggests that learning might have a personal outcome, an implicit purpose beyond the accumulation of knowledge. When a new addition to the curriculum is offered – like politics or peace studies – it is often assumed to have a particular and biased philosophical point of view, and that it is a threat rather than a help to the individual's moral development. And yet one can see the possibilities of fundamental moral purpose in almost any part of the curriculum. Any kind of learning can help towards the delineation of a new way of thinking or a different level of self-knowledge as easily as it can be used towards the bolstering of an existing belief.

The child's view of childhood and the adult's view of childhood are often strikingly different. To a child knowledge of the self and knowledge of the world are one; they have to be. The exploration of the world is a personal one. They desire to know what is good and bad, what to praise and what to avoid. The period of childhood is not a period of unalloyed pleasure; children do not think of it as the happiest time of their lives.[9] But to adults the period of childhood is too easily seen in sentimental terms because of its intensities and moments of happiness. In a wide range of autobiographies it is clear that childhood is always recalled as a time for secret worlds, for fantasy, as a time when children tried to create the imagery that would enable them to understand their world in their own way.[10] Children might, in a romantic sense, have the advantage of looking at the world in an unspoiled way, but if they are, in Wordsworth's sense, the 'father to the man', it is because they take on the burden of understanding, not because they can escape into some dream of perfection. What does 'fade away' is the close engagement with trying to make sense of the world, with trying to understand it.[11]

Children's earliest instincts about learning do not include a crude distinction between learning about the self and learning about the environment. The intensity of the scrutiny given to the world derives from the need to be able to come into a relationship with it, to understand and to respond, to control it and to accept what cannot be controlled. The sense of others, the realization of clear opposition between the good and bad, between the nice and the nasty, and the desire to know where they fit, dominates early developments of learning. This is when story and mythology, with their complete structures and with a strong moral sense of the ideal, are so important. The sense of clear distinctions between good and bad might seem like a naive simplification compared to the unsafe ambiguities of the everyday world, but it is the platform on which a personal point of view needs to be based. When curiosity about the outside world grows, the sense of structure becomes overwhelmed by an accumulation of facts. This is when children understand the fragility of their own position in the world. Far from being the centre of all events, or the hero of all adventure stories, or the person who needs to imitate the actions he sees on a screen, the child steadily accumulates new experiences which he tests against what he has already perceived.

Out of the accumulation of facts and ideas comes the realization that simple moral structures cannot contain such complex information. Children then accept that truth has different meanings to different people. It is when they understand this that children grow into the desire for moral certainty, for rediscovering the moral intent implicit in any subject, and then they try to fit all that is learned into a consistent and clear pattern of truth. The difference between the earlier desire for structural clarity and the later desire for unambiguous morality is the difference between a vision of the world as certain and the certainty of a personal point of view. The latter certainly derives from trying to impose a pattern that is not just a personal reaction to what is seen and observed, but one that others should share and, to our bewilderment, do not.

There are many examples of moral fervour used for all kinds of immoral ends, of information being manipulated to bolster an opinion rigidly held. There are many people who never go any further in learning, in almost any capacity, than a fanatical insistence on a certain point of view. The very limitation of an idea can seem to be a kind of advantage; not understanding the alternative point of view is certainly more comfortable. But the ability to see all sides of a question is not in itself the mark of wisdom: it can be little more than the accumulation of different facts. The person with no view at all is the one who makes no judgements at all, whose open curiosity about opinions is merely the habit of a collector. The most important stage of learning is that in which people understand the possibility of other points of view and can make judgements that relate to their own and other people's lives.

The learning of self-knowledge and irony can be taken as the culmination of personal wisdom but also as the highest stage in each semi-independent experience of learning. In becoming acquainted with a new subject it is at first difficult to see what the point is, what possible outcomes have relevance. A new subject either fits into an already established series of convictions or does not disturb it. But a growing curiosity and knowledge of the subject makes it extremely complicated, to the point at which the expert can be inarticulate under the burden of knowledge. There is also a moment when simple mastery of a half-forgotten subject makes talking about it more lucid than the facts. But a real expert in any subject, who has real mastery of it, is able to talk about it with great simplicity. Mastery of new information is a process not unlike understanding oneself, moving from simple outlines to the accumulation of facts, from simple moral fervour to a sense of irony.

About wisdom it is easy to seem wise; but to achieve it is a different matter. We would all recognize that the end of learning contains that sense of irony and perspective that combines deep personal conviction with a framework that includes a sense of forgiveness for human nature's limitations. The relationship between the individual and the world remains the most important part of learning from the beginning to the end. The morality of individual conscience and conviction is balanced by a sense of the universal which respects that sense of individuality. All is not relative, any more than it is for the young child trying to make sense of what the world means; but it becomes a matter of more complex relationships in which the inner world refines the most important elements that it observes.

Learning does not take place without emotion. The importance of attitude and motivation reveals that. But emotion can also undermine learning. There are constructive and destructive impulses constantly at war, with rational decision undermined by personal prejudices or antipathies. Just as the learning of facts and ideas is a matter of connections, of categories and memories, the emotional side of learning is a matter of associations. The tendency to create a mythology around the good and the bad, between 'us' and 'them', is a sign of a constant personal engagement in self-justification. A patient under psychotherapy, for example, shows the same tendency to exaggerate, to make crude distinctions between the very good and very bad. This kind of attitude is not only observed in analysis, in trying to make sense of the complex inner forces of the self, but is held subconsciously in the actions that demonstrate the hold that personal feelings have over judgement. The power of emotions over attitudes and actions is obvious, if not always acknowledged.[12] The awareness, or lack of awareness, of the self remains a basis on which learning takes place.

There is always an element of self-consciousnes in any learning. While the teacher delivers herself of information or a book is absorbed, the strand of self-awareness, of mood, of distraction, of day-dreaming, continually emerges. The ears go on listening to the sounds of a truck, the kettle or birds; the sounds of other people in the library are a constant background to the immediate perception. The eyes themselves are constantly focusing and unfocusing, in a series of jumps, even when looking at a page of text.[13] So the possibilities of distraction when listening to a teacher are endless. This is a result of the brain not being very adept at concentrating for long periods – it has been established that the attention span in the most committed is never more than twenty minutes.[14] When the lecture is over and the notes have been assiduously taken, the amount that is subsequently retained by the listeners is a tiny proportion of what they heard being unburdened to them.[15] The audience is aware of the teacher, the implicit meanings, the other people, the sun on the wall and, most of all, of a multitude of individual stray thoughts. Much of what is learned lies beneath the surface of information. Private associations are constantly made. The fact that the mind wanders off on other subjects is not just day-dreaming but the subconscious forming of new associations and new ideas.

One of the most important parts of learning a new subject is the developing attitude towards that subject.[16] Even when a deliberate attempt is made to change how students think, as in behaviour modification, the greatest change that takes place is in the students' attitudes towards the subject.[17] The 'love of one's subject' is a fundamental condition of knowledge; it might be inverted, but some strong feeling is nearly always involved in learning. It is partly because of this that so many disciplines that appear to be intended to be applied, such as statistics, soon become fascinating in their own right. Even within the most exacting and pure discipline the element of personal emotion is always present. The love of learning, for its own sake, is a matter both of growing self-awareness and of awareness of the joys of being lost within a subject, rather than being master of it.

Self-knowledge and self-deception both play a major role in learning. The power of inner drives is such that knowledge remains a need rather than a luxury. There are many purposes in knowledge, often hidden. In almost any learning there is a tendency to avoid certain kinds of information and to be emotionally interested in others. Almost everything that we learn is tuned by our own tastes, changed, obscured or even deliberately obliterated.[18] Much of the avoidance of learning is subsconscious. Even the most simple of stories will be reconstructed in a personal way that suits each individual differently.[19] And the greater the social value of what is learned the more likely it is that the information will be subject to an idiosyncratic, personal reconstruction.[20] Even in a context that has no social or personal meaning, as in an experiment about isolated words, the emotional reaction of subjects and the consequent memory depend on the emotional overtones of the words themselves, as when words like 'fairy' or 'pubic' are introduced.[21] The extent of deliberate or undeliberate reconstruction of information so that it fits into a personal framework can reach startling proportions.

The personal point of view, the inner world into which all new information must fit, is rarely consistent. The strain of the illogical and the contradictory runs throughout learning. It is common for people to hold two sets of beliefs which completely contradict each other. The rearrangement of facts for the convenience of one point of view is only one side of personal learning; more common is the rearrangement of material into sets of views, when one chooses to take one set at one time, and another point of view at a different time.[22] Even when confronted by a set of logical statements people respond not by thinking out the logic but by using a kind of personal 'rule of thumb', an emotional reaction according to their already established assumptions. To be remembered easily a fact must fit within the generally established representation of the world that the individual possesses.[23] Even the single sentence, which because of its ambiguity, seems to demand an alternative interpretation half way through causes difficulties.[24]

The most disappointing aspect of human knowledge is not so much its deliberate misuse in the hands of wicked propagandists, but the capacity for self-deception on which propaganda relies. The capacity to be indifferent to the outcomes of learning and deliberately to ignore evidence is shown most tellingly in the example of the treatment of the Jews in Nazi Germany. Many normal, comparatively civilized people were able to carry out horrible and grotesque acts.[25] Many people's normal lives remained undisturbed by what was going on around them. They were able to deceive themselves and retain the most terrible paradoxes: for example, that the Jews were no longer alive . . . but not necessarily dead.[26] They were able to act against their better judgement, able not only to deceive themselves but also to entertain mutually exclusive beliefs. They were able to ignore uncomfortable facts as if they did not exist. But while the holocaust remains the most extreme symbol of such irrationality it is not only one among many, but a symbol of a universal truth about learning. The shadow of self-knowledge is self-deception. There are many who think that a belief is absurd and yet believe it themselves. It is as if they are able to compartmentalize their minds so much that the associations and consequences of belief are lost. When a belief is held for a particular motive, as in wishful thinking, it is almost a deliberate act. But the inner contradictions in belief show how undeliberately human beings can avoid thinking.

Learning can be manipulated for oneself as well as for other people. Just as language gives the power of communication and mastery of ideas, and yet through cliché becomes itself the master of what we wish to say, so learning can be used not only to understand but also to hide from understanding. The difficulties with learning do not arise out of the obscurities of the highest reaches of symbolic logic but from the fact that learning can be driven by irrational emotions. We cannot avoid learning. It is therefore through understanding how the individual learns that we see both the capacity for wisdom and the ability to behave in an irrational manner.

Self-knowledge depends on the clear understanding of the world of other people, and of other people's points of view. The most difficult aspect of self-knowledge is to make room for new information, and to allow it to make a difference; to make room for the success of others and to have the creative capacity to take pleasure in it. That acceptance of a larger framework than one's own, the realization that there are also realms of knowledge outside one's own control, becomes the mainspring of action, and make the crucial difference between the creative and open-minded and the negative and controlling.

NOTES AND REFERENCES

1 This is despite the fact that many research studies relate the extent of investment in education to a country's commercial success.
2 Cullingford, C. *Children and Television*. Aldershot: Gower, 1984.
3 The Socratic insight about learning remains as significant as ever: that the process of exploring oneself is combined with the disinterested concern for society, and that such a process contributes to the development of a just society. Education is therefore at the heart of any civilization as well as at the heart of finding a meaning in life.
4 It was instructive to note the change from the simplicities of the firm statements of a national curriculum and its assessment, to the more complex outcomes that emerged from the discussion of professionals.
5 Curriculum theory, in its simplest form, sought, like behavioural objectives, to clarify the immediate tasks and outcomes of each subject and each classroom. See the critiques, e.g. Lawn, M. and Barton, L. *Rethinking Curriculum Studies*. London: Croom Helm, 1981.
6 Bruner, J.S. *Towards a Theory of Instruction*. Cambridge, MA: Harvard University Press, 1967; taken up in 'Man: a course of study'.
7 Trilling, L. *Beyond Culture*. London: Secker and Warburg, 1966.
8 Bantock, F.H. *Dilemmas of the Curriculum*. Oxford: Martin Robertson, 1980.
9 Although they tend to look back at any age as being rather nicer than the present; even at the age of eight.
10 Burnett, J. (ed.) *Destiny Obscure: Autobiographies of Childhood, Education and Family from the 1820s to the 1920s*. London: Allen Lane, 1982.
11 See Huizinga, J. *Homo Ludens: A Study of the Play-element in Culture*. London:

Routledge and Kegan Paul, 1942, and Caillois, R. *Man, Play and Games*. London: Thames and Hudson, 1962.

12 The 'id' in Freudian terms, or in Jungian terms the domination of the animus.

13 Called 'saccadic' jumps. See, for example, Kennedy, A. *The Psychology of Reading*. London: Methuen, 1984.

14 Attention span is almost always found to be less than one would have thought.

15 Bligh, D. *What's the Use of Lectures?* Harmondsworth: Penguin, 1972.

16 Hence the interest in the subject, or discipline 'for its own sake'. Newman, J. on the idea of a university in *The Scope and Nature of University Education*. London: Longman, 1859.

17 Merrett, F. and Wheldall, J. 'Does teaching student teachers about behaviour modification techniques improve their teaching performance in the classroom?' *Journal of Education for Teaching*, **8** (1), 67–75, 1982.

18 See Hovland, C.I., Janis, I.L. and Kelley, H. *Communications and Persuasion: Psychological Studies of Opinion Change*. New Haven, CT: Yale University Press, 1953.

19 Bartlett, F.C. *Remembering: A Study in Experimental and Social Psychology*. Cambridge: Cambridge University Press, 1932.

20 Krech, D. and Crutchfield, R.S. 'Perceiving the world'. In Schramm, W. (ed.) *The Process and Effects of Mass Communication*. Urbana: Illinois University Press, pp. 116–137, 1955.

21 Bruner, J.S. and Postman, L.P. 'Emotional selectivity in perception and reaction'. *Journal of Personality*. **16**, 69–77, 1947.

22 Kahneman, D., Slovie, P. and Tversky, A. *Judgement under Uncertainty*. Cambridge: Cambridge University Press, 1982.

23 Bransford, J.D. and Johnson, M.K. 'Contextual prerequisites for understanding: some investigations of comprehension and recall'. *Journal of Verbal Learning and Verbal Behaviour*, **11** (6), 717–726, 1972.

24 Compare the 'garden-path' theory.

25 Arendt, H. *The Trial of Adolf Eichman*. London: Secker & Warburg, 1969.

26 See Pears, D. *Motivated Irrationality*. Oxford: Oxford University Press, 1984.

CHAPTER 16
Learning and Society

The laws of Nature are nothing but the immutable habits which . . . follow in their actions and reactions upon each other.

William James, *The Principles of Psychology*, Vol. 1.

For many people learning is associated with the accumulation of knowledge. To be able to remember, to quote and to cite the relevant texts is an obvious display of the capacity of the mind. For many others, however, who know that it is as easy to store information in libraries, file cards or computers, the brain can be better used in other ways, not to store but to analyse, not to remember but to work as smoothly as a well-balanced piece of machinery. These two attitudes to learning – the display of memory and the demonstration of wit – dominate the way in which people regard the use of learning in society. Neither has very much to do with the possible effect we have on society and on other people's as well as our own place in it. The problem for learning is that at its most refined it seems at first glance to have little to do with the complex practical realities of the everyday.

Even in those places where there is most need for the application of learning, prestige is afforded as much to those who have displayed their power of abstract thinking as to those who are outstandingly successful people of action. Every 'new' subject in the curriculum is introduced because of its relevance, because there is a need to rethink the way in which the curriculum responds to social changes, but a new subject tends to be resisted and despised *because* of its relevance.[1] Prestige, in terms of better resources, better staff/student ratios, easier teaching loads and more respect, accrues to traditional academic subjects at the expense of practical ones. In this sense we are always old-fashioned. We might be amused at the curriculum of the 1830s or the examination syllabus of the 1950s, but exactly the same principles that applied then apply now. What is being tested, or admired, is the capacity to demonstrate abstract thinking. The most perfect subject for displays of thinking is the most complete: the subject that is not in danger of being changed by the accumulation of different facts, or by the difficulties of real events. It is easier for society to admire a subject that has little or nothing to do with the direct application of practical skills, just as it is far easier to be highly advanced at a young age in subjects like mathematics or music than in those that demand moral judgements. Admiration for the traditional disciplines is as strong as ever, not only because of the careers of those established in these traditions but also because it is part of human learning to be enamoured of displays of learning.

Real decisions about actual problems are a different order of reality. To learn to tackle them is both more demanding and less admired. Many new subjects, such as linguistics or psychology that have been added to the traditional curriculum, have become traditional in their turn. They have created their own vocabulary, their own sense of order and a stability that those who enter the discipline are taught to accept before they are allowed to continue. This technique of the orthodox becomes so carefully controlled, so assumed to be empirical, that what is called the 'mathesis of thought' takes place, in which the study of the subject is replaced by the formalizations of theory about the study of the subject.[2] What begins as a genuine curiosity about another part of the human experience becomes almost inexorably a set of concepts that become stable.[3] Even psychology is sometimes supposed to be more academically respectable when it attempts to be scientifically empirical, even when that means that human beings themselves are unsatisfactory objects for study.

There are at least two reasons for the general dislike of the practical. One is that the most powerful academic tradition of learning is based on the model of science. The notion of completeness derives from the perfect experiment in which nothing is left out, and something tangible is proved beyond doubt. The experiment will have been based on previous work, will be an advance on it or a refinement of it, and will therefore lead to more work to be done; cells will inexorably be broken into atoms, atoms into particles, particles understood in terms of the constituent quarks, quarks broken down into tzintza, and so on. The rule of the empirical, or a set of hypotheses that can be tested in experiments, is not, however, confined to scientific experiment but applied to other realms of human knowledge. This is where the difficulties begin. Social 'scientists' try to analyse human nature by subjecting their hypotheses to tests. This means that they discover what is testable. And in the terms with which we are most familiar there is little of human nature that will lend itself to such treatment. What is therefore respectable to research is not always worth researching. What is worth researching is not always academically respectable. It has all the jagged edges of the incomplete, is loaded with many variables, with ambiguity and guesswork. Its limitations are, in fact, far too much like those of real life. The judgements that people make of each other and the bases of their behaviour do not lend themselves to measurement.

If the various tendencies to apply scientific methodology are one reason for the belief in academic excellence, the other is a more fundamental mythology about learning: that people learn what they are told. When a teacher stands in front of a class and talks, it is easy to assume that the pupils will learn and inwardly digest all that they are told. Politicians speak with similar hopes that, having stated something, it will be understood in the way that they wish, that it will persuade or convert the audience into a new kind of belief.

One of the best examples of this belief in the capacity of the mind to absorb what is said is television. In the debates about the 'effects' of television on children, or what children learn from television, there is a desire to believe not only that children pay close attention all the time but also that they absorb all they hear and see.[4] Those who are against television cite a programme of violence and suggest that the audience will remember a particular scene and go out and imitate it. Those who are employed by television companies and who spend their talents and time trying to put out the best programmes have the same fundamental belief, that their own half-hour, on which they have spent hours of work and more hours arguing for it in committee, will transform the audience that sees it. This belief in simple effects, through imitation or disinhibition, transcends the fact that children watch an average of more than three hours of television every day. It overcomes the realization that there is little on television that causes states of high tension, euphoria or unmitigated fear. We know how little is remembered soon after it is seen. But the underlying assumption about learning prevails: that what is seen is what is learned; that stimulus equals response. It is as if there was a need to believe this, as if the transmission of information is both easier to understand and more gratifying than the reception. In trying to understand the ways in which the audience learns from television the common method of enquiry is the scientific one, in which the essence of a good experiment is the successful exclusion of variables, such as personal characteristics and the context that makes the experience real.

Given some of the unexamined mythologies about learning, it is no surprise that it is in its applications that learning is most difficult to understand. Even in the subjects that are designed to enhance the performance of the professions, the almost inevitable tendency of the institutionalization of learning is towards withdrawal from the problems that professionals meet. Even in the setting up of problems or case studies, as Schoen points out, there is a deliberate simplification, a technical rationalization that attempts to ignore all that is conflicting or confused.[5] The context of real decisions is different from the context of academic research.[6] In one the solution always changes; in the other there is one solution. In one the sense of personal engagement is the most important aspect; in the other it is the sense of the complete answer. Schoen found that when people were given the chance to pursue their own individual answers to a problem, in their own ways, without the framework of imposed academic constraints, they were able to perform three times as well. But the security of a given point of view, the sense of authority, of the certainty of what is tried, is a temptation that many find almost impossible to resist. Those who find no order in themselves like to have it imposed on them.

Adults, as well as infants, like to have a sense of order. A natural conservatism and a love of security in established norms characterize many approaches to learning. Once a habit of mind is ingrained, most contradictory sets of facts will be forced to fit into the established habits or response. Self-justifications for the most brutal of behaviours become more easy to understand as one sees the way in which all facts are turned to the advantage of a point of view. This implies that change is not brought about easily or quickly. Far from being a matter of propaganda or the possibilities of rhetoric, changes in political outlook and belief are complex and obscure. One man might capture the mood of a moment, or articulate the unexpressed ideas of many, but the actual change in point of view happens far more obscurely. A direct attack on people's assumptions, on a habit or a belief, almost invariably has far less effect than an overheard remark.[7]

The changes that individuals undergo are not a matter of logic, the inexorable stages of maturity or just a matter of the information they receive. They are more like 'sea changes' in their obscurity: the result of a powerful inner movement that takes place both by chance and because people do not deliberately rationalize their points of view. When a general opinion becomes publicly expressed it can undergo a series of changes and manifestations through the way it is taken up and passed on. No one could have foretold, although hindsight gives us this realization, that when Kant[8] began to explore a philosophy based more on the ideal of the individual than on chance associations, such a change of emphasis would lead, through Hegel's expression of ideal nationalism, to the 'triumph of the will' in Hitler's National Socialism.[9] But then no one would think that philosophy would in any form have practical consequences, even when transformed beyond itself. The changes in belief in a nation and in an individual remain slow, inexorable and a matter of chance.

In organizations we can see similar changes taking place as a result of the mixtures of personalities, their particular visions, the structural arrangements and the procedures imposed. The more we understand the way in which any organization works the more we see the difference between the changes willed on us by the person in command and the actual changes in spirit and level of work. Any organization is a unique balance of a physical environment, intellectual processes and emotional climate. The sense of space influences the spirit of invention and sense of identity; the threats to the individual obscure the lines of communication. Organizations change as a consequence of changes in individual self-concepts. They are expressions of a number of value systems and are always liable to change, almost as if organizations were as distinct and changeable as individual human beings. It is possible to see how different organizations manifest their own ethos, being interpreted in terms of power and conflict, in terms of distinctions between group identity and open-mindedness, in terms of inter-dependence and adaptation, or in terms of belonging and polite-ness.[10] But the learning factors within an organization are emotional and fragile, as much a matter of attitude and style as of an authoritative individual imposing her will. They are quite unlike a series of management objectives disseminated like infor-mation. The various systems that make up an organization, the cultural and economic, the social and governing, all overlap.

If organizations are the social consequence of learning, so are more obscure groupings according to shared tastes or attitudes. When the individual acquires his own attitudes towards a series of events he does not do so only from teachers, or from those forms of communication that have designs on him. The peer group, the love of a common identity and the desire for acceptance all lead to a series of mutually accepted codes that project an assumption or opinion. To please the group, consciously or subconsciously, the individual changes behaviour and adapts to what is expected in tone, in the dialect used (the dialect of the group) and, most significantly, in the assumptions made. A simplified and shared opinion about an event becomes a more complete association with it.

There are many studies that reveal how powerful are the half-hidden assumptions and limitations of a group. Not only are there certain recognizable signs of a group, in dress, accent or taste, but there are powers in the conformity of a group that imply a pressure of change on learning and information. There are a number of different levels of response to pleasure and work, from individual engagement to the acceptance of a collective attitude. The level of interest is partly a function of the desire to continue learning, or not, or the result of the habit of learning; but it is also a part of a shared attitude towards learning. Many people do not know their own capacity to learn. They do not want to know because of the very norms of the group from which they learn. Habits are easily caught. The learning of certain *attitudes* can be like an epidemic that permeates societies, large and small.

We know how much in learning depends on the attitude to-wards the teacher, or the source of learning. We also know that the circumstances in which learning takes place make a difference. As a typical, if slight example, it is recognized that the willingness to listen to and accept what a salesman says is not just a question of the need for the product or his loquacity and charm, but a result of the way he dresses. Wearing a tie doubles the success rate.[11] But willingness to accept the way other people are dressed is only a slight indication of response compared to attitudes towards accent and the use of language. Judgements can be based superficially on the accent used, but they are nevertheless affected by the associations that have been built up over many years with particular modes of expression. The educated person is expected to use a particular form of expression; the signals of learning are like the signals of money or class.

Some groups deliberately use distinct modes of language. Given the attitudes involved as a result of being 'branded on the tongue', it is easy to understand why the work of Bernstein should have caused such a furore.[12] The advantages of home background, and the symbols with which they are expressed, although distinct from each other,[13] make a powerful combination, so that it is sometimes difficult for anyone to avoid coming to the conclusion that different levels of learning are manifested by different socio-economic groups.[14] The use of different styles of speaking according to different circumstances affects all people, in a mimicry of others that is for some almost unavoidable, or in more gentle adaptations to other people's tones of voice. But such changes in behaviour can also influence changes in attitude.

The terms used to express opinions sometimes seem more powerful than the opinions themselves. Like an academic discipline a group will impose a jargon of phrases that are not only not commonly understood but also an imposed password for their peers. Latinisms or the word 'one' are types of demarcation between one sub-group and more universal currencies of language. Sometimes the fear that there might be so many dialects that they will be mutually unintelligible seems well founded.[15] The power of language to communicate is shadowed by the power of language to divide. Without language no ideas could be expressed, nor any sense of personal identity come to fruition. But language can also be a dangerous weapon, not only in the power of rhetoric, but also in the power of cliché, the power to lie, to obfuscate, to make things not what they are.[16] The example of 'newspeak', as formulated in Orwell's *1984*, where words are changed around to obscure their real meaning, is not utterly different from the use of terms such as the Ministry of Defence or Department of Employment, devoted to war and unemployment, or in a phrase such as 'limited strategic capability strike-back option', which means killing millions of people. Language is affective at a number of levels. It is not only a means of conveying ideas but is communication itself. If has the power to hold, as if there were a magic to it, in poetry and in spells.[17] And it has the power to rationalize, to clarify, to detect. When we mention the learning that comes from overheard remarks and from different linguistic attitudes we show how fragile is the mastery that language has over us, and how fragile our mastery over language.

Anecdote often has a greater influence on the opinions of government than a carefully elucidated mass of data. We are all more easily influenced when we think that no one is trying to influence us. The advertisement that insists on its message might be rejected, but the endorsement of a product by a friend is easily taken on board. Thus opinions are formed in ways that bear little relationship to logic or rational conclusions. The sea change that takes place in society or groups is also the kind of change that takes place in opinion forming, although an opinion, once formed, is hard to change. But people can find themselves easily led, can assume that there are correct ways to behave even without thinking about them. Their favourite politicians seem to win every argument; the preferred teacher always has the same authority. There are standard ways of behaving that fit into a pattern. To break out of a standard pattern of behaviour that governs a group is very difficult. Seconds elapse before people realize that the shooting in the street is not part of a television serial. Minutes go by before people realize that they should help someone who is threatened with rape. This is not the result of langour or selfishness, or the desire not to be involved, but a psychological difficulty in connecting with a different world. What is 'normal' becomes like a suit of clothes, a customary fit one does not easily change.

The desire to remain within a point of view extends to odd circumstances. When a game of frisbee was started during the rush hour at a railway station in the United States the hurrying passengers stopped and threw back the frisbee if the person before them did so, or if the person before them threw the disc to the ground rather than in the air, they did the same. Whatever action became the norm the others followed.[18] But the tendency to copy others, visible in the lack of reaction to a sudden incidence of violence, is even more marked if there appears to be something 'official' in the behaviour. Milgram's experiments are still an interesting example of the capacity of people to obey a course of action that they know to be absurd.[19] When passers-by were asked to come and help in an experiment they were told that they were to manipulate a machine which would give electric shocks to the victim. They were told there had to be someone neutral to administer the tests, which would determine the effect of pain on memory. The machine was complicated with different dials and had a handle that was supposed to administer electric shocks in either small doses or very large ones, depending on how far it was turned.[20] If the 'victim' was unable to answer a question electric shocks were to be given. It was as well that the 'victim' was an actor; the majority of subjects would cheerfully have given lethal electric shocks and would have done so even when they had talked to him or touched him. The sanction of the official seemed to be enough to justify their actions. Given the general milieu they could not connect the consequences of their action with the circumstances in which they were doing it.

Attitudes are therefore not just formed through a range of influences but are themselves a way of learning, or manipulating learning. Gossip can become a means of re-organizing experiences, including those of other people.[21] It is possible to set up barriers to learning as well as to pick out just those things that one would like to learn. Rumours are a way of fitting remembered material into pre-existing patterns.[22] When expectations about information are strong there will be a marked bias towards anything that is presented. Hungry people will relate almost anything to food;[23] they will perceive a stranger differently according to what they have just been doing.[24] Deep-seated associations will make people actually misinterpret what they see, as in the famous example by Allport and Postman when people they interviewed, after seeing a picture of a white man threatening a black man with a razor, remembered it as a black man threatening a white one.[25]

Predisposition to learn can actually inhibit what is learned. From the point of view of the individual all new facts are a form of evidence that bolsters an already formed belief.

It is this misapplication of learning, and the human tendency to avoid learning in the real sense, that explains how easily people are subject to prejudice and to manipulation. Societies as a whole can be said to learn, and change as organizations change, becoming healthy or despairing, and affecting each individual in them. But societies depend on the ways in which the individuals have approached and applied learning, and on the way the individual responds to communication. Almost any use can be made of a 'message'. The story of a hijack can be used to inspire someone to copy the methods, to think of applying the example. The murder that opens a religious tract used to be cited as giving a bad example of violence to those who wished to model their behaviour on it. But the distinction between different uses of information depends on the habits and application of learning. And that depends on the individual and the level at which the individual is thinking. It is easy not to learn. It is as easy to misapply learning. But learning cannot altogether be avoided. The hope we have remains dependent on our capacity to learn, and to understand learning.

NOTES AND REFERENCES

1 Goodson, I. *School Subjects and Curriculum Change*. London: Croom Helm, 1982.

2 Tyler, S.A. *The Said and the Unsaid: Mind, Meaning and Culture*. London: Academic Press, 1978.

3 Ornstein, R.E. *The Psychology of Consciousness*. New York: Harcourt Brace Jovanovich, 1977.

4 Cullingford, C. *Children and Television*. Aldershot: Gower, 1984.

5 Schoen, D. *The Reflective Practitioner: How Professionals Think in Action*. London: Temple Smith, 1983.

6 One distinguished academic went to a computer centre which prided itself on a decision-making program. They welcomed him and offered to help until they realized what he wanted: 'You mean this is a *real* problem?'

7 See Cullingford, C., 1984, op. cit., Chapter 13.

8 Kant, I. *Kritik der Reinen Vernunft*. Königsberg, 1781.

9 Kedourie, E. *Nationalism*, 3rd edition. London: Hutchinson University Library, 1966.

10 Mulford, W. 'Consulting with educational systems is about the facilitation of co-ordinated effort'. In Gray, H.L. *The Management of Educational Institutions*. Lewes: Falmer Press, pp. 179–218, 1982.

11 Gaffman, E. *The Presentation of Self in Everyday Life*. London: Allen Lane, 1971.

12 Bernstein, B. *Class, Codes and Control*. London: Routledge and Kegan Paul, 1975; and the literature following it, e.g. Stubbs, M. *Language and Literacy*. London: Routledge and Kegan Paul, 1980.

13 Labov, W. 'The study of language in its social context'. In Fishman, L. (ed.) *Advances in the Sociology of Language*. The Hague: Mouton, pp. 152–216, 1971.

14 Cazden, C.B. *Child Language and Education*. New York: Holt, Rinehart and Winston, 1972; Klein, J. *Samples from English Cultures*. London: Routledge and Kegan Paul, 1965; and Edwards, A.D. 'Social class and linguistic choice'. *Sociology*, **10**, 101–110; 1976.

15 Whorf, B.L. *Language, Thought and Reality*. Cambridge, MA: Massachusetts Institute of Technology Press, 1956.

16 Hence some of Plato's strictures against the language of poetry.

17 As in the sense 'this is the word'.

18 Latané, B. and Darley, J.M. *The Unresponsive Bystander: Why Doesn't He Help?* New York: Appleton, 1970.

19 Milgram, S. *Obedience to Authority: An Experimental View*. London: Tavistock, 1974.

20 The 'Buss aggression machine', which simulates the giving of electric shocks, was much used in experiments of this kind.

21 Sabini, J. and Silver, M. *Moralities of Everyday Life*. New York: Oxford University Press, 1982.

22 Allport, G.W. and Postman, L.P. *The Psychology of Rumour*. New York: Holt, Rinehart, 1947.

23 McLelland, D.C., Atkinson, J.W., Clark, R.W. and Lowell, E.L. *The Achievement Motive*. New York: Appleton, 1953.

24 Bruner, J.S., Goodnow, J.J. and Austin, G.A. *A Study of Thinking*. New York: Wiley, 1956.

25 Allport, G.W. and Postman, L.P., op. cit.

CHAPTER 17
Conclusions

'Would you tell me, please, which way I ought to go from here?'
'That depends a good deal on where you want to get to', said the Cat.
Lewis Carroll, *Alice in Wonderland*, Chapter 6.

The greatest human achievements, such as the plays of Shakespeare, are a reminder of the capacity of the mind to learn and communicate. The difference between such possibilities and what we normally achieve is so wide that we must often wonder why it is that we do not make more use of our capacities. The answer lies not just in circumstances or in the distribution of innate gifts but in the way in which we actually use, or do not use, our ability to think. The mind is powerful and often demonstrates its power, but it is often used in an inappropriate way. There seems to be a gap between the capacity of the brain and the uses to which this capacity is put.

It is a temptation to wish that thinking people could be as efficient as computers, but when we work with computers we soon learn how limited they can be, as well as useful, and how unlike the human mind, with its leaps of imagination, its emotional habits and its idiosyncratic associations. Learning is not a steady accumulation of knowledge, nor is it demonstrated simply by the facts of memory. It is affected by attitudes to ourselves and others. There are periods, which worry teachers and parents, when nothing appears to be learned. But something is being learned all the time, for all the pauses or the repetitions. Even unlearning, or learning *not* to learn, is a perverted form of learning. One of the most important parts of the process of learning is learning how to learn. Of all the precious skills acquired from home and school a desire to learn and a developing curiosity are among the most valuable. For children also easily acquire the pathological skills of *not* learning, of avoiding learning. Even by the age of eight they can be fatalistic about their own incapacity to learn.

Learning is a more obviously active process for children than for adults, not only because they have more new information to take in but also because they are so closely engaged in the experience. They have not learned how to fit new facts into pre-arranged attitudes, or how to ignore what is different or uncomfortable. They do not spare their brains. For them language is an action, a personal discovery and exploration. Their curiosity is not limited to the convention of the 'task in hand' but is drawn to all the major parts of experience; they learn about the teacher and not just what is taught. The concept of 'match' and 'mismatch' should not be limited to the idea of information appropriate to the age and sequence of learning but should extend to the different assumptions that children make about learning. There can be mismatch between their views of themselves and others' views of them, between their perception of the world and that of others. It is not so much the different paces of learning that cause difficulties as the different styles.

There was a time when children were regarded as miniature adults. They were dressed in smaller versions of adult clothes and were expected to carry out adult tasks. Today we have developed a view of childhood that praises the freshness and individuality of the innocent point of view. The tradition in educational thought, usually traced to Rousseau, that children are born perfect and only spoiled by the corruption of the adult environment, remains a strong one. It is sometimes difficult to understand children in their optimism and curiosity, in their happiness and misery, without seeming to be sentimental about them. We need to combine our understanding of children's spontaneity with an acceptance of their dignity as complete human beings, with their own point of view and their own insights. Neither the view of children as stunted adults nor the picture of them as charming innocents does justice to the processes of learning. We need to remember that there is no demarcation line between childhood and adulthood, any more than there are clear distinctions between the 'seven ages' of mankind.

There are two important points about ourselves that need to be understood, even if they go against some prevailing assumptions about learning. The first is the realization that children's thinking is not a simple, cruder, less efficient version of adult thought, but a striving for understanding that is complex, varied, perceptive and interesting. The second point is that adult thought itself is not quite as 'adult', as rational, as it is sometimes assumed to be. Much of our time is spent not in thinking but in being entertained without demands, without the kind of concentration we can only keep up for short periods. The vanity of thinking is that we assume that there is no other type than the clear, cerebral, ratiocinative analysis of concentrating on the matter in hand. We might *wish* that all human beings were like computers in their efficiency, processing given information, but we know that we actually learn through our emotions, through associations and habits, as much as we do through readiness to meet the demands of being intellec-tually tested.

We must avoid being sentimental about childhood. The idea of unspoiled innocence awaiting corruption is a comparatively recent one that can lead us into underrating the capacities of children. The adult experience of learning is different because of the desire to make it so; the fear of accepting something new can become the most rigid of mental 'sets'. Children's need to under-stand the meaning of the world in terms of structure and rules can easily become hardened into a simple set of assumptions. Adults, with all the sophistication at their command, can have the most simplistic views of the world, knowing that is it much more comfortable to feel sure. For every complex problem there is a simple solution that is wrong.

The grace of children is that they *can* learn and want to learn. They might not always do so in expected ways, and they will certainly take some idiosyncratic steps. They might answer questions in a way that is designed to shock or surprise, or answer arbitrarily. They also learn how to deceive. But in the end they will always speak the truth about what they think, if they are expected to. They have not acquired the sophistication of self-deception or of the display of what is felt *should* be thought rather than what is. Such honesty is a natural part of children's constant scrutiny of the world, not so much innocent an anthropological. Children are willing enough to answer questions about their perception; but they are not often asked.

Children naturally acknowledge the variety of styles of learning. They are aware that they perform differently according to their interest, and know what it is *not* to want to learn. They learn at a variety of levels, not all of which are recognized. They discover attitudes, take on new ideas, absorb new information, are influenced by new concepts and experiment with new opinions. The mistakes that they make, in small or large matters, are themselves a crucial part of their learning. But this does not imply that they are playing games for their own sake. Learning always has an underlying purpose. The need to understand is innate. Those subjects that seem obviously interesting to children are those with a clear inner relevance, the subjects in which they become 'inside' the argument. Learning is a complex matter. It is, of course, hard to prove or measure the different levels of thinking. But this does not mean that we should sacrifice our understanding for the sake of a notion of what is 'empirical', or sacrifice truth to statistical formalism.

Underlying the complexities of learning are some general principles that apply to any age. The acceptance of any new idea, for example, goes through a familiar evolutionary cycle. First comes indignant rejection, then reasoned objection, followed by qualified opposition and tentative acceptance. Afterwards the idea is given qualified endorsement, then judicious modification followed by cautious adoption and then impassioned espousal. Such a cycle shows the reluctance of people to take on any new idea easily. They begin, after all, by not knowing and being satisfied with not knowing (subconscious incompetence). They then wonder 'what's in it for me?' (conscious incompetence). They then become uncomfortably aware of the new idea (conscious competence) and finally acquire the confidence that comes with using the idea (subconscious competence).

Just as individuals learn how to manage change, so institutions undergo changes of a kind that are subtle and hard to describe. We can recognize the probable catalyst for new ideas but we know that leaders reflect ideas as well as impose them, and that it is hard to say exactly *why* new assumptions or new ideas can rapidly be accepted in whole societies. Such underlying changes in institutions are more a significant sign of learning than manipulations of structure. Indeed the temptation to change a system can be a sign of wanting to avoid change, as expressed in the parody of the bewildered Roman, Petronius: 'We trained very hard, but it seemed that every time we were beginning to form into teams we were re-organized. I was to learn later in life that we tend to meet any new situation by re-organizing and a wonderful method it can be for creating the illusion of progress, while producing confusion, inefficiency and demoralization.'

Institutions and systems are themselves reflections of human nature. It is a moral issue that we should devote more attention to understanding people and, in particular, how we learn. Such insight might well lead to a re-appraisal of the way we go about enabling children to learn. We might find that there are far better ways of using the capacities we have than the ways we tend to follow. Learning is not only the accumulation of experience, of a growing sense of irony, it is also a means of learning what to ignore. For the young child the development of categories, of labels, or seeing exactly which piece of information is to be taken seriously, is a means of discrimination and insight. Such a sense of knowing what is to be ignored can later become a means of defence, of refusing to change. The capacity of human beings is immense. The question is how we learn to use it.

The question for teachers is how we help others develop their capacity to learn. Nothing is more practical in teaching than knowing how people learn. Learning is not a theoretical issue. We need to understand the learning process not only because, as teachers all, we need to know ourselves, but also because we need to express our curiosity in how other people learn. The diagnosis of an individual child's learning difficulties is the most practical starting point for action.

Every sentence that describes learning contains practical implications. These are not applicable only to a specific age. Those insights that apply to very young children apply to us all. For learning is not only a constant process, both rich and varied, never static, whether for better or for worse, but also a process with many different layers, including the inner world of imagination, perception, intelligence and relationships.

There are some fundamentals about learning that emerge again and again, and are true of all ages:

● Children need conversation. They need as many chances to have *sustained* personal dialogues as possible.

- Children need to experiment, to discover, through constructional play, how things work, and how they can be manipulated; and they need to be allowed to make mistakes.
- Children learn from each other. They are natural teachers as well as natural learners.
- Children need teachers to take the trouble, and have the patience, to *explain* as clearly as possible.
- Children like having distinct things to learn, they like being told, with some formality.
- All children need to be noticed with as similar an amount of attention as possible, so that they do not retreat from learning.
- Children need to understand conventions and rules, and how they can be turned upside down. They respect conventions better for seeing them from a different point of view.
- Children like to categorize, to discriminate, to sort materials into lists and groups, and they like games (such as Twenty Questions) that are based on definitions.
- Children need stories, both heard and read, and the more the better.
- Children need to learn to argue a case, not only so that they can organize evidence, but also so that they can explore their feelings through a point of view.
- Children need to pursue a particular interest in some depth, to master it as best they can, to make one subject their own.
- Children need to understand other people's points of view, so that they can appreciate their own experience and the world around them.
- Children need to write, to communicate their own ideas and feelings, not to meet a teacher's wishes but to express themselves.
- Children need to work out their own style of working, to be aware of study skills.
- Children should always work with a sense of purpose. There must be a *reason* for every part of the curriculum.
- Children need to learn through parody. They understand the original by making their own version of it.
- Children constantly need their perceptions developed, as part of their intelligence.

All the practical ideas and many more than are suggested here are implicit throughout the book and have wide implications. This puts an obligation on teachers, for we are all teachers, whether formally or not. Children are learning all the time, not just when we wish them to. They detect clues and analyse other people's expectations and behaviour all the time. This is part of the reason why teaching can be such an exhausting activity. It is hard work to care about others enough to be firm with them rather than lazy. It is harder work to explain than to ignore. It is harder work to insist that they do things properly than to convey indifference. But hard work has its rewards.

Teachers need to have a common purpose and vision that can be communicated. It is not always fashionable to care for others, but none of us really survives as a human being without doing so. And teachers are learners too. They, like their pupils, need their own space to learn, their own interests and excitements for their own sake. For the teacher with high standards, the task of teaching can seem impossible. Researchers in their classrooms commonly detect many instances of children not having demands made of them, of carrying out inappropriate tasks and wasting time. Only those who aim for perfection would recognize such failures. But teachers also need time. Children sometimes need to carry out tasks that *seem* fairly routine. Teachers sometimes need more of the individual attention that they should give to children.

We are all involved in teaching as we are in learning, just as we teach ourselves, deliberately. The failures are often failures of nerve, of lack of self-belief or lack of energy. Those who believe in their own capacity to learn and who understand the fragility of learning are best equipped to help others and themselves.

Name Index

Name Index

240

Subject Index